Theories of Famine

D1323358

Theories of Famine

Stephen Devereux

New York   London   Toronto   Sydney   Tokyo   Singapore

First published 1993 by
Harvester Wheatsheaf
Campus 400, Maylands Avenue
Hemel Hempstead
Hertfordshire, HP2 7EZ
A division of
Simon & Schuster International Group

Typeset in 10/12 pt Times
by Keyboard Services, Luton

Printed and bound in Great Britain by
T.J. Press (Padstow) Ltd

British Library Cataloguing in Publication Data

A catalogue record for this book is available from
the British Library

ISBN 0-7450-1417-8 (pbk)

1 2 3 4 5   97 96 95 94 93

338·19

To Gillian

Contents

Figures

Acknowledgements

In 1986, the Food and Agricultural Organization (FAO) of the United Nations commissioned a report on the causes of famine from the Food Studies Group, University of Oxford. That report, *Origins of Famine*, was co-authored by Roger Hay and myself, and it provided the basic text for this book, which has since been extensively revised and updated. The views expressed here are not necessarily those of the FAO, nor of Roger Hay, though his influence remains strongly felt.

I also wish to thank the following for their constructive comments, in conversation and in writing, on various drafts of this book: Lucia da Corta, Alex de Waal, Thomas Downing, John Field, Betsy Hartmann, Dominique Harvie, John Hoddinott, Tony Jackson, Stephen Jones, Adrian Leftwich, Michael Lipton, Frances Stewart and Getachew Woldemeskel.

Over the six years that this project has taken to reach fruition, I have also gained a great deal from discussions with Jane Corbett, Jean Drèze, Barbara Harriss, Judith Heyer and Peter Walker, among others. I should also acknowledge an intellectual debt to Professor Amartya Sen, whose lectures and writings inspired my interest in this subject.

Grateful acknowledgement is made to the BBC and the contributors to the debate on the 'Politics of Hunger' for permission to reproduce material from the debate. Every effort has been made to trace copyright holders, but if any have been inadvertently overlooked the publisher will be pleased to make the necessary arrangements at the first opportunity.

While I have benefited greatly from the contributions of all those named above, they are not implicated in any deficiencies of the final product.

We find it difficult to understand that in those barbarous times there were some people who had too much to eat and others who had nothing.

Ariel Dorfman, *The Last Song of Manuel Sendero*

PART 1
The nature of famine

1

Introduction

The purpose of studying famine is to contribute to its elimination.
Michael Mortimore (1989, p. 30)

This book is a search for the causes of famine. That famine persists in the modern world, a world of greater affluence and more advanced technology than ever before, is an anachronism and an obscenity. Clearly, it is not enough that agricultural production, communications and transport systems are now capable of producing and distributing more than enough food to meet the world's nutritional needs. Something is missing. Lack of political will is often a factor. Yet famines have also occurred, very recently, despite the best efforts of those afflicted, their governments and donor agencies to prevent them. In these cases, it is arguable that deficient *theory* was partly to blame. Problems were misdiagnosed or not foreseen, leading to inappropriate or late intervention. Many people died, often unnecessarily.

If famine is to be prevented, it must first be understood. But this book is not a policy guide for civil servants, nor is it a manual for aid agencies. It is a theoretical review, because effective policy depends on good theory, and the theory of famine is confused.

For example: one evening in December 1990, six experts and practitioners in the field of world hunger sat around a table in the BBC studios, London, for a 'Food Night' debate on the 'Politics of Hunger'. The panelists were: Lord Peter Bauer (London School of Economics), the Reverend Samuel Kobia (National Council of Churches, Kenya), Robert Hindle (World Bank), Susan George (Transnational Institute), Glenys Kinnock (One World Action) and Vishnu Persaud (Commonwealth Secretariat). The chairman, Donald Mac-Cormick, began by asking each panellist in turn 'that most fundamental question of what actually causes world hunger'.

Lord Bauer: I think the cause of famine, starvation and acute hunger is not overpopulation, or bad weather, or debt, but government policies: the policies of Third World governments made possible by Western aid. Official Western aid – which is taxpayer's money – does not go to the pathetic figures of aid propaganda; it goes to their rulers, and mostly these rulers are responsible for the dreadful condition of their subjects.

Rev. Kobia: I think that poverty and underdevelopment are the main causes of hunger. That means families which are unable to grow or have enough money to buy food to feed themselves. And as we know, this is a situation which could be traced back to colonialism, because colonialism was not in the business of helping people to be able to feed themselves, and this has continued up to this time.

Hindle: Well, the causes are obviously complex, but let me highlight three of them that I think are most important. One, obviously, is war. If one stops and thinks about the countries in Africa now where there are severe hunger problems, they're all countries at war. Second, I agree with Mr Kobia that poverty is a problem. People who do not have income do not have access to food, so frequently when food is available, people cannot get to it. And third, there clearly – certainly in Africa – has been a problem over the past two decades, when population growth rates have far exceeded food production rates, and this has led to an increasing lower per capita availability of food in Africa.

George: First of all, it's not climate, because people always have known that drought would come and when they were able to do so they would have harvests and reserves so they could get through those difficult periods. I don't agree that it's population. Every country in the world where the population rate has gone down, it has been *after* a certain level of food security has been achieved, so that's putting the cart before the horse, in my view. I think that it is quite possible to feed everyone if we lived in a just world. We would only need about 2 per cent, even less, of total world harvests to abolish and eradicate every nutritional problem in the world. So there is no absolute lack of food. But it is a question of poverty. And what lies behind poverty, if poverty lies behind hunger? Well, injustice and inequality. And that I think is at every level.

Persaud: Well, I would say it's a failure of international co-operation, for one thing. I mean, all countries can't be at the same stage – some are poor, some are rich – and we have a world where we have the capacity to really feed everybody. We have the technology, but the will has not been there to do it.

Finally, Glenys Kinnock added that famine 'is about democracy and the environment'. Six experts, twelve explanations! Hunger and famine are caused, apparently, by: Third World government policies, Western aid, poverty, underdevelopment, colonialism, war, population growth, injustice, inequality, the absence of democracy, environmental problems and a failure of international co-operation reflecting a lack of political will.

All these explanations will be considered in the chapters that follow. This study falls into three main parts. The remainder of this first part takes a broad sweep through the thinking on definitions of famine (Chapter 2) and introduces some basic issues (Chapter 3), where the development of major debates in famine theory from Malthus to the present is briefly considered.

Part 2 reviews theories of famine which dominated the literature until the 1980s. Chapters 4 and 5 share a common contention, that famine follows a decline in the production of food at a national or regional level, until there is insufficient food to sustain life. Chapter 4 focuses on climatic shocks (drought, floods), which result in crop failure. Chapter 5 concentrates on the other side of the 'people–natural resources' equation, and examines the effects of population pressure on food producing capacity. These two theories, climatic and demographic, see food availability decline (or 'FAD') as the critical determinant of famine. The next two chapters consider economic theories of famine, the first focusing on 'demand failure', the second on 'distribution failure'. Chapter 6 sets out Sen's 'entitlement approach', which places poverty at the centre of the analysis; while Chapter 7 considers the role of market failure during food crises.

Part 3 is concerned, not with 'theories' of famine causation, but with 'political economy' explanations, which do not fall neatly into particular theoretical frameworks. Chapter 8 returns to the relationships between people and their environment, and asks how natural resource (mis-)management contributes to the risk of famine. In Chapters 9–12, development strategies, government policies, war and international relations each receive similar attention. Chapter 9 takes a historical perspective, reviewing arguments that processes of development create enhanced conditions of vulnerability, sometimes temporarily, sometimes permanently, for certain 'marginalized' groups of people.

Chapter 10 considers various ways in which governments have contributed to famine causation, whether deliberately or inadvertently, or else failed either to prevent food crises or to alleviate their effects. A particularly strong expression of government power is civil strife or war, and Chapter 11 spells out the disruptive consequences of war on food production, storage and distribution systems. The lethal combination of drought, war, displacement and famine is found in most contemporary African famines. The final chapter in this part is concerned with the international dimension of famine – the oligopolistic global grains trade, and the successes and failures associated with the internationaliza-tion, in recent decades, of food aid and famine relief generally.

Part 3 also includes five case studies of twentieth-century famines, which illuminate aspects of the political economy of famine. Although major food crises since Bangladesh 1974 have been confined to Africa, most of these case studies are not African and are not contemporary. Famines are chosen to illustrate particular themes. Without implying that any famine can be explained by a single cause, government policies are clearly pre-eminent in explaining the Ukrainian famine of 1932–4 and China's Great Leap Forward famine of 1958–61 (Chapter 10.4 and 10.5). The Bangladesh 1974 famine is treated as a case study in international policy failure (Chapter 12.4), but is also discussed in the chapter on food markets, because of the role played by grain hoarding and trader speculation in exacerbating the crisis. The Dutch famine of 1944 is analyzed as an archetypal war-induced food crisis (Chapter 11.4). The African famines of the 1970s and 1980s are characterized by great causal complexity, and these are referred to throughout this book, in several contexts – drought, 'failure of development', ecological crisis, market failure, war. The Sahelian famine of the early 1970s (Chapter 9.5) illustrates the first three of these five factors.

The fourth and final part of the book consists of a concluding chapter, which briefly restates the main points of each theory and argument.

This book does not offer a new theory of famine. The objective instead is to review the multiple explanations offered for famine causation, to contextualize and criticize them in the light of recent theoretical debates and empirical evidence. If there is one general conclusion that this review emphasizes, it is that there is no single 'correct' theory of famine. Many of the paradigms discussed in this book could be applied to most famines, and each would probably provide some explanatory power – but each on its own would tell a partial story at best. The causes of food crises change as societies and relationships between societies evolve and develop. Famines are as complex and intricate as the communities which suffer them.

2

What is famine?

Famine is like insanity, hard to define, but glaring enough when
recognised.[1]

If asked to define 'famine', most people in the West would probably volunteer
variations on: 'mass death by starvation'. Famine is perceived as an abnormal
event with distinctive and dramatic characteristics. Yet it has proved strangely
difficult to provide a robust distinction between famine and other symptoms of
deprivation – such as chronic malnutrition, 'seasonal hunger' or isolated cases
of starvation – all of which are endemic among the poor, especially (but not
only) in Third World countries. Most attempts to define famine merely
describe its commonest causes and effects, and the boundaries between
definition, description and explanations of famine are often blurred.

Since a famine is quite unmistakable, some analysts have questioned the
need to define the word at all, suggesting that to do so is spurious or merely
academic. Sen (1981, pp. 39–40) argues that: 'While there is quite a literature
on how to "define" famines, one can very often diagnose it – like a flood or a
fire – even without being armed with a precise definition.'

Nevertheless, a review of common definitions is an appropriate starting
point for this study, for three reasons. There is, first, an academic justification
for establishing a rigorous definition of a phenomenon under study. Second,
many widely accepted definitions are weak or misleading because they reflect
an implicit theory which is deficient or incorrect. Finally, definitions often
provide the criteria on which resources such as food aid are released or
withheld in response to a perceived threat of mass starvation. So, a definition is
important at least for diagnostic purposes – a famine has to be identified as such
before institutional responses are triggered. It is therefore vital that, if they are
to have practical use, definitions are sound.

The definitions commonly encountered can be divided into five groups: (1) the simplest, dictionary-type definitions; (2) definitions that reflect the theory that famines result from a decline in the supply of food; (3) definitions based on food consumption deficits; (4) 'behavioural' definitions; that is, definitions based on observed responses to widespread hunger; and (5) 'insider' definitions, which reflect the perceptions of famine victims themselves.

2.1 Dictionary definitions

The simplest definitions of the word 'famine' emphasize two features: that famines are associated with severe shortages, especially of food, and that they are causally associated with hunger and starvation. The 1980s editions of four popular dictionaries defined 'famine' as follows:

- 'An extreme scarcity of food; *broadly* any great shortage.'
- 'Extreme general scarcity of food: scarcity of anything: hunger: starvation.'
- '1. A severe shortage of food, as through crop failure or overpopulation. 2. Acute shortage of anything. 3. Violent hunger.'
- 'Extreme scarcity of food in a district etc.; dearth of something specified (*water famine*; famine prices, prices raised by scarcity); (archaic) hunger, starvation (*die of famine*).'[2]

Dictionary definitions, of which the above examples are typical, merely describe a few *symptoms* of famine ('scarcity of food', 'dearth', 'hunger'). When they do go further and suggest *causes* of famine ('crop failure', 'overpopulation'), they are selecting arbitrarily from a number of possible causal factors, and just as arbitrarily ignoring all the others (war, poverty, market failure and so on). So one difficulty which dictionaries have failed to resolve is to provide a definition of famine that is both comprehensive and concise.

Another problem with standard definitions of this type is that they fail to convey either the scale or the catastrophic nature of famine. They could apply equally to starvation of one single person, and this does not constitute famine. They could apply either to longstanding consumption inadequacy or to short, sharp episodes of food deprivation. Most dictionary definitions are therefore rather unhelpful in distinguishing famine as a discrete phenomenon from starvation as a state in which food consumption is inadequate. A good working definition of famine must describe a subsistence crisis afflicting particular groups of people within a bounded region over a specified period of time.

2.2 Food shortage definitions

Dictionaries are not the only source of definitions which imply that famines are caused simply by critical food shortages. Many academics share this view:

A temporary, but severe, local shortage of food is called a famine. It is generally the result of an almost complete crop failure in an area of subsistence or near subsistence farming. (Ferris and Toyne, 1970, quoted in Dando, 1980, p. 63)

a famine is a food shortage leading to widespread death from starvation; [alternatively, a famine is] a societal crisis induced by the dissolution of the accustomed availability of, and access to, staple foods on a scale sufficient to cause starvation among a significant number of individuals. (Watts, 1983, pp. 13, 17–18)

What these definitions fail to explain is why a localized food shortage is not redressed by imports of food from elsewhere. A second group of definitions addresses this question by implying that the failure of markets, together with the non-arrival of food aid, is either the cause of famine or must accompany a failure of crop production for a famine to develop. In other words, not only local food *production* systems, but also food *distribution* systems, must fail simultaneously. This dual prerequisite is explicit in the following two definitions:

Famine may be defined as the regional failure of food production or distribution systems, leading to sharply increased mortality due to starvation and associated disease. (Cox, 1981, p. 5)

A famine is usually agreed to be a general, acute, and extreme shortage of food within a region, which is not relieved by supplies of food being sent in because of inadequate distribution. Famines cause death from starvation and disease, which follow the extreme shortage of food, calories and nutrients. (Lowenberg *et al.*, 1974, quoted in Dando, 1980, p. 62)

These statements are more than definitions in that they imply a theory of famine. They suggest that food shortage is a necessary prerequisite of famine. However, they are misleading because they leap backwards from the '*fact*' of starvation to the *assumption* of a food shortage. This assumption does not allow for the possibility of famine in areas which have no food supply problem at all. Sen's famous opening sentences in *Poverty and Famines* puts such definitions into context:

Starvation is the characteristic of some people not *having* enough food to eat. It is not the characteristic of there *being* not enough to eat. While the latter can be a cause of the former, it is but one of many *possible* causes. (Sen, 1981, p. 1)

The crucial point is that, although a shortage of food may be one causal factor in the chain of events leading up to a famine, it is neither a necessary nor a sufficient condition for a famine to occur.

2.3   Famine as mass starvation

Another common group of definitions equates mass hunger and starvation with famine. The focus here is on the physiological plight of famine victims – famine is described in terms of inadequate food *intake*, rather than inadequate food *availability*. In the view of Mellor and Gavian (1987, p. 539), 'famine is an extreme on the hunger continuum'. Rivers *et al.* (1976, p. 355) state bluntly that: 'Starvation is a semantic prerequisite for the definition of famine.' According to Aykroyd (1974, p. 2): '"mass-starvation" and "famine" mean much the same thing'. Woldemariam's (1984, p. 9) definition describes the effects of food consumption deficits, without attempting to identify the causes of famine:

> Famine is a general and widespread, prolonged and persistent, extraordinary and insufferable hunger lasting for several months and affecting the majority of the rural population over a more or less extensive area, resulting in total social and economic disorganisation and mass death by starvation. In defining famine, we are not concerned with specific hunger, but with general hunger. . . . Famine is general hunger affecting large numbers of people in rural areas as a consequence of the non-availability of food for a relatively long time.

Many definitions based on food consumption deficits fail to distinguish between famine and other forms of hunger and starvation. By contrast, Woldemariam (1984, p. 4) explicitly spells out this distinction:

> Ordinary hunger is not famine; undernourishment is not famine; malnutrition is not famine; even though all these terms are used interchangeably as if they are synonymous.

Sen (1981, p. 39) adds starvation to this list of 'what famine is not':

> Famines imply starvation, but not vice versa. . . . Starvation is a normal feature in many parts of the world, but this phenomenon of 'regular' starvation has to be distinguished from violent outbursts of famines.

The distinction between starvation and famine is usually made in terms of the numbers of people affected. It is generally agreed that famines affect sizeable populations over a relatively large area, while starvation afflicts individuals or small groups of people. Paddock and Paddock (1967, p. 50) illustrate this contrast in graphic terms:

> Perhaps when a man keels over and collapses from lack of food, then that can be accepted as the dividing line between malnutrition and starvation. . . . Perhaps when whole families and communities keel over, then it can be called a famine.

Sen (1981, pp.40–1) introduces a third distinction, the 'time contrast', between starvation and famine:

> In analysing starvation in general, it is important to make clear distinctions between three different issues. (1) *lowness of the typical level* of food consumption; (2) *declining trend* of food consumption; and (3) *sudden collapse* of the level of food consumption. Famine is chiefly a problem of the third kind.

This discussion suggests that 'extreme', 'widespread' and 'catastrophic' cases of hunger or starvation should be described as famine. How extreme will be determined by the area, the duration and the number of people affected. At what point, though, does serious starvation assume the crisis dimensions of a famine? Seaman and Holt (1980, p. 284) suggest that fine distinctions like these are rather arbitrary, and that 'famine may simply represent a continuum of size and be beyond definition: some authors have emphasised this by the use of terms such as "chronic" famine.' Others talk of malnutrition as 'endemic famine', or of famine as 'epidemic malnutrition' (Foege, 1971, quoted in Dando, 1980, p. 60), but this juggling with jargon only confuses the issue.

The line between famine and other manifestations of food crisis has been drawn by Alamgir (1980, p. 7) in terms of 'excess mortality' (more deaths per unit of population than would normally be expected). 'One can now distinguish famine from starvation, hunger, and malnutrition . . . famine implies hunger, starvation, malnutrition, and something more – excess death.'

A final distinction, that of *irreversibility* in the decline in food consumption, is offered by Mengestu *et al.* (1978, p. 1). They define famine 'as occurring when a decline in the flow of food to households becomes irreversible so that, without outside intervention, people starve to death.' Although this statement lacks the scale element which is successfully captured by other definitions, a useful feature is the introduction of a dynamic element to the notion of 'declining flows of food'. Famine mortality *may* follow a sudden shock to food production or supplies, but only after some time, during which 'outside intervention' can assist the afflicted population to recover. But it is not only interventions such as food aid which help people survive famine. They have their own 'coping strategies', as D'Souza's (1988, p. 7) definition recognizes:

> famine can be defined as a reduction in normally available food supply such that individuals, families, and eventually whole communities are forced to take up abnormal social and economic activities in order to ensure food. If these activities are unsuccessful, then starvation will follow.

In summary, there seems little difficulty in distinguishing 'malnutrition' and 'undernutrition' from starvation and famine. Chronic malnutrition describes nothing more than a poorly balanced diet, lacking in essential nutrients, while 'undernutrition' is the physical syndrome associated with prolonged food deprivation. Neither constitutes sufficient evidence for famine, which is a wide-ranging crisis, not simply a biological syndrome. Nor is there much difficulty in distinguishing 'hunger' from starvation. Hunger is an individual's perception of the need to eat – the obese can feel hunger as much as the poor. Starvation is a continuation of hunger to the point where life is threatened. Finally, if the perception of famine as a crisis of mass starvation is valid, then it is scale which would seem to separate starvation and famine.

The definition that comes closest to incorporating all these arguments is Woldemariam's, which began this section. This definition combines the physical effects of starvation on the *individual* with the extent of its impact on a *population*. Unfortunately, it is too long and descriptive to be regarded as a succinct statement of famine's essentials, and too restrictive in that it refers only to rural people. The complete statement is not entirely 'theory-neutral' either; it states that famine is caused by the non-availability of food.

A major practical drawback to Woldemariam's definition is that it has limited diagnostic or predictive merit, since it merely describes the worst possible outcome of a famine, long after the time has passed when a more sensitive definition might have helped to prevent it. As de Waal (1987, p. 256) argues, 'the role of the definition as "pithy description" leads to its focusing on extreme or paradigm cases of famine, which is of little help in marginal or borderline cases.' There is also an emerging debate about whether starvation and excess mortality are necessary components of famine definitions at all, as will be seen.

2.4 'Behavioural' definitions

The next category of definitions draws attention to the social and economic disruption (mentioned in Woldemariam's and D'Souza's definitions above), which typically accompanies a famine, and thus identifies famine in terms of the responses of communities afflicted by it. These definitions regard famine as a 'community syndrome' rather than (simplistically) as the result of a 'natural disaster'. Although they also derive from the perceptions of 'outsiders', they do try to see famine from the victims' point of view. Currey's (1981, p. 123) definition (originally devised in 1976) was the first of its kind:

> Famine might be more effectively defined as the community syndrome which results when social, economic and administrative structures are already under stress and are further triggered by one, or several, discrete disruptions which accelerate the incidence of many symptoms, or crisis adjustments, of which one is epidemic malnutrition.

Alamgir (1980, pp. 5–6), arguing in favour of this approach, notes that: 'The multiplicity of definitions of famine indicate that it is a complex socio-economic phenomenon. Its essence cannot be captured within a simple definition. The community syndrome approach, therefore, assumes great importance.' Alamgir's (1980, pp. 6–7) own definition spells out some of the social and economic, as well as biological, consequences of famine:

> famine is considered to represent a general state of prolonged foodgrain intake deficiency per capita giving rise to a number of accompanying substates (symptoms) involving individuals and the community that ultimately lead, directly or indirectly, to excess deaths in a region or in a country as a whole. These substates include: increase in interregional migration, increase in crime, increase in incidence of fatal disease, loss of body weight, changes in nutritional status, eating of alternative 'famine foods', mental disorientation, 'wandering', uprooting of families, separation of families, transfer of assets, and breakdown of traditional

social bonds. Among these, crime, disease, loss of body weight, changes in nutritional status, and eating of alternative 'famine foods' can combine to produce significant excess deaths.

Unfortunately, these are *ex post* descriptions rather than definitions which might be used for *ex ante* prediction and prevention of potential famine situations. They are also rather vague. Currey's and Alamgir's statements might equally describe the effect on a community of war or civil disturbance. On the other hand, the notion of 'community syndrome' does introduce a valuable sense of dynamism and a social context to the way famines typically develop – that is, as a process which occurs over a period of time. This is developed in another descriptive definition, proposed by UNRISD (United Nations Research Institute for Social Development) (1976, p. 3), which refers to three phases in a famine's 'episodic career':

> the word 'famine' is used to refer to a societal crisis induced by the breakdown of the accustomed availability of and access to basic foods, on a scale sufficient to threaten the lives of a significant number of people. . . . The crisis thus defined is limited in time, being of an episodic career with three distinct phases: an initial period of gestation in which a number of factors converge in attenuating food supplies; a period in which the inaccessibility of food reaches critical dimensions in terms of human survival and creates modes of behaviour which diverge extensively from the accustomed routines; and a period of recovery when one or more contributory factors or trends cease to operate and there is a return to the accustomed (or modified) patterns of access to food; or else dissolution of settlements and migration of groups or individuals subject to famine take place.

Perhaps the most complex definition within the 'behavioural' family is that developed by Cutler (1985b), which is significant for introducing a social class dimension, in order to identify the likely victims (and beneficiaries) of famine:

> Famine is an abnormal event, characterised by a breakdown in social relations giving rise to epidemic starvation and excess mortality. It is caused initially by a severe disruption in normal economic activity, principally but not exclusively brought about by vagaries of climate, which leads to expectations of future scarcities of food among producers, traders and consumers. This in turn leads to modes of social behaviour such as asset sales, hoarding, speculation and the erosion of traditional social bonds which themselves contribute to the development of famine conditions. When famine conditions have become fully established, so that large numbers of vulnerable people have become stripped of their assets and options and have begun to starve, there will be widespread mortality in excess of normal levels unless the authorities or other outside agencies intervene with effective relief and rehabilitation aid. Excess mortality is concentrated among certain classes, social groups and household members who are particularly vulnerable socio-economically or culturally. A corollary of this is the profit which can be made from famine by other dominant classes, social groups or households.

This is one of the most detailed definitions to date but, like those of Currey, Alamgir and UNRISD, is mainly descriptive. It sketches in graphic detail the development and effects of a famine, but fails to explain why any particular 'disruption in normal economic activity' *necessarily* results in 'excess mortality'. There is, of course, no such causal inevitability, and it must be concluded that Cutler's description lacks the conciseness or precision which a clear and usable definition should provide. Moreover:

> Some might object that such a definition underplays historical and structural factors in the development and eruption of famine. But whatever its limitations, this statement shows how difficult it is to define famine. It also underlines the need for a multicausal analysis and understanding of famine, and it usefully combines some of the factors isolated above. It certainly represents a way of thinking about famine which confirms the need for interdisciplinary work. (Leftwich and Harvie, 1986, p. 35)

A final definition in this category, by Walker (1989, p. 6), has the advantage of being succinct, emphasizing the nature of famine as a process rather than an event, and de-emphasizing starvation and death as necessary preconditions (what Rangasami (1985, p. 1748) describes as 'the elevation of mortality'). Its limitations are those of the much longer definitions cited above – in particular, vagueness in that it cannot isolate famine from other processes which might cause 'accelerated destitution':

> famine is a socio-economic process which causes the accelerated destitution of the most vulnerable, marginal and least powerful groups in a community, to a point where they can no longer, as a group, maintain a sustainable livelihood.

2.5 'Insider' definitions

So far we have listed the perceptions of outsiders about the nature of famine. Very few writers have asked victims themselves how they perceive famine. This ethnocentricity is responsible for much that is wrong with famine definitions and famine 'management'.

Almost all 'outsider' definitions stand united behind Sen's (1981, p. 39) observation that 'Famines imply starvation.' The implicit conceptual model is that 'impoverishment leads to involuntary lowered food consumption which leads to starvation and death' (de Waal, 1990, p. 6). This model can be challenged empirically on two grounds:

> One is that during famines, many people choose not to consume food rather than sell vital assets. The other is that most famine mortality is not directly related to undernutrition but is caused by outbreaks of disease. (de Waal, 1990, p. 1)

De Waal (1989, p. 20) therefore argues that 'the current English notion of famine as mass starvation unto death is inappropriate, and should be discarded' in favour of African and Asian definitions, since these reflect more accurately the experience of the victims of famine themselves. For one thing, people afflicted by famine distinguish between several types, intensities and consequences of famine – their definitions are more subtle and complex than ours. 'Those who suffer from famine have a more exact vocabulary than those who analyse it' (Swift, 1989, p. 8). Comparing local definitions from Africa and Bangladesh, de Waal (1989, p. 10) concludes:

> In both Africa and Bangladesh the concepts grow out of actual experience of famine, and in neither case is there a positivistic criterion of measurable changes in food availability or death rates. Most importantly, neither of these concepts of famine use the presence of deaths from starvation as a criterion at all.

'Insider' definitions recognize many shades of poverty, hunger and starvation. In Bangladesh, according to Currey (1981, p. 123), 'the culture defines three types of famine: scarcity is *akal* (when times are bad); famine is *durvickha* (when alms are scarce) and nationwide famine is *mananthor* (when the epoch changes).'

The title of de Waal's study of the 1984–5 famine in Darfur, Sudan, *Famine that Kills*, provocatively separates famine from mortality, identifying as distinct cases famines that result in death and famines that do not. In Darfur, de Waal (1989, p. 76) argues, famine means 'not merely starvation but also hunger (that is, all manners of suffering), destitution and social breakdown. When people are dying, manifestly because of the hardship and disorder associated with a famine, it is a "famine that kills".' The Arabic word *maja'a*, used in Darfur for 'famine', incorporates three concepts: hunger, destitution and death. English requires all three for famine, especially death. Famine names in Darfur suggest at least three different severities, with hunger common to all, but destitution rather than death being the focus:

> the concept of famine in Darfur is primarily one of destitution, and not mortality and starvation. . . . Europeans believe that famine implies death by starvation, Africans who are exposed to famines do not. (de Waal, 1987, p. 257)

Thus a pastoralist from Niger, questioned about a famine which occurred during the 1950s, replied: 'No one died, but the price of millet rose: when the sack of millet costs 6000 francs, isn't that a famine?' (Laya, 1975, p. 88).

The idea that a famine can be said to have occurred even without starvation and excess mortality may seem odd to Westerners conditioned by the media to think of famine in terms of starving Africans in refugee camps. And yet, if a relief programme ever was completely effective, nobody would actually die, but nor would most observers doubt that a famine had occurred. If it is accepted that famine is a process, one final outcome of which may be starvation (unless prevented), then there is no paradox in Rangasami's (1985, p. 1748) assertion that 'mortality is not a necessary condition of famine.'

Of course, starvation and death *are* common features of many famines, but the problem is that definitions based on these criteria exclude situations where every element of a famine is present *except* death from starvation. As Walker (1989, p. 35) emphasizes:

> Famine does not necessarily imply a massive death toll through starvation. In communities where it is recurrent, it is the process which *may* ultimately lead to a high death toll which is seen as defining famine, not the deaths *per se*.

This distinction is important, and not simply a semantic sleight of hand. Crude 'outsider' definitions have resulted in crude understanding and bludgeoning interventions (or non-intervention) by agencies whose effectiveness could be dramatically improved with the subtler approach which an 'insider' perspective would provide. The contrast between 'insider' and 'outsider' definitions is starkest when it is recognized that victims see widespread death as the end result of a famine process, while outsiders see it as the beginning.

2.6   Conclusion

Conventional 'outsider' definitions of famine reveal a preoccupation with three attributes which supposedly differentiate famine from other manifestations of hunger or poverty. These are: 1. A critical food shortage; 2. Starvation; 3. Excess mortality. Yet many recent famines fail to meet even these basic criteria. In the 1970s and 1980s alone, famines occurred:

1. *With no food shortage* (Bangladesh, 1974): according to Sen (1981, p. 137), '1974 was a local peak year in terms of both total output and *per capita* output of rice.'
2. *Where excess mortality was not caused by starvation* (western Sudan, 1984–5): de Waal (1989, p. 192) argues that 'famine mortality in Darfur . . . was mostly or wholly disease-driven and not starvation-driven.'
3. *With no increase in mortality* (Sahel, 1972–4): according to de Waal (1989, p. 27), 'it is even possible that fewer people than normal died during the famine.'

Where do our definitions of famine stand now? Alamgir's (1980, pp. 6–7) delineation of what constitutes a 'good' definition of famine sets three apparently reasonable objectives:

> A definition of famine should fulfil the following objectives. First, one should be able to distinguish clearly between a famine and a nonfamine situation. Therefore, emphasis on excess mortality is important. Secondly, the definition should identify the prior indicators of famine, which will provide a basis for governments and potential victims to be forewarned and relief instruments activated. Finally, it should indicate the immediate cause of a set of famine substates that ultimately lead to excess mortality.

Alamgir's first criterion is based on the premise that a famine is clearly distinct from other situations. But is it? As Walker (1989, p. 53) has observed:

> states tend to react only to the final mass starvation phase of famine. They view the phenomenon as a temporary aberration, a view in direct contradiction to that of the victims, who see it as an extension of the norm.

If Walker is correct, then attempts to isolate and define famine as a unique event are doomed to failure, misled by the focus on 'excess mortality', which is only one possible final outcome of the famine process, not its defining characteristic. Famines that result in excess mortality are a subset of all possible famines.

As far as Alamgir's second criterion is concerned, it is clearly the case that agencies and governments concerned with famine are working with hopelessly inadequate definitions, one effect of which is to delay their interventions, often fatally. The Ethiopian famine of 1984–5 provides a tragic recent example. Gill (1986, p. 26) has documented how 'the Western world . . . responded only when people were dying, not to the warning signals and not to the challenge of trying to avert famine.' Only a few months before the famine peaked, a member of a UN mission in Ethiopia (quoted in Gill, 1986, p. 50) accused the Ethiopian government of 'crying wolf': 'You have been telling the world of this problem in 1982 and 1983, but we've not seen the people dying like flies yet.' In the light of this 'no corpses, no food aid' myopia (not to mention callousness), we must agree with de Waal (1987, p. 256), who concludes pessimistically that 'there is no good definition on which to make a diagnosis' of impending famine.

Alamgir's third criterion is the identification of 'famine substates', again with a view to timely intervention. Food aid and other resources which are made available when famine is 'declared' are typically not available when the precursors of famine – the processes listed in 'community syndrome' definitions, for example – are observed. Again, this reflects limited perceptions by external agencies about the nature of famine. As D'Souza (1988, p. 7) observes, 'if one asserts that famine in its early stages is characterized by social and economic responses, then it cannot be detected by anthropometric or nutritional means, or even defined in those terms'. A definition of famine which relies on indicators such as changes in bodyweight will result in relief arriving far too late. In this context, the growing empirical literature on famine coping strategies, which charts the behaviour of famine victims in response to deepening threats to their survival, has much to offer.

Alamgir's criteria are rarely met in the literature on defining famine. They can never be met, because they themselves reflect an 'outsider' conceptualization of famine. This explains why there is a surplus of definitions and a scarcity of consensus. Famine victims, who have a broader and subtler conception of famine than do famine observers, must be consulted if a precise and, above all, useful definition is to be found. The views of famine 'insiders' are worth incomparably more than those of textbooks and dictionaries.

Notes

1. Taylor, unpublished manuscript, quoted in Currey (1981, p. 123).

2. Longman's Concise English Dictionary (1985), Chambers English Dictionary (1988), Collins English Dictionary (2nd edition, 1986), Concise Oxford Dictionary (7th edition, 1982), respectively.

3

The evolution of famine theory

> Famines are enormously complex social and biological phenomena and it is quite hopeless to expect a generic theory of their origins or consequences.
>
> Michael Watts (1987, p. 205)

Theories of famine have existed for as long as famine itself. They have produced a considerable body of literature. Much of it is the result of intense debate, and all of it reflects the disciplinary and ideological biases of its authors. Before proceeding to a detailed review of these writings, this chapter briefly addresses some general questions which divide or unite the famine literature.

3.1   Act of God or act of man?

Perhaps the single issue which still polarizes the literature is whether famine should be regarded as an 'act of God' or 'act of man'. The conventional view was that famines are unusual events inflicted on their victims by a malign fate or some freak of nature. The alternative view is that, while famines may be triggered by a discrete *natural* event, they are the tragic consequence of *human* activities.

The 'act of God' approach tends to isolate the phenomenon of famine from other social, political and economic issues, and to place it in the same category as 'natural disasters' such as earthquakes, floods, hurricanes or volcanic eruptions. This view has some important implications. For example, vulnerability to famine must then be seen as the consequence of living in an area prone to drought or flooding, rather than being the result of poverty, government policies or undeveloped markets. There is little that can be done and it is probably best that people move elsewhere. This view also supports the belief that should famine strike, once relief has been supplied, the situation returns to a pre-famine 'normality'.

The 'act of man' view, by contrast, places famine on a continuum with hunger, poverty and social deprivation, and argues that famine is a consequence of human activity (or inactivity) which can be prevented by modified behaviour and/or economic and political interventions. It is the result of processes in which human beings actively engage, for which they may be held responsible and which they can almost always prevent. It is therefore necessary to look beyond the immediate causes of catastrophes like droughts or floods, and to explore the processes which, in adverse circumstances, may culminate in destitution, starvation, epidemics and death.

This book is biased towards the second view. This is not to suggest that all famines are *maliciously* 'man-made', in the sense that premeditated action is taken deliberately to cause the death of others by starvation. Nor is it suggested that climate plays no autonomous role at all. What is certain, however, is that few if any recorded famines can be blamed entirely on forces outside human influence. At best, famines are the product of human interactions with nature. To attribute them to nature or God alone is simplistic and fatalistic.

There are at least three related reasons for taking this view. The first is that there are very few famines in which the rich have starved. It is therefore necessary to focus attention on why the poor suffer disproportionately from famine. Clearly, the reasons must be socioeconomic and political. Unless poverty can be attributed to God or a freak of nature, then no more can famine.

The second point is that no recent famine could not have been averted by taking food from somewhere else. Famine is almost always preventable, and its prevention is man's responsibility. At the global level today, Carlyle's statement about England in 1852 is all too true: 'in the midst of plethoric plenty, the people perish' (quoted in Lipton, 1977, p. 27). The world has not reached the stage where the classical Malthusian view – not enough food to go around – holds at a global level. There is no inevitable 'trade-off' between rival consumption needs. No American or European goes hungry because aid to Africa deprives them of essential food. More and more famines are 'man-made', by default if not intent, and fewer can be attributed to natural catastrophe.

Finally, the correlation between climate and famine is weaker than that between poverty or war and famine. Famine has been banished from all but the poorest and most strife-torn societies, irrespective of their susceptibility to drought or flood. Australia and the United States have droughts but no famine. Rainfall in most of the Middle East is no greater than in the Sahel, but famine today is unknown in the Arab world and Israel. Again, famine must be seen as a problem of maldistribution and disrupted access to food, rather than one of inadequate food production and availability.

Having accepted society's role in contributing to famine, a related question which divides the literature is whether famines should be blamed on the victims themselves or on other groups of people (such as governments) instead. This debate will come up again and again, in various contexts, throughout this book. Famine victims are accused of contributing to their own downfall by having too many children (Chapter 5) and by over-exploiting their natural environment (Chapter 8). Among the outsiders accused of 'setting people up' for famine are grain traders (Chapter 7), colonialists (Chapter 9), local governments (Chapter 10), hostile foreign governments (Chapter 11) and international agencies (Chapter 12).

Another issue on which there is much disagreement concerns the *nature* of famine. Is famine a process or an event? Is it a distinct and recognizable 'crisis of mass mortality' or a creeping process of impoverishment and destitution, one ultimate consequence of which may be 'excess deaths'? These questions have to some extent been addressed in the discussion of famine definitions (Chapter 2), but they inform famine theorizing as well. Most writers continue to treat famine as a discrete event, which is analytically separable from longer-term processes, even if influenced by them. This is as true of Sen's 'entitlement approach' (Chapter 6), which is widely regarded as the most sophisticated theoretical framework yet developed for understanding famines, as of any other theory.

3.2   Supply failure or demand failure?

As will be seen in Chapter 6, one academic consequence of Sen's 'entitlement approach' was to spark a fierce (though ultimately sterile) debate about the relative roles in famine causation of supplies of food and demand for food. In order to contrast his ideas with earlier theories which focused exclusively on sudden or secular collapses in food production, Sen coined the phrase 'food availability decline' (or 'FAD') for these theories, which he regarded as incomplete and often wrong. The definitive hypothesis of FAD theory is that people starve because of a local, national or regional decline in food availability, for whatever reason, to a level below the minimum necessary for the affected population's survival. Sen, by contrast, emphasizes differences in access to food – effective demand for food, in economist jargon, rather than aggregate supplies of food.

Chapters 4 and 5 will review two common antecedents of food availability decline – climatic shocks and demographic pressure. Other processes and events (the erosion of natural resources, wars) are also linked with FAD theories of famine (see Chapters 8 and 11). While a famine theory based solely on a global decline of food availability is patently absurd (though the 'world food crisis' of the early 1970s is still erroneously cited as a cause of the famines in Africa which followed), the explanatory power of localized declines in food availability bears closer attention. Most contemporary famines are triggered either by drought causing harvests to fail, or by war (including food blockades), which disrupts food production and distribution. Even in the modern world, a local FAD can, in the absence of trade or aid transfers, develop into a local famine. It might be argued, then, that FAD becomes increasingly powerful as the unit of analysis is reduced in scale – from country to region, from region to community, and from community to household. As this happens, however, FAD begins to look less like a theory about aggregate food *availability* and more like a theory based on differential *access* to food – which is precisely Sen's point.

FAD theory has dominated famine analysis, prediction and relief policies since the time of Malthus. Although now under considerable attack, its influence remains profound, both in international donor agencies and in popular perceptions of famine causation. FAD provided the theoretical basis for actions implemented after the 1974 World Food Conference, which had the highly ambitious objective of eradicating hunger and famine by the turn of the century. Indeed, the idea that famine is caused primarily by a decline in food supplies has been responsible for at least five pieces of 'applied theory', which continue to dominate anti-famine strategies.

3.2.1　Famine prediction

Many 'famine early warning systems' are based on the assumption that local foodcrop production can be used as a proxy for the amount of food available to families in a given region. A forecasted change in crop yields or output therefore serves as an indicator of a change in vulnerability to famine. This can only be valid under very restrictive conditions. Most families in areas prone to crop failure have non-agricultural sources of income on which they rely for food purchases in bad years. (*Non*-agricultural incomes are vital in rainfed farming systems where foodcrop and 'cash crop' production are highly covariant.) In drought-prone rural Botswana, for example, livestock income and remittances from migrants provide more stable and dominant sources of access to food than crop sales.

3.2.2　'Food balance sheets'

'Food balance sheets' are widely used in the assessment of food import requirements for a region or country. Average or per capita food supplies (production plus stocks) are compared with average or per capita food 'needs'. In practice, severe methodological problems are associated with estimating both food production and subsistence consumption requirements. Moreover, this methodology assumes that available food is evenly distributed among consumers. In reality, the rich eat more, and the poor less, than the average consumption level. Food balance sheet figures are thus not only statistically unreliable, but potentially very misleading. It is possible for the risk of famine to be higher in societies with a 'good' food balance sheet, if the *distribution* of food and wealth is highly unequal, than in societies where a lower calories:population ratio suggests greater vulnerability.

3.2.3 Food aid assessment

The quantification of famine relief requirements is also typically based on estimates of the 'food gap' between supply and needs (calories required minus calories available). A more correct – though admittedly more difficult – calculation would be the difference between nutritional needs and effective demand for food, disaggregated both geographically and socioeconomically.

Famine relief is dominated by a single policy instrument – the supplementation of local food supplies with foreign food aid. This rests on the assumption that food shortages cause famine. The remedy is obvious – make good the shortage. It also assumes that food will not be available locally, but food shortages, when they occur, are usually spatially concentrated. Recently, efforts have been made to promote 'triangular food aid' arrangements, whereby donors buy food in one country to sell or donate to hungry people in a neighbouring country. This policy stimulates local production and trade and also provides food aid recipients with local cereals and other foods, rather than Western foods which may be culturally and nutritionally inappropriate.

3.2.4 National food reserves

Many countries hold national food security stocks as a bulwark against famine. Government marketing agencies release this food onto markets or distribute it (free or subsidized) during crisis years or the annual 'hungry season'. The objective is to stabilize food availability in the face of production fluctuations and prevent undue rises in food prices, thereby protecting the access to food of poorer consumers. This is a useful and important component of an effective anti-hunger strategy. However, national food reserves are not, in themselves, an adequate guarantee against famine.

3.2.5 'Carrying capacity'

Perhaps the single most ambitious exercise undertaken with a FAD basis was the FAO's (1984) estimates of global food prospects. The world's land surface was divided into agro-ecological cells. The agricultural potential at three levels of technology for the crops most suited to each cell was calculated. This was then converted into nutrient equivalents, and 'carrying capacities' (defined as the number of people each cell could support) were calculated. Lastly, these figures were compared with existing and projected population numbers for each cell, so that 'food deficit' regions could be targeted. However, the possibility of trade was explicitly excluded from the methodology, so that wealthy food importers like Japan and the Middle East were misleadingly categorized. Moreover, consumption projections were based entirely on posited needs. Effective demand, which is deficient among the poor and greater than subsistence needs among the rich, was ignored.

This summary suggests that FAD theory is intimately associated with many of the conventional principles of food policy and famine management. If this theory is found to be wanting, much of the practice which is based upon it begins to look exceedingly thin.

In fact, FAD theory has several major weaknesses. In the first place, it is incomplete. FAD discusses only supply factors, but a shortage can occur for either supply or demand reasons: 'a shortage in this sense (essentially the existence of excess demand in the market), can occur without FAD, i.e. without any *decline over time* of food availability, since the market demand can sharply rise over time' (Sen, 1986b, p. 126). So FAD cannot explain famines that have occurred when food supplies appeared adequate. FAD ignores the effects of changes in real purchasing power brought about by an increase in food prices or a fall in individual incomes, either of which can produce famine in a situation of unchanged or even *rising* aggregate food availability.

Second, even in the case of famines which *are* characterized by reductions in per capita food availability, FAD says nothing about who is most vulnerable. FAD focuses exclusively on the total quantity of food in an area, divorced from individual demands for or access to that food stock. At best FAD can identify a geographical region which might be vulnerable to famine following, say, a drought. This is not very helpful in terms of targeting those families (rural or urban? farmers or pastoralists?) and individuals within families (adults or children? males or females?) who are most at risk. In its overriding concern with food supply and its failure to consider effective demand, FAD completely ignores the distributional effects of food supply shocks, which translate into starvation for the poor but allow the wealthy to survive (and even to prosper). Sen's (1981, p. 154) basic objection to FAD is that 'it does not go into the relationship of people to food'. Given that food, like income, is unequally distributed at the best of times, no famine affects all members of a population identically:

> The Food Availability Decline (FAD) approach . . . says little about who is dying, *where* they are dying and *why*. It fails to answer the cruelest irony: 'why is it that producers of food are the first and most seriously affected by drought and famine and why do so few town dwellers die from hunger while rural areas are decimated by starvation and death?' (Bush, 1985a, p. 61.)

Third, for FAD to be convincing the analysis must assume a closed economy (given that a food deficit is defined in the context of a bounded famine region). While historical famines may well have been caused by lack of food following a local crop failure, nowadays there is no necessary reason why a drought or crop blight should result in famine. Such a 'theory' explains only a production disruption; it is unable to explain why a local food deficit is not offset by inflows of food from surplus regions elsewhere. In the modern world, a food availability decline becomes a famine only if there is no compensating intervention by traders, the government or an outside agency.

Kumar (1985, p. 1) provides an empirical example, in an analysis of the extent to which a decline in food production might explain the recent Ethiopian famines. Kumar accepts the World Development Report (1984) estimate that per capita food production in Ethiopia fell by 18 per cent from 1969–71 to 1982, but notes that other countries fared even worse. Over the same period, this statistic fell

> by 27% in Portugal, by 25% in Algeria and by no less than 38% in Trinidad and Tobago. Yet none of these countries has faced starvation and the explanation must lie principally in their ability to expand economic activity so as to import sufficient food to distribute to the population. Therefore, in assessing a country's capacity to feed itself, an analysis of its ability to expand its own food output faster than its population growth is less important than an analysis of its overall ability to command enough food.

The urgent need to dismiss FAD as 'bad theory' is further demonstrated by the fact that food production per capita in the developing countries as a whole has risen steadily since at least the 1940s, yet famines have continued to occur. Although Africa is an exception to this trend, famines occurred in south-east Asia during this period as well, where per capita food production has not been falling.

Famine rarely happens in wealthy countries, not just because the population is wealthier and protected by social security, but also because markets are more integrated and economies more open. A combination of supply *and* demand factors explains the non-occurrence of famines in contemporary Western Europe and North America. Similarly, both supply *and* demand factors explain the persistence of famines in the Third World. The victims do tend to be poor, of course, but they also tend to live in isolated rural communities, where markets behave sluggishly at the best of times, and where supplies of food are highly volatile and determined more by local climatic and environmental factors than by the equilibration of supply and demand across the entire country. It follows that the most damning criticism of FAD theory is that it diverts attention from possibly the most salient fact of all – that famine is first and foremost a problem of poverty and inequality:

> Famine, a short-term phenomenon, is inescapably linked to persistent long-term poverty. Rich people don't starve. The idea of famines wiping out whole societies,

> as though the consequences of bad weather were meted out in equal measure to all, is far-fetched and can usually be traced to sensationalist history writing rather than a real record of what happened. . . . Even in famines there is always some food. Who has ever seen a starving military officer or merchant, let alone aid worker? It is a question of who has access to that food. (ICIHI, 1985, p. 63)

This perspective raises searching political questions – questions that FAD studiously avoids. As Sen (1982, p. 459) argues, 'the food problem is not concerned just with the availability of food but with the disposition of food. That involves economics, politics and even law . . . There is, indeed, no such thing as an apolitical food problem.'

3.3   Famine theory: multiplicity and simplicity

Famine victims are not well served by famine theory. Too many explanations overlook the complex web of factors which set people up for disaster, and focus instead on the most obvious and immediate symptoms of food crisis. This leads to correspondingly simplistic relief interventions, such as emergency food aid, which may save lives but entrenches vulnerability to future crises.

It might seem paradoxical that theories of famine have been so plentiful and yet so inadequate. One reason for this is that (published) famine theorizing spans at least three centuries, during which the world has undergone profound changes. Early observers of famine lived in a world in which opportunities for trade in food were relatively limited and where a local failure of food production might well be sufficient cause for starvation.

Malthus, for example, lived in England at a time when it seemed inevitable that population growth on his island would eventually exceed any possible increases in agricultural output. The international grain trade and aid flows of today could not possibly have been foreseen. The prevalence of small units of economic organization in those days, without extensive and integrated markets, may provide sufficient reason for the dominance, until recently, of supply-side theories of famine. Even now, it remains the case that those most vulnerable to famine live in communities where obtaining food is the result of their own productive activities, whose trading activities are mostly limited to local exchanges, and whose links with the wider world are very restricted. Poverty and isolation leave them very vulnerable to local fluctuations in production and prices.

None the less, the revolutions in agriculture and transport during the nineteenth and twentieth centuries, which have made it possible to produce and distribute food on a global scale with unprecedented speed and ease, also generated the conditions in which a new theory of famine was required – one which emphasizes failure of access to food as a dominant cause of famine. Despite its limitations, Sen's entitlement approach arguably constitutes this new theory, a framework on which future famine theorists will build.

This recent about-face in famine theory has happened much more abruptly than the socioeconomic and political processes which necessitated it. The development of famine theory has lagged way behind changes in the scale and organization of economic activity, and in the structures and capacity of political systems and international institutions. While these were evolving very rapidly, particularly during this century, our understanding of famine stagnated. We were stuck with Malthusian and climatic simplifications even though societies had grown more complex and interrelated. 'Single cause' explanations are no longer valid, but no one has yet suggested a 'multiple cause' model which incorporates all the factors that combine to create famine conditions and yet is useful outside academia as well.

A related reason for the multiplicity of theory arises from the extent to which observers have brought a disciplinary bias to their writings – anthropology, climatology, economics, epidemiology, geography, political science, to name a few. This has resulted in a proliferation of 'single factor' explanations of famine, a fact that seriously inhibits our understanding of famine as a complex phenomenon:

> The major shortcoming of the literature on famine . . . lies in the incompleteness and one-sidedness of explanation, and in particular the failure to show how different factors in practice interrelate to produce the mechanism of famine in different kinds of famine situation. Existing studies tend to deal only with those particular aspects that fall within the professional discipline of the author.
> (UNRISD, 1976, p. 6.)

As a generalization, which view individual writers hold tends to be compatible with the discipline in which they were trained. If an economist writes about famine, then famine is caused by market failure or lack of purchasing power. If a climatologist writes about famine, then famine is caused by drought or desertification. When a Marxist sociologist explains famine, colonialism and international capitalism are to blame.

In addition to disciplinary bias, ideology has played its part too. Within most categories of explanation there has been a 'right-wing/left-wing' debate. On the right, food supply shocks are characterized as acts of nature, the fault of the victims, or of ignorant, corrupt and despotic Third World governments. The left generally emphasizes demand-side factors and, in particular, the powerlessness and exploitation of poorer classes and communities (through colonialism, the market, uneven development processes and so on). The result has been an unhealthy and unnecessary polarization of views, with each side denying the validity of anything the other says, rather than a serious attempt to synthesize the best arguments of each camp into a holistic theoretical framework.

A final reason for the multiplicity of famine theory is that many explanations which have been offered are descriptions of causes, rather than systematic theories. (As a banal example, 'drought causes famines' is only true for those famines where drought played a role.) The most cursory examination of any famine reveals it to be a complex phenomenon which cannot be adequately explained by one single factor. Conversely, multiple explanations have often been offered without relating them to an underlying theory. However valuable and illuminating many of these insights have been, they have resulted in a large body of fragmented literature which is now extremely difficult to synthesize.

3.4   Towards a taxonomy of famine theories

There have been a number of attempts to impose order on the chaos of famine theory. Most 'taxonomies' have evident difficulty in dealing with the diversity of theory in a neat, categorical manner. This is to be expected, since the theories divide along various ideological, disciplinary and conceptual lines (as discussed above), and often overlap with each other.

Dando's (1980, p. 87) famine typology, while not an attempt to classify theories, does provide a framework for analyzing the causes of particular food crises. He describes 'five basic famine types':

1. *Physical* famines occur 'in regions where the physical environment was naturally hostile to intensive forms of sedentary agriculture but man developed techniques which enabled him to temper natural hazards in all but their extreme form'.
2. *Transportation* famines occur 'in highly urbanized, commercial or industrial food deficit regions dependent upon distant food sources and supplied normally by a well developed transportation system'.
3. *Cultural* famines occur 'in food surplus regions induced by archaic social systems, cultural practices and overpopulation'.
4. *Political* famines occur 'in regions that are nominally self-sufficient in basic food stuffs but where regional politics or regional political systems determine food production, food distribution and food availability'.
5. *Overpopulation* famines occur 'in drought-prone or flood-prone, over-populated, marginal agricultural regions with primitive agricultural systems, whose inhabitants' perennial food intake was only slightly above starvation levels'.

The virtue of Dando's taxonomy is that it allows different famines to be explained by different causes, rather than insisting on a single dominant theory which should be applied to all famines, at all times and in all places. This means that it avoids disciplinary and (to a lesser extent) ideological bias. By focusing on social systems (rather than social sciences!), it isolates the sources of vulnerability to food shortage which different communities might face. The limitation is that it isolates various disruptions in food *supplies*, thereby supporting a 'FAD' view of famine causation.

Table 3.1 A taxonomy of famine theories

1. **Food Availability Decline** (FAD)
   1.1 Population increase (Malthus)
   1.2 War
   1.3 Climatic factors

2. **Ecological Mismanagement**

3. **Socioeconomic and Political Dislocation** in the Course of 'Change' or Development

4. **Economic Theories**
   4.1 Market failure (Alamgir)
   4.2 Exchange entitlements (Sen)

5. **Government Mismanagement** / Political or Institutional Failure

6. **Anthropological or Sociological Explanations**

7. **Multi-causal or Eclectic Approaches**

Source: Compiled from Leftwich and Harvie (1986, pp. 29–35).

Leftwich and Harvie's (1986) taxonomy (Table 3.1) categorizes theories along mainly disciplinary lines. It is interesting that they include war, along with population and climate, under 'food availability decline' approaches. This taxonomy does not distinguish between immediate events or 'famine triggers' and longer-term processes such as 'socieconomic and political dislocation in the course of "change" or development'. Perhaps such distinctions are impossible in a single list of causal factors, so that a robust and useful classification is not possible at all.

Downing (personal communication) suggests that it might be useful to categorize partial theories and explanations of famine along a set of 'continua', recognizing the alternative views that have been taken by various observers. A slight adaptation of his ideas produces the following dichotomies:

Natural disasters	Social processes
Declining natural resource endowments	Declining political/economic influence
Transitory food shocks	Increasing vulnerability
National/regional analysis	Household/individual analysis
Supply failure	Demand failure

To the above might be added the distinction between 'precipitating factors' and 'underlying processes'. Sen (1982, p. 447) focuses on one of these dichotomies and identifies two sets of approaches to 'the food problem':

> One group emphasises the natural sciences and engineering, and relates the food issue to technological issues of various kinds. The other group concentrates on

social issues, including political economy, and sees the food problem primarily in social terms. At the risk of oversimplification, the two classes of approach may be called 'nature-focussed' and 'society-focussed', respectively.

Each of these taxomonies and dichotomies attempts to impose a logic on the major lines along which famine theory has moved and continues to develop. They provide maps to guide the reader through a labyrinth of argument and debate. However, none of them is entirely satisfactory. An alternative taxonomy of famine theories or explanations is not offered here, although the structure of this book might imply one. Part 2 discusses what might strictly be called 'famine theory'. The theories discussed are climatic, demographic (Malthusian), and economic ('entitlements' and market failure).

Vulnerability to events that precipitate famine is profoundly influenced by social and political processes. Part 3, therefore, considers the political economy of famine – the 'mismanagement' or over-exploitation of natural resources, unfavourable patterns of development leading to marginalization for some groups, inappropriate or malign government policies, the impact of war and refugees, and the international trade and aid dimension. These factors add layers of explanation to the formal demographic, climatic and economic theories, and are, therefore, equally important. In most cases, several 'underlying processes' or political events act in combination with the factors identified by the theorists to produce famine conditions, so ignoring them simply because they do not fit neatly into any one theory is a recipe for partial understanding and misguided policy interventions.

PART 2
Theories of famine

4

Climate and famine

A drought on a desert island is no disaster, nor is a flood in an uninhabited mountain valley. It is the relationships between humans and these trigger events which determine whether a disaster will occur, and, if so, how big it will be.

Lloyd Timberlake (1985, p. 20)

The path from drought (or flood) to crop failure to starvation is so simple and direct that, in the popular imagination, 'drought equals famine', at least for many recent African tragedies, and nothing more need be said. In this chapter we do not deny the observed association between climate-induced crop failure and many (but not all) famines. Instead, we challenge the credentials of climate as an adequate 'theory', and place it in context as an important factor, rather than overriding determinant, of famine causation.

4.1   Climate and 'natural famine regions'

Since famine is so frequently associated with 'natural disasters', it is hardly surprising that a large literature exists which explicitly ascribes famine to crop failure following a major climatic 'perturbation', such as drought or flood. Geographers, climatologists and other physical scientists have taken the lead in ascribing famines to the vagaries of the earth's climate. A common theme during the 1970s was the suggestion that climate produces 'natural famine regions'. Cox (1981, p. 8) describes two global 'famine belts':

One, extending from the British Isles across Europe and Soviet Russia to northern China, corresponds to a region in which food production failures may occur because of dampness, cold, and shortened growing seasons. The second, extending from Africa and the Mediterranean Littoral eastward through the dry and monsoon lands to China, is a belt of drought-induced famine.

These explanations, which are now regarded as rather outdated, saw climate as a 'fixed boundary condition'; an exogenous factor over which people had little or no control:

> As such, climate was considered a major, if not dominant, constraint to economic and social development in many locations around the world. The view was that either a region received enough rain for agricultural production and yields and production would be high, or it did not and production would be low and erratic. (Glantz, 1987, p. 1)

The 'famine belts' theory can be immediately critiqued as incomplete. Why do famines not occur in some 'drought belt' countries, such as those in the Middle East, which share a proneness to low and variable rainfall with countries in the Horn of Africa and the Sahel? In this context, it is illuminating that Cox (1981) explains the virtual elimination of famine in the northern 'famine belt' during this century in terms of the modernization of transport infrastructure, together with greater government capacity to intervene to buffer food production variability. This reference to the evolution of transport and political structures tacitly concedes that climate alone may not be a sufficient explanation for famine. But Cox does not hold out much hope that this progress towards famine elimination will continue:

> The world may well be emerging from a half-century moratorium on famines triggered primarily by climatic factors. . . . This period of favorable conditions and relative adequacy may now be at an end . . . The specter of famine appears again to be with us. (Cox, 1981, p. 5)

Until the mid-1980s, climatic prophets of doom like Cox believed that vulnerability to famine was likely to increase world-wide because of 'ecological imbalances' brought about by massive climatic changes, notably the *cooling* of the northern hemisphere, which 'has been implicated as a possible causal mechanism of drought in the Sahelian Zone of Africa' (*ibid.*, p. 9). Dando (1980, p. 104) extends the argument to suggest that transfers of food from surplus producers in the northern hemisphere to deficit regions will disappear, leading to global shortages. 'The earth is cooling . . . Small changes in climatic variables produce significant environmental changes for food production and also reduce North America's ability to provide food relief in times of famine.'

This argument is unconvincing, and has in any event been superseded by the contradictory 'global warming' theory (which, curiously, offers very similar prognoses; see below). Even if 'global cooling' were true, though, the apocalyptic conclusion does not necessarily follow. Commentators who pursue purely climatic explanations fail to distinguish between the climatic crisis of drought and the socioeconomic crisis of famine. No famine can be explained by its trigger factor alone, particularly something as 'scientific' (that is, removed from its social, economic and political context) as a drought. Drought causes crop failure; but *vulnerability* to drought causes famine.

The 1985 ICIHI report on famine in Africa also seeks associations between the incidence of famine and changes in climate, but is more circumspect in its projections. Addressing the debate over whether declining rainfall in the Sahel is permanent or cyclical, it notes that predictions drawn from the evidence of less than two decades are highly controversial. 'Obviously, there has been a lot less rain than usual in the last few years but whether that marks the low point of a normal cycle, or is indeed a break with all past weather patterns is still open to doubt' (ICIHI, 1985, p. 82). Those who believe that the downturn in rainfall is permanent have expressed grave concern about the predicament of people living in the dryland farming areas of sub-Saharan Africa, south Asia, and South America. 'Scientists' forecasts agree broadly about a trend for this decade and the next, and likely to push into the 21st century. Droughts will probably turn into famines more often' (Torry, 1986, p. 201).

In the late 1980s, growing awareness of the phenomenon of 'global warming' produced a resurgence of climatic determinism: 'likely changes to the environment, particularly in global climate, could affect millions of our fellow human beings: how they live, where they live, whether they live' (Tickell, 1989, p. 3). Whereas writers on 'global cooling' predicted a direct negative link between weather changes and food production, 'global warming' pundits concentrate on the demographic consequences of rising sea levels.

> the expected rise of the sea level because of global warming threatens to reduce the planet's habitable area on a grand scale, perhaps forcing the evacuation of low-lying cities and agricultural land throughout the world. . . . The 1-meter increase projected over the next century will displace millions of people in the delta regions of the Nile and Ganges rivers, for instance, exacerbating land scarcity in the already densely populated nations of Egypt and Bangladesh. (Jacobson, 1988, p. 6 and p. 7)

What is new and more urgent about this wave of anxiety is the recognition that human actions have a great deal to do with the 'greenhouse effect', the destruction of the ozone layer and so on. An added imperative is provided by the fact that climatic changes (specifically, rising temperatures and sea levels) are happening extremely rapidly, perhaps faster than human capacity to control or respond to them. What is predictable and conventional about these very valid concerns is the fact that, as always with predictions of climatic catastophe, the 'specter of famine' is invoked. Threats to human survival are expressed in terms of threats to global food production.

> those dependent on such annual events as the monsoon or summer rains might find new irregularities in the weather system. Recent droughts in the Sahel have illustrated the vulnerability of people living in or on the fringes of arid zones, and

current population levels might prove unsustainable. The present temperate areas, where most of the world's industry and agricultural production now lie, would not escape. The food surpluses which at present act as a buffer stock to cope with deficits elsewhere, could disappear quickly. (Tickell, 1989, pp. 12–13)

But the immediate threat to agricultural production and food security would come from the creation of millions of environmental refugees, dispossessed of their land by the sea, and with nowhere to go to start farming again. With agricultural surpluses reduced or eliminated in countries such as the United States, feeding these displaced millions would be impossible, and mortality rates from starvation and diseases would be high. In this 'worst-case' scenario, famine would be a secondary rather than primary consequence of global warming, with social disruption preceding rather than following food crises.

4.2   Drought and famine

Drought can be defined from a variety of perspectives, including meteorological, agricultural and economic. Glantz (1987, p. 15) defines meteorological drought as 'a specified percentage reduction in precipitation over a given period of time', and he quantifies this as a 25 per cent fall in a region's long-term annual average rainfall. An agricultural drought can be defined as 'the lack of adequate soil moisture to sustain crop growth and production' (Wang'ati, quoted in Glantz, 1987, p. 15). 'This requires a certain distribution (not just a total amount) of moisture throughout the growing season' (Hansen, 1986, p. 231). From an economic perspective, drought occurs when rainfall deficits result in a shortage of those economic goods (mainly crops and animals) which depend on rainfall. Finally, recognizing the fact that droughts are deviations from a norm, Rasmusson (1987, p. 8) proposes a relativistic rather than absolutist definition:

Drought implies an extended and negative departure in rainfall, relative to the regime around which society has stabilised. Thus, drought conditions in one region may be considered normal conditions in a more arid region, or during a more arid epoch.

Apart from the purely 'scientific', meteorological definition, it is notable that drought is usually related to human activities. In this sense, droughts in the unpopulated parts of the world are not considered to be relevant or significant at all. 'Drought is defined in terms of human needs' (Hansen, 1986, p. 232). The road from drought to famine follows from this 'people-centred' conceptualization. Drought is perceived as a 'natural' event; famine as its human consequence.

There are a number of ways in which a drought (or flood) exposes a community's vulnerability. Its immediate effect is to reduce food production, but its impacts on employment opportunities and on food and asset prices are equally significant. Crow (1986, p. 6) sketches these three routes from crop failure to the threat of starvation:

Climatically-induced reductions in output may affect a household's ability to get food by:
(i) reducing their own production (and any sales thereof);
(ii) reducing their ability to get cash or kind wages through work;
(iii) reducing the purchasing power of what wages they do get (and assets they have accumulated) by raising the price they have to pay for food.

But starvation and death do not follow immediately, if at all. Lacking food or the resources to buy sufficient food, drought-afflicted individuals still have a number of ways of ensuring their survival (such as gathering wild foods, borrowing and rationing). Droughts are not unforeseen events which catch vulnerable people totally unawares:

To the extent that drought is recurrent throughout the Sudanic savannas and that rainfall variability is part of the climatic order of events, it is to be expected that those who depend directly on the land for their livelihood demonstrate a sound knowledge and judgment of climatic variability and environmental risk. (Watts, 1987, p. 180)

Farmers and pastoralists in semi-arid areas have devised a range of sophisticated adaptive responses, insurance mechanisms and coping strategies which prevent all but the most severe and protracted droughts progressing towards outright famine. 'These strategies, tactics, and mechanisms intervene between drought (or any other perturbation) and famine (or any other calamitous outcomes)' (Hansen, 1986, p. 239). The danger of *prolonged* drought is that these strategies will be exhausted before the next adequate harvest comes in.

The Sahelian and Ethiopian famines of the early 1970s, for example, were preceded by five to seven years of consecutive poor harvests, the result of unusually catastrophic droughts. These lasted several years, from 1968 to 1973, during which the watertable dropped, thousands of wells dried up and Lake Chad shrank to one-third of its normal size (El-Hinnawi, 1985, p. 10). In this famine, the chain of causality from drought through crop failure to cattle death, human hunger, mass migration and mortality seems irrefutable.

In our view, however, the drought does not explain the Sahelian famine by itself. Later in this book (see Chapter 9), this famine is discussed as a case study in political marginalization and uneven economic development, processes which combined to 'set people up' for the drought when it came. These factors are more helpful in understanding the determinants of vulnerability to famine in the Sahel than a focus on 'nature' in isolation. None the less, it is certainly true that, following the 1970s famines, low rainfall continued throughout the next decade, leading up to the food crises of the mid-1980s:

The Sahel countries have experienced continued rainfall shortages over the past fifteen years. In 1983 and 1984 they recorded their lowest total for a century. . . . As the desert advances, river beds dry up, making irrigation impossible. This, together with the lowering of the water table and the continuing drought, renders agricultural production untenable. This in turn sharpens the competition for land, family labour inputs and other available resources between export crops and food crops. Prolonged drought undermines the adaptive and adjustive mechanisms of the people and the ecology, leading to famine. (Nnoli, 1990, pp. 132–3)

As Nnoli suggests, several years of drought, or a secular decline in rainfall, also speed up processes of soil erosion and desertification. In western Sudan, as throughout the Sahel, these effects interact with each other, so that short-term climatic events (droughts) are magnified by and accelerate the longer-term processes (land degradation):

Water limits economic opportunity like no other environmental factor, and rainfall deficits have been the norm for 18 years running. Aggravated by degrading soils and retreating climax vegetation, drought effects have reached a new benchmark. Drought affecting rainfed farmers and herders will result in food crises as never before. (Torry, 1986, p. 219)

Worse still, a vicious cycle often develops between drought and human activities (a theme that is taken up in Chapter 9). Drought caused by 'natural' rainfall variability induces agricultural and pastoral responses which, by undermining the physical environment and contributing to desertification, in turn produces droughts which are of 'man-made' origin.

The extent of human influence is controversial, but the possibility that current droughts are another example of man-modified environments undercuts the 'naturalness' of drought and the utility of continuing an arbitrary separation of crises according to their supposedly natural or social causes. (Hansen, 1986, p. 232)

So we must conclude that there is an evident association between climate and famine, but whether droughts and floods are a *sufficient* explanation of famine is another matter. Sceptics acknowledge the importance of climatic perturbations as a 'trigger' for many famines, but argue that such explanations are superficial. The attraction of climatic theories lies in their simplicity. As Dando (1980, p. 59) points out: 'Meteorological factors ... are more readily understood than social causes of famine.' This point is developed by UNRISD (1976, p. 1).

though a natural disaster may well be the triggering cause of a famine, the reason why a famine results from the natural disaster is the inadequacy of the socio-economic system concerned to cope with the occasional or unusual harshness of the natural conditions. To consider famines simply as natural disasters manifests a fatalistic tendency to place the whole responsibility upon nature when in fact society itself, by the manner in which it exercises control over natural resources and access to food supplies, is a prime contributor.

Woldemariam (1984, pp. 125–6) offers two arguments against the equation of drought and famine. First, he notes that drought occurs in the southern

United States, Britain and other industrialized countries, yet '[t]hese countries are free from the menace of famine today.' Second, there are many Third World countries where drought is 'a permanent condition', but permanent famine does not ensue because the local people have adapted to these harsh conditions. 'It appears, therefore, that drought alone does not explain famine . . . It is only under certain conditions that drought can become one of the factors of famine.'

Although a major drought occurs in the United States approximately every twenty years, 'American farmers don't starve, their politicians and bank managers see to that' (ICIHI, 1985, p. 64). Just as wealthy individuals are rarely victims of famine, so wealthy countries can buy their way out of disasters like drought and crop failure. 'The political unacceptability of famine in the United States ensures that provision is made to cover the costs of calamity by spreading it through the tax system and by ensuring government supervision of agriculture and conservation' (Bush, 1985a, p. 111).

Hay (1986, pp. 76–7) sees the 'preoccupation with drought' as one of many analytical defects which obscure the true causes of the African famines of the 1970s and 1980s:

> The droughts which have plagued Africa during the last decade are not new. Their effects are, however, unprecedented. . . . The preoccupation with drought as an exceptional event drew attention away from the more important underlying processes which were and are at work and which inevitably and inexorably work their way out into the open as increasingly serious famines during years when rainfall was less than average.

A 1984 report for Oxfam makes the point that drought-induced famines in the Sahel are rarely associated with aggregate shortages of food: 'the Sahel's primary crisis even in drought years is not one of production, but of distribution' (Twose, 1984, p. 12). It is not the incidence or severity of drought that is increasing in the Sahel, but the vulnerability of certain groups of people to the effects of drought: 'although droughts themselves are not unexpected and do not appear to be getting more serious, the ability of large sections of the population to cope is declining' (*ibid.*, p. 19).

Hansen (1986, p. 234) argues that, in Africa, 'drought is not the singular cause of famine but only one of several contributing factors.' Woldemariam (1984, pp. 127–9) believes that there is a causal chain of processes leading up to a famine, of which drought is often, but not always, one element. A drought may or may not cause crop failure, which may or may not result in food shortage, which may or may not be alleviated by supplies from elsewhere:

> Even if it is established that drought invariably precedes famine, we cannot from this conclude that drought and famine are causally related. What begs for explanation is the period between the time when drought is recognised and the commencement of the period of starvation. It is this period of waiting passively that *allows* the process of famine to develop to its full capacity of destruction.

The direct link between drought and famine has been broken in areas where societies have become less isolated and self-sufficient, as in northern Nigeria. 'Early in this century a widespread drought was much more likely to result in famine, but improved transportation (especially long-distance trucking) later permitted the importation of food from other areas' (Hansen, 1986, p. 234).

More generally, theories of famine that persist in privileging the drought-famine linkage have overlooked the rapid incorporation this century of even the remotest rural communities into nation-states and global economic and political networks. These theories are lagging behind reality. They reflect a conceptual myopia that sees no human intervention between drought and famine. Drought *may* be an act of nature, but famine is decidedly an act of man. So, simply stating that droughts or floods cause famine is not a *theory* of famine – it is only a description of one factor in a string of possible causes of famine. 'Famine is not a natural phenomenon. It is not always preceded by a drought although a relative change in the climate may act as a "trigger" for the *possibility* of famine. Famine is *man* made' (Bush, 1985b, p. 9).

On the other hand, just because drought is not *invariably* associated with famine does not mean that drought and famine are not causally related. Droughts which struck most continents in 1982–3 were followed by famines only in those countries – all in Africa – which were most *vulnerable* to drought (Glantz, 1987, p. 3). Elsewhere, reviewing two books which take a 'social' or 'political' approach to natural disasters and the problem of desertification, Bush (1985a, p. 59) observes that 'it is the poor who suffer most from drought . . . we need to *explain* why drought becomes famine and why certain sections of the population, and why some communities rather than others, suffer most from it.'

The key factor emerging here is vulnerability. 'Starvation, therefore, must be seen as an economic, social and political problem and not only as a problem of food production and drought. It has become evident that what were generally considered "natural disasters" are not strictly natural any more' (Lemma, 1985, p. 45). In the modern world, 'natural' disasters are, properly speaking, 'social' disasters, in that they reflect differential abilities to cope with crises. Bush (1985a, p. 61) echoes the case against naive 'catastrophe' explanations of famine: 'it is the interaction between people and their natural environment (the way that they respond to, create and shape their "ecosystem") that determines the possible causes and effects of famine.'

4.3   Seasonality, vulnerability and famine

Two ecological characteristics dominate the environmental context of famine: seasonality of climate and major reliance by human populations upon subsistence and local market food production systems. Virtually all naturally-triggered famines have occurred in regions which combine strongly seasonal patterns of temperature or moisture with a high degree of variability of these factors from year to year.

(Cox, 1981, p. 6)

There is a direct connection between seasonality and vulnerability to hunger. Climatic seasonality is most pronounced in semi-arid rural areas where rainfall distribution is unimodal or bimodal, so that only one or two harvests are possible each year, each being highly dependent on an adequate quantity and favourable distribution of rain. Where food reserves are low, one or two consecutive crop failures can lead directly to starvation for those who cannot afford to buy food. Of course, critical shortages would not arise if surpluses could be accumulated over two or three years. But grain and other foodcrops are perishable, and on-farm storage methods in Africa and Asia are not very efficient, so that post-harvest losses are significant. Mortimore (1989, p. 32) goes so far as to conclude that '[f]amine is really about the failure of storage.'

Production seasonality translates into economic seasonality through the market mechanism. Food and asset prices move counter-cyclically through the year, so that the value of assets is lowest during the annual 'hungry season', when the need for food is greatest. A clear indicator of a household's relative food security is the extent to which it is subject to the economic pressures created by climatic seasonality. Poor farmers who need cash for obligations such as taxes will be forced to sell some of their produce immediately after a harvest, even if they are left without enough food to get through the 'hungry season'. Spitz (1980) describes this dilemma within poor self-provisioning households as a conflict between 'the forces of extraction' and 'the forces of retention'. Conversely, wealthier farmers and traders with surplus cash can profit from seasonality by buying up grain at low post-harvest prices and selling it back to the poor later in the year, when market supplies of food are much reduced and prices have doubled or trebled.

Seasonality increases both the power of the wealthy and the dependence and vulnerability of the poor. Low granary reserves just before a harvest induce 'distress sales' of assets by the poor to raise money for food, initiating a decline in their stocks of wealth which can become a 'poverty ratchet': 'an irreversible downward movement into deeper poverty as assets are mortgaged or sold without hope of recovery' (Chambers *et al.*, 1981, p. 5). Among these assets is labour power, and poor people are frequently forced by 'seasonal hunger' to work for food or cash in the fields of wealthier farmers, neglecting their own farms as a result. This process of gradual dispossession of peasant resources exposes their vulnerability to an acute extent:

Short of outright starvation and death, the most serious effects of seasonal stress are processes in which the stress incurred during one season (and especially one of drought or other disaster) leads to a reduction in the control by the peasant family over its means of production, thus adversely affecting its ability to withstand the stress incurred in subsequent seasons. (Raikes, 1981, p. 69)

A poor community with limited reserves can easily slide into food crisis – especially the poorer elements of that community – if the harvest fails. Recent research suggests that the distinction between 'seasonal hunger' and famine is blurred rather than discrete. During a particularly severe 'hungry season', poor families have been observed to follow the same sequence of responses as entire communities do during major famines, up to and including 'distress migration' (Campbell and Trechter, 1982; Watts, 1983). Perhaps the real distinction between seasonality and famine, therefore, is simply scale of impact.

In summary, the 'hungry season' is often a precursor to famine, and it may continue to perform this role in Sahelian Africa in future. But agricultural seasonality itself is not a 'cause' of famine; rather, by perpetuating low productivity, indebtedness, chronic malnutrition and morbidity among the rural poor, it increases *vulnerability* to famine. As Chambers *et al.* (1981, p. 223) succinctly state: 'seasonality presents contexts which bring poverty to periodic crises.'

4.4   Conclusion

Theories of famine based exclusively on catastrophic climatic events have been subjected to considerable criticism. None the less, seasonality continues to undermine household food security, and drought regularly triggers food crises, particularly in sub-Saharan Africa. Climate cannot therefore be totally ignored.

Three conclusions have emerged from the above discussion, which help to place the role of climate in perspective. The first is that climatic shocks are neither a necessary nor a sufficient cause of famine. Droughts occur without famine and famines occur without droughts.

Second, for drought to cause famine, many other conditions must simultaneously be fulfilled. For instance, vulnerability to drought is maximized where livelihoods are directly dependent on stable and sufficient rainfall. Self-provisioning food producers in drought-prone areas are often most at risk. Conversely, factory workers in Birmingham, or academics in Cambridge, do not suffer hunger following a failure of the year's rains. Also, in common with other theories that focus on food supplies, the 'drought equals famine' equation implies isolation from sources of subsistence beyond the drought zone – remittance income, national food markets, multilateral food aid. Famine is not only about the failure of food production; it is also about the failure of 'coping strategies' and other alternative sources of food.

The third conclusion is that academic approaches to famine causation are less polarized than in the past. A consensus is emerging which favours an integrated, multi-causal explanation of famine. This holistic view explicitly recognizes the strong links between 'natural' and 'man-made' or 'ecological' and 'political' factors – or, to return to Sen's terminology, 'nature-focused' and 'society-focused' approaches – instead of separating them into competing camps or theories. One such interdisciplinary approach is 'climate impact assessment'. It developed out of geography, climatology and human ecology, and attempts to integrate the analysis of climatic events (or 'natural hazards') with their human consequences, as Downing (personal communication) explains:

> The usual paradigm describes the state of the environment (an event like a flash flood, an episode such as a drought, or a process such as soil erosion) in terms of its frequency of occurrence and magnitude. The 'event' is related to ongoing processes and impacts in the biogeochemical cycles (nature and agriculture). Human societies and populations are described in terms of their vulnerability to perturbations, perception of hazards, and responses (both long-term adaptations and short-term adjustments).

While retaining a focus on the contribution of 'nature' to famine causation, this approach avoids the simplifications of earlier 'scientific' explanations of famine, and must therefore be welcomed. More bridges still need to be built, though, between the physical and social sciences, if famine is to be completely understood and then comprehensively defeated.

5

The population monster

Some people are going to have to starve. . . . We're in the position of a family that owns a litter of puppies: we've got to decide which ones to drown.

US Secretary of Agriculture, 1946[1]

'Too many mouths to feed' ranks alongside climatic shocks as one of the most enduring popular explanations for famine. Malthus's theory of demographic dynamics was perhaps the first coherent theory of famine causation to be advanced. Like 'drought equals famine' and other supply-side arguments, conventional Malthusianism is currently unfashionable. However, neo-Malthusian refinements of the original propositions have some explanatory power, as will be seen.

5.1   Malthusian theory

The best introduction to Malthusian approaches to poverty, famines and population control remains the famous passage from which the entire school of thought evolved. Explaining his 'Principle of Population', Malthus (1798, quoted in Dando, 1980, p. 59) suggested two 'postulata':

First, that food is necessary to the existence of man. Secondly, that the passion between the sexes is necessary, and will remain nearly in its present state. . . .
Assuming, then, my postulata as granted, I say, that the power of population is indefinitely greater than the power in the earth to produce subsistence for man. Population, when unchecked, increases in a geometrical ratio. Subsistence increases only in an arithmetical ratio. A slight acquaintance with numbers will

show the immensity of the first power as compared with the second. By that law of our nature which makes food necessary to the life of man, the effects of these two unequal powers must be kept equal. This implies a strong and constantly operating check on population from the difficulty of subsistence.

Although Malthus's view of the world now seems rather naive, his theory retains some influence in contemporary policy-making, partly because of its attractive simplicity. The mathematics of the argument is that food production can increase at most by an arithmetical progression (1, 2, 3, 4, 5 . . .), while population simultaneously increases in a geometrical progression (1, 2, 4, 8, 16 . . .), such that population increase rapidly outstrips food production growth. There is no empirical basis for this argument, and Malthus's own obviously 'slight acquaintance with numbers' has led many writers to dismiss his pseudo-precision as merely a numbers game. Sen (1982, p. 448) describes Malthus's 'particular fascination' with arithmetic and geometric progressions as 'an attempt to get profound insights from elementary mathematics – a tendency not altogether unknown in modern economics as well'.

Malthus's postulata opposed an earlier viewpoint, as expressed by the French Physiocrats, that population growth would actually *increase* the agricultural surplus. The larger the population, they argued, the larger the aggregate surplus that could be produced. Malthus's theory was based on the classical economists' theory of diminishing returns to labour, such that population growth would gradually reduce and ultimately eliminate the agricultural surplus per head. A fuller exposition of the basic Malthusian theory can be presented in five steps, as follows:[2]

1. Population and the demand for food increase at a parallel rate.
2. This rising demand for food can be satisfied either by more *extensive* cultivation (increasing the amount of land used for food production), or by more *intensive* cultivation (raising the output per unit of land already in use).
3. Land is both scarce and of variable quality. More fertile land is cultivated first, but population pressure causes less fertile land to be brought into cultivation, so that the marginal productivity of both land and labour declines as a result of *extensive* cultivation.
4. Attempts to increase output by *intensive* means – applying more labour to land in cultivation – will also fail. The marginal productivity of labour will fall, because of diminishing returns.
5. Because of these inevitable diminishing returns to both land and labour, food production will always grow at a slower rate than population. Eventually, these limitations on potential food production will act as a binding constraint on population growth, with famine being the mechanism of control.

By this logic, population must stabilize in the long run at the constrained equilibrium level, given a fixed level of resources and fixed technology – 'there is a maximum population size at which the net rate of population growth must be zero' (Watkins and Van de Walle, 1983, p. 7). A contemporary variant on this 'Malthusian equilibrium' argues that ecological systems respond to their environments in ways that maintain a balance between resources and requirements. Instead of over-exploiting their environment, natural populations practise sustainable resource utilization. In human societies, for example, cultural restraints such as abortion, contraception and China's 'one child family' policy control population growth, supposedly in recognition of the limitations on global food supply. Watkins and Van de Walle (1983, p. 8) explain the Malthusian underpinnings and implications of this argument:

> There are thus two equilibria: that between birth rates and death rates, and that between population size and resources. . . . Finely tuned homeostatic mechanisms permit a comfortable balance between prudent populations and their resources, a low-pressure equilibrium in which per capita resources are above, and perhaps well above, the minimum necessary for survival. Cruder versions of the story rely more heavily upon mortality to bring feckless populations back into line: they depict a high-pressure equilibrium in which per capita resources are close to the minimum necessary for survival, and in which the threat of starvation is ever present.
>
> In the systems of homeostatic adjustment mechanisms, it is only if neither impediments to the stream of births nor death rates from causes unrelated to resources are sufficient to maintain the necessary balances that appeal will be made to what is in effect Malthus' court of last resort: deaths from famine, or chronic mortality related to chronic scarcity. Malnutrition, then, is the logical ultimate constraint in the system of homeostatic mechanisms which has been postulated to keep a population within the bounds of its resources.

Contrary to Malthus's belief, however, recent empirical studies suggest that famines may not act as 'natural population checks' at all. For one thing, the numbers of people who actually die in famines, though tragic in human terms, is usually a very small proportion of the national or even local population. For another, the evidence strongly indicates that population in famine-afflicted regions returns fairly quickly to pre-famine levels. Demographic crises (famine, war, epidemics) trigger demographic responses – a post-crisis 'baby boom', or, in Bongaarts and Cain's (1982, p. 52) phrase, 'a compensatory surge in fertility'.

One factor explaining this is that the people most vulnerable during famines are the very young and the very old, while adults of reproductive age are most likely to survive. Field (1989, pp. 10–11) discusses three examples. Following the famines of Bengal 1943–4 and China 1958-61, populations recovered fully within two decades. 'Population was right back on trend line, even above it, as if the famine had not occurred.' The case of Bangladesh 1974 – a smaller famine in mortality terms – is even more dramatic:

The famine deaths in Bangladesh in 1974, 1.5 million (2% of the population), were outstripped by a population growth rate of 3%, meaning that these excess deaths were compensated for in less than one year. To the extent that overpopulation is a serious problem, famine is not a solution.

5.2   Critique and contra-Malthusian models

The two fundamental flaws in Malthus's reasoning were his failure to allow for technological improvements in agriculture, which would raise agricultural productivity and thereby offset diminishing returns to labour and land; and his failure to foresee the transport and communications revolutions, which would increase both the amount of land available for cultivation and the ease with which food could be traded from food surplus to food deficit countries.

The classical economists assumed decreasing returns to agriculture in the long run and increasing returns to manufacturing industry. This was only partly correct. 'They were right about the rate of increase of manufacturing output; had they applied the same reasoning to agriculture, their contribution would have been fully useful' (Perlman, 1982, p. 78). Neo-Malthusians do accept the potential for productivity-enhancing technical innovation in agriculture, but argue that this only delays the inevitable time when population exceeds the earth's physical capacity for feeding everyone.

Opposing Malthusian reductionism are various so-called 'contra-Malthusian' models, which argue (like the Physiocrats, but in a stronger form) that population growth actually *enhances* the potential for increases in food production per head. Boserup's theory is perhaps the best known of this type:

> In contrast to the models of the neo-Malthusians, Ester Boserup . . . argues that population, resources and technology are linked together in a progressive manner. Population pressure provides a useful economic stimulus to technical innovation. . . . Her claim is that population pressure is a general pre-condition for agricultural progress, and agricultural progress allows unprecedented levels of population concentration to be achieved. (Richards, 1983, p. 4)

Specifically, Boserup argues that the negative impact of diminishing returns is only one effect of population growth on agricultural production. The positive effect of population concentration is that it makes financially feasible investments in infrastructure (water and irrigation, energy and transport) and in improved production technologies, which would be uneconomical for a smaller population. These 'economies of scale' may more than offset the negative effects of decreasing returns to land and labour in agricultural production, as Ghatak and Ingersent (1984, p. 257) explain:

> As population pressure increases, progressively more intensive systems of land use

are adopted, combined with consequential changes in methods of cultivation and the choice of tools, in order to offset any tendency for food output per capita to decline, due to diminishing returns. In more formal terms, the model postulates that although in the short run there may be diminishing returns to agricultural labour, in the long run the aggregate agricultural production function will always shift upwards in response to population pressure, at whatever rate is required to maintain output per capita. The shift variable is agricultural technology, as expressed by the system of land use, the method of cultivation and the choice of tools. Thus Boserup explicitly rejects the classical notion of a *continuous* agricultural labour productivity function: in her view the true function is discontinuous and the reason for discontinuity is technological change.

In Boserup's own words (1983, p. 208): 'Malthusian and neo-Malthusian theories ... have overlooked or underestimated the positive effects which increasing population may have on infrastructural investment and techno-logical levels.' There is no basis, historically, for Malthusian pessimism: 'technological improvements promoted further population growth and further population growth promoted further technological improvements in a beneficial upward spiral, instead of the vicious downward spiral on which the Malthusian school focused its attention.'

Critics of this contra-Malthusian model question the behavioural assump-tions and the unidirectional causation behind the argument. They argue that Boserup's chronology of agrarian systems suggests an historical transition from communities with marked leisure preferences to more 'industrious' societies. 'Underlying this argument is the assumption that in primitive agriculture the motivation for work is the attainment of a fixed *income* target (with the income consisting primarily of food) rather than income (or utility) *maximisation*' (Ghatak and Ingersent, 1984, p. 259). In fact, there is little empirical evidence to suggest that people have 'fixed income' objectives, even in a 'subsistence' environment of relative or absolute poverty.

Two other criticisms of Boserup are often made. First, her model has greater plausibility in explaining how food production can increase along with population growth in a sparsely populated than a densely populated country, where the scope for increases in agricultural productivity is limited and is contingent on the fortuitous discovery and dissemination of technical innovations. Second, the costs of adopting such innovations in agriculture are not properly considered.

None the less, the general point which Boserup and others correctly emphasize is that Malthus's predictions simply failed to foresee the agricultural and transportation 'revolutions' which were soon to occur in Great Britain, which preceded and perhaps made possible the Industrial Revolution itself. Boserup's model focuses on improvements in land and labour productivity – raising the *intensity* of utilization of agricultural resources. It is also argued that Malthus underestimated the potential for *extensive* increases in food production, which was facilitated by the development of sophisticated transport and communications infrastructure. Not only did this enable population pressure in Great Britain to be relieved by migration to North America and the colonies, it also allowed specialization in production and trade, so that food deficit countries could import from food surplus trading partners to meet their consumption needs.

These points are easily made with the benefit of hindsight. A more technical criticism concerns the Malthusian assumption that land at the 'extensive margin' of cultivation is necessarily inferior in terms of fertility than land already being cultivated. In reality, improvements in transport, communications and agricultural technology have steadily reduced the costs of bringing previously inaccessible or uneconomic land into cultivation, at least in the West. In the Third World (Malawi, Tanzania, Zimbabwe and elsewhere), experiments with pan-territorial pricing have demonstrated that a prime constraint on agricultural production is not lack of fertile land, but poor marketing structures and the high costs of transporting produce to markets and cities. It follows that building roads and improving marketing infrastructure can provide more effective antidotes to famine vulnerability than attempts to limit population growth in isolated rural areas.

Finally, it should be noted that both the Malthusian and contra-Malthusian models have been accused of assuming a uni-directional (though opposite) causal relationship between population and food supply. Ghatak and Ingersent (1984, p. 265) suggest instead that the two factors work together in a mutually reinforcing way:

> Whereas Malthusians assume that an autonomous food supply growth rate (cause) limits population (effect), contra-Malthusians assume that an autonomous increase in population (cause) induces a corresponding increase in food supplies (effect). Uni-directional causation is open to the criticism that it rules out *feedback*. An alternative hypothesis is that as growing food supplies induce population expansion, so population growth induces further growth in food supplies. . . . A resolution of the opposing viewpoints of Malthusians and contra-Malthusians might be found in a model of this kind.

5.3   Neo-Malthusianism

Although Malthusian theory may appear to lack predictive or descriptive power in the modern world, neo-Malthusianism, in various guises, is alive and well. As Watkins and Van de Walle (1983, p. 7) explain: 'The notion of an equilibrium between population and resources is pervasive and persuasive. . . . The Malthusian logic which insists that food supplies ultimately constrain population growth is compelling.'

The highly sensationalized 'shortfalls' in world grain production in the early 1970s, plus Africa's experience of continually falling food output per capita and repeated famines, fuelled the neo-Malthusian view that the world was rapidly approaching the limit of its capacity to provide food for all. Addressing 'The complexity of the food problem', Brown (1975, p. 11) invoked a number of simplistic Malthusian explanations:

> Looking at the world of the early seventies, one is struck with the sobering realisation that it appears to be losing its capacity to feed itself. The reasons for this include, on the demand side, the impact of rising affluence and the rapid population growth. The annual increase in the demand for food is now immense, yet the earth is no larger today than it was a generation ago. . . . Currently the resources used to expand food production – land, water, energy, fertiliser – are all scarce. There are opportunities for expanding cultivated area, but most of the good crop land in the world is already under the plough, and much of the additional area that could be brought into use is marginal.

This 'limit' theory is reflected in Meadows *et al.* (1972), which, 'by parameterising current population growth, present dietary levels, and yields at twice the current yield levels, concluded that the world would run out of food supplies by the middle of the twenty-first century' (Yotopoulos 1978, p. 2).

The solutions, given this prognosis of 'excess demand', are self-evident: food supply must be stimulated (this provides the ideological justification for Green Revolution-style innovations such as 'high-yielding varieties' of cereals), and the demand for food should be reduced. The Club of Rome Report recommended that 'the only feasible solution to the world food situation requires . . . an effective population policy' (quoted in Alamgir, 1980, p. 2), among other measures. Brown (1975, p. 13) reached the same conclusion: 'Looking beyond the immediate crisis, we will have to rely much more on curbing demand if we expect to achieve a reasonable balance with the supply of food at an acceptable price. Curbing population growth can make a difference.'

This depressing prediction of imminent global food shortages by demographic prophets of doom such as Brown has been challenged by many who believe, in effect, that the intensive and/or extensive margins of cultivation are much further away than neo-Malthusian pessimism suggests. Borgstrom (cited in Dando, 1980, p. 96) has estimated the 'carrying capacity' of the world as being as high as 19 billion, if grain now used as animal feed was used instead as food for people, and if trade smoothed out differences in regional food supplies. Finally, Hallett (1981, p. 278) cites Colin Clark, another contra-Malthusian, 'who maintains that it is the growth of population which forces mankind to seek new ways of increasing food production, that attempts to control population are unnecessary, and that food production can be increased to feed any possible population.'

An argument often advanced in support of the 'excess population' arguments is that developments in modern medicine have reduced infant mortality and death rates, raising life expectancies to such an extent that demographic structures in most countries have been radically altered. Aykroyd (1974, p. 166) observed that: 'Health services can operate effectively in countries which are not being "developed" to any large extent in other ways.' The result is that 'death control' is being practised in countries where birth control is not yet widespread, and fertility rates are still high. Furthermore, since preventive medicine such as immunization 'acts more strongly on "unhealthy" populations than on those which have already benefited from it for some years' (*ibid.*, p. 167), this is presented as another reason for the gap between population growth rates in Western industrialized countries and the Third World. However, UNICEF (1985, p. 22) believes that reductions in infant mortality need not exacerbate the population 'problem' at all, and may help to solve it, since parents will adjust their decisions on family size accordingly:

> all the evidence suggests that a reduction in the number of child deaths would also help to bring about a greater reduction in the number of child births. . . . The greater the chance of a child's survival, the less the parents need to insure against loss by bearing more children than they actually want.

Woldemariam (1984, p. 141) specifically rejects any explanation of famine which invokes what he describes as 'the population growth myth':

> the problem of famine is not necessarily and solely related to population growth. Many countries in Western Europe, Tsarist Russia and China have histories of famine. Now, in these same countries, in spite of much larger populations, famine does not occur. This, certainly, is sufficient to exclude population growth as the cause of famine.

5.4   Modern demographic arguments

Although neo-Malthusian arguments are now criticized as vigorously as were their Malthusian predecessors, this does not mean that there is no relationship at all between population pressures and vulnerability to hunger and famine. What, then, are the links between Malthus and current theories of famine? Several debates remain unresolved.

The first concerns the relationship between population *density* and vulnerability to famine. In a discussion of potential famine regions, Borlaug (1975, p. 16), predicted that 'the critical area for the immediate future is South Asia, where the greatest population density exists.'[3] This proved to be factually inaccurate. With hindsight, it now appears that Asia had just seen its last major famine (Bangladesh, 1974), so that Africa rather than south Asia became the main famine arena of the 1980s. Also, while it is true that Bangladesh (at 663 people/km^2 in 1983) has the highest concentration of people in the world, compare this with Ethiopia (33/km^2) or the Sudan (just 8/km^2), and the supposed association between population density and famine risk is broken immediately.[4]

Borlaug's focus on the 'person:land' ratio in poor countries misses the point. More pertinent might be some measure of the 'person:economic prospects' ratio. Population density must be expressed *in relation to* economic opportunities (*arable* land, average incomes, modes of production) if it is to have any meaning. Excessive population density – 'too many people' per unit of land – is persuasive as a possible cause of famine only if the number of people is linked to the area's natural resource endowments, transport and marketing infrastructure, production systems and so on. Also crucial is the *distribution* of resources such as land: an area of relatively sparse population can suffer a kind of Malthusian crisis if a few people control most of the productive land (say, private estates or plantations), or if some people have been pushed onto unproductive land. Within Blantyre District, Nyasaland, for example, Vaughan (1987, p. 72) notes that 'there was continuous movement of population' for several years prior to a famine which struck the district in 1949, and that

> most of this movement was away from the congested highlands into the less
> crowded but more agriculturally marginal areas. Although European observers
> made the easy equation between congestion and vulnerability to food shortage, it
> was in fact in these newly colonised and less crowded areas that the 1949 famine
> struck with most severity.

So population density *per se* matters far less than its geographic and economic distribution, which largely predetermines the survival prospects and living standards of people at birth. Dutch children, though born into one of the world's most densely populated nations, are less likely to experience famine than pastoralists in sparsely populated Mauritania. Even within Ethiopia or Sudan, children born to affluent urban merchants or civil servants are less vulnerable than children born to poor peasants in remote villages.

Since World War II, 'agricultural populations in the developed world have halved. In the developing countries, in contrast, the agricultural population has increased by 45 per cent' (Grigg, 1985, p. 63). This kind of statistic explains more about vulnerability to famine than national head-counts. It suggests that some sources of income and food offer greater security than others. Urbanization offers one way out of highly risky self-provisioning agriculture, even if the employment opportunities for rural migrants to Third World cities are limited.

The second debate emerges if population *growth* is distinguished analytically from population *density*. Neo-Malthusians often present figures for population growth and density as if the two are closely correlated. For example, Dando (1980, pp. 90–1), predicts 'a globe-girdling tropical "Future Famine Zone", about which he comments: 'These nations and other poorer countries within this zone contained two-thirds of the world's population in 1978, produced only one-fifth of the world's food and accounted for four out of every five births.' A related confusion concerns two neo-Malthusian hypotheses about population dynamics and changes in incomes. The first is that population *density* and the growth of agricultural output (and, therefore, of rural incomes) are inversely related. The second claims that the same inverse relationship holds for the *rate of growth* of population and the growth of agricultural output and incomes. Recently, neo-Malthusians have focused increasingly on the rate of population growth as a constraining force on food availability per capita, rather than simply on population density. This contention has some validity, as will be seen.

The next line of thought, which has its origins in Malthus, is the relationship between population and economic growth. There are several ways in which, it is argued, rapid population growth can slow economic growth in general, and increase individual vulnerabilities in particular. The first relates to the fact that fixed wages are paid for work, irrespective of family size. Accepting the proposition that the most poorly paid workers also tend to have the largest families, their quality of life per head is likely to be diminished as a result. The significance of differential family sizes is emphasized by Van Schendel (1981, p. 15), and also by Leibenstein (1982, p. 113):

> Population growth by itself is likely to cause large-scale downward mobility. This may take the form of a downward aggregate shift, but the fastest-growing group would almost always be the dispossessed.'

> If income cannot grow in proportion to family size as population increases, then falling below the famine level becomes a possibility. In other words, even if in nonfamine years a given family size yields adequate calories, the larger the family the greater the chance of the family getting into the high vulnerability zone.

This part of the argument might be countered by saying that a larger family may have more economically active members than a smaller one. But large families also tend to have high 'dependency ratios' (few workers, many consumers), and these households are likely to be the most vulnerable. As long as infant mortality rates are high, birthrates will be high, because it is the surviving children who matter, so dependency ratios will remain high too. De Janvry (1981, p. 142) adds that 'a fast-growing population means that a high percentage of the population is young, and thus not in the labour force, and is imposing high rearing, feeding, and educational costs on society, which is thus drained of its investable surplus.'

The second negative impact of population growth occurs if it results in excessive fragmentation of landholdings through generations of partition among heirs. In his study of a village in Hausaland, West Africa, Watts (1981, p. 205) reports that 'population densities have risen sharply. The result has been a decline in the average size of farm holdings which, in conjunction with thc relatively poor quality of the soil, has meant that the poorer peasantry are increasingly incapable of fulfilling basic biological requirements in most years.' This observation does not contradict the now widely accepted view that small peasants often make more efficient use of land than large farmers; it only emphasizes that landholdings can be subdivided to such an extent that subsistence becomes untenable.

Griffin (1981, pp. 310–11) suggests a third negative impact of 'rapid demographic expansion' on the poor, in an argument directed against 'trickle-down' theories of economic growth. 'The primary effect of rapid demographic expansion is to lower the share of labour in national product and thereby to increase inequality in the distribution of income. . . . It is in this sense that population expansion is one of the causes of immiserising growth.' A constantly growing 'pool of surplus labour' in rural areas cannot all be absorbed into industrial employment, nor can workers facing competition from the unemployed exert upward pressure on wages to raise their living standards.

So perhaps the population 'problem' can be characterised as a type of 'prisoners' dilemma'[5] paradox, in so far as behaving according to individual or household rationality seems to reduce social welfare as a whole. Utility-maximizing reproductive behaviour by each household collectively results in lower food output per head, deepening income inequalities, and a retardation of the demographic transition to a stable population, high income society.

But if it is true that high dependency ratios and the partition of inheritances erode a household's resource base so that poor families become poorer over time, surely this undermines the 'individual rationality' assumption of the 'prisoners' dilemma' scenario? If so, the question remains: why do the poor continue to have the largest families? The reasons are too complex to explore in depth here, but an important factor for this discussion is that poor parents see children, particularly adult sons, as their primary protection against risk.[6]

> During crises, mature sons present opportunities for spreading risk and reducing household vulnerability through diversified earnings, temporary migration for work, and as labour reserves in case the principal earner in a household falls ill or dies. . . . Societies that are currently famine-prone are, by definition, high-risk environments. Famine also signals the absence of adequate risk insurance. Thus, the long-term (or less immediate) demographic response to famine to which we refer is the persistence of high fertility. (Bongaarts and Cain, 1982, pp. 53, 54)

In other words, it is not rapid population growth which causes famine, but the persistence of famine which encourages rapid population growth. Bongaarts and Cain (1982, p. 57) conclude their discussion of this complex interaction pessimistically:

> The possibility that famine and rapid population growth perpetuate and feed on one another is, of course, most disturbing. The behavioural response to extreme insecurity – that is, unconstrained reproduction – could have more tragic long-term

implications than the more visible and immediate suffering and misery associated with famine mortality. With persistent high fertility and continued rapid population growth, not only is the likelihood of future, perhaps more severe, famines greater than it would otherwise be, but the prospects for true development recede, as government policy is diverted by the effort of feeding a burgeoning population.

These theoretical advances reveal the real directions of causality in the context of population, poverty and per capita food supply: 'the causal relation seems more logically to run from poverty to overpopulation than the other way around' (de Janvry, 1981, p. 142). It follows that the neo-Malthusian obsession with population growth focuses on the wrong side of the equation. As de Janvry emphasizes, the most effective (and equitable) means of 'controlling' the fertility of the poor in the long run is to raise their living standards:

> The rural poor thus have large families because it is economically rational for them to do so. Improvements in the material conditions of life diminishes these functions and gradually transforms children into only 'consumer goods', which leads to a decline in birth rates and to a demographic transition.

5.5   Policy implications

The debate about the links between population, food production and risk of famine has a direct bearing on the policies adopted by governments and by institutions working in the fields of development and famine relief. Four policy lines will be briefly considered here. The first seeks to limit population growth – if necessary, by coercion. The second is 'triage', or 'lifeboat ethics'. The third suggests limiting 'excessive' food consumption by the rich, to release extra supplies of food for the poor. The fourth aims to improve levels of living, partly to reduce vulnerability to famine and, at the same time, to increase parents' incentives to limit family size.

The first strategy for tackling an 'excess demand for food' follows from the Malthusian diagnosis of an 'excess supply of people'. Accepting this diagnosis provides the justification for fertility control, by whatever available means. Comparatively few people would object to contraceptives and family planning advice being offered as a service to people who are free to choose whether or not to use them. But some outsiders who think they know best have devised various schemes for intervening in the fertility decisions of people poorer and more vulnerable than themselves, ostensibly with the intention of breaking the 'population growth poverty trap'.

In recent years, India, Bangladesh and China have all adopted this policy (or had it thrust on them) in one form or another. China's 'one child family' policy is notorious. Female infanticide has risen dramatically because of a preference for sons, as have cases of abortions and enforced sterilization. At the household level, the policy flies in the face of economic rationality. 'Ironically, China's one-child policy was introduced at the same time as agrarian reforms that have actually increased people's need for children. Greater private economic incentives in the countryside, where 80 percent of China's people live, are leading to a breakdown of the collective security system' (Hartmann, 1987, pp. 150–1). As Hartmann explains, the dissolution of agricultural communes means that children are needed in the family fields more than ever before. Medical treatment and retirement benefits, which previously were provided through the communes, must now be paid for, 'which especially threatens the elderly with no sources of cash income. As a result, children are vital for old age support.'

In the case of Bangladesh, Hartmann and Standing (1985, p. 17) describe how food aid has been used to induce women to be sterilized, in districts where crop production had been devastated by floods. 'In the course of monitoring food relief programmes, field workers from British voluntary agencies discovered cases where emergency food aid provided through the UN World Food Programme had been withheld from destitute women unless they agreed to be sterilised.' Often these women had no idea of what the operation involved, and did not realize that they would never be able to have children again.

Quite apart from the moral problems associated with these tactics, the evidence suggests that population control by coercion, blackmail or deception is financially costly, often dangerous for the health of the women involved and of limited aggregate effect. It is also analytically flawed and therefore counter-productive: given that children are a form of risk insurance, denying poor people the right to have children 'for their own benefit' is likely to leave them more vulnerable than before, not less.

Even more cynical than coercive population control is the suggestion that famine-prone areas are unsalvageable because of the vicious circle set up by poverty and population growth. One strategy which stems from this position is non-response to famine (no food aid), to allow a 'Malthusian final solution' to equilibrate population with resources (see 'lifeboat ethics', below).

However, more discriminating neo-Malthusian variations have also been proposed. One such is a form of 'triage' (from the French verb meaning 'to sort'). Triage is a method for allocating scarce medical resources in wartime, by classifying the wounded according to their chances of survival. In the context of food aid policy, triage has a long and ignoble history. In 1967, for instance, Paddock and Paddock suggested that the United States should practise triage in its allocation of food aid to famine-prone nations. If the United States were to allocate its food aid 'efficiently', it would have 'to sort out countries according to those which have a future and should have food aid, and those without a future whose people must be sacrificed for the well being of the world community.'[7] Neo-Malthusians have even found a 'moral' justification for their recommendations, one which is strongly reminiscent of Darwinian natural selection theory:

> Malthusians argue that it is more humane to let poor hungry people and nations succumb to their inevitable destiny. A natural relationship between the human race and the natural world must be maintained; starvation and famine must be allowed to perform their population control functions. (Dando, 1980, p. 98)

Closely related to triage is Hardin's 'lifeboat ethics', which starts from the same presumption that famines in the Third World are inevitable because of the rapidly worsening population/food ratio in those countries. 'Hardin's argument against famine relief may be summarised metaphorically as two lifeboats on a survival course, one lifeboat full of affluent well-fed people and the other lifeboat crowded with starving passengers. Those who can, swim towards the lifeboat with food' (Dando, 1980, p. 194). However, 'if we try to save the drowning by bringing them aboard, our boat will be overloaded and we shall all drown. Since it is better to save some than none, we should leave the others to drown' (Singer, 1977, p. 47). The policy implications of this banal metaphor are obscene:

> the rich nations of the earth must not provide food aid, no financial help to develop national economies, limit immigration from food-deficit to food-surplus countries and reduce other assistance until the overpopulated poor countries have lowered their population within the carrying capacity of their countries. (Dando, 1980, pp. 195–6)

The lifeboat analogy (which Dando does not endorse) is misleading, since it implies that the rich and poor 'lifeboats' are completely autonomous. This simplification ignores both the reality of trade relations between rich and poor countries, and the various theories of interdependency and underdevelopment, versions of which argue persuasively that Third World poverty is at least partly due to the unequal power relations which characterized the period of colonial exploitation. If this view has any validity, a policy that abrogates the West's responsibility towards the Third World is both callous and unjust. Hardin's assumption that 'rescuing' the starving will lower the survival prospects of all is also misleading. Singer (1977, p. 48) refutes Hardin's lifeboat metaphor succinctly, and proposes an alternative analogy:

> the world presently produces enough food to give all its inhabitants an adequate diet. Unfortunately that food is very unevenly distributed. *In the United States and Western Europe alone, more food is wasted by being fed to farm animals than the total world food shortfall.* Through his high meat diet, which provides him with about twice as much meat as his body can use, the average American indirectly consumes enough grain to feed four Indians. Under these circumstances the lifeboat analogy seem grotesquely inapt. It is rather as if we in the rich nations were on a luxurious yacht, feasting gluttonously and playing deck quoits to ward off obesity, while we avert our gaze from those drowning in the sea around us.

'Triage' and 'lifeboat ethics' are equally immoral. There is no justification other than self-interest for dividing the world into rich and poor regions, and inventing excuses for rich countries not to help the poor. The *New York Times*, commenting on triage theory, described it as 'one of the most pessimistic and morally threadbare positions to be advanced since the demise of the Third Reich' (quoted in Alamgir, 1980, p. 8).

A third policy line advanced by some aims at reducing the food consumption of the rich. Hallett (1981, p. 271), for instance, states: 'There is considerable medical evidence that people in the developed countries eat too much', as though this were a primary cause of Third World hunger. The Second Report to the Club of Rome argued that 'the strains on the global food production capacity would be lessened if the eating habits in the affluent part of the world would change, becoming less wasteful' (quoted in Alamgir, 1980, p. 2). Brown (1975) and others also believe in reduced consumption by the rich as a solution to global food supply constraints.

This reasoning would be valid if supply-side explanations of famine were accepted without question. But it misses the crucial point – that malnutrition and famines are not primarily caused by aggregate *supply* constraints, but by limited *incomes* or 'entitlements' to food (see Chapter 6). Overproduction and overconsumption of food in North America and Western Europe have had little noticeable impact on hunger elsewhere, and there is no reason to believe that a reduction in food consumption by the West would have any effect on consumption in famine-prone areas of the world.

Besides, the argument is also internally inconsistent. If famines could be abolished simply by reducing excess consumption in the affluent West to feed the poor South, then there is no problem of aggregate food *shortage* at all – only a problem in the *distribution* of food. The *New Internationalist* (September 1985, p. 25) exposed the flaw in this logic powerfully, if facetiously: 'Americans represent only six per cent of the world's population, yet they consume 35 per cent of the world's resources – the same as the entire developing world. So is the real world population problem that there are too many Americans?'

The fourth and final policy line derives from de Janvry's (1981, pp. 142–3) observation that, in the long run, population control policies seem to have had only limited success until standards of living rise above the point where famine poses any real threat. Alternatively, parents have to believe that reduced fertility is good for society as a whole. In either case, people should not be forced into behaviour that raises their own vulnerability:

> if the social valuation is that population growth is excessive, the crux of the solution lies in reconciling individual rationality (according to which poverty and subsistence production induce large families) with social rationality. Only when this reconciliation obtains can population programs be effective. Historically, this has been achieved in two ways: (1) through increased income levels that ensure the meeting of subsistence needs and of social security for the bulk of the population (this has been the basis of the demographic transition in the center nations); and

(2) through social mobilisation, whereby social rationality supersedes individual rationality in decision making on family size.

The complex relation between demographic pressures and risk of hunger, and the way priorities have shifted in recent years, is illustrated by the World Bank's position on this issue. An interesting sequence of statements is offered to conclude this section. In its 1981 report, 'Accelerated Development in Sub-Saharan Africa', the World Bank (1981, pp. 112–14) argued explicitly that rapid population growth was retarding economic development in general, and food production per capita in particular:

> The consequences of rapid population growth for economic development and welfare are very negative. . . . For example, if the population grows at 3 percent and per capita incomes grow between 1 and 2 percent, there will be an annual increase in food demand of about 4 percent. But in the last decade, agriculture grew at less than half this rate (1.8 percent annually). . . . The above scenario for the remainder of the century envisages pressure on the land, extremely rapid urbanisation with declining quality of life, and little increase in the share of population provided with basic services.
>
> Thus, it is crucial to take steps now to reduce fertility. There is widespread recognition that efforts at family planning can be effective, even prior to modernisation . . . emphasis on modern contraceptives to provide birth spacing appears to have great potential in accelerating Africa's demographic transition. These considerations suggest that population policy in Africa should be largely concerned with slowing population growth.

A 1983 World Bank Staff Working Paper was more cautious:

> Many factors, including policy, influence the speed and pattern of economic growth. Population is only one of these factors. . . . It would be wrong to attribute the growing food deficit of Africa to population pressures *per se*. Only 5 percent of the total land area of the continent is now cultivated. Buringh et al. . . . estimates that 24 percent of the total land area is potentially cultivable. The land frontier in this sense is much further away in Africa than in Asia (where 16 percent of total area is now cultivated against a potential cultivable area of 20 percent). (Faruqee and Gulhati, 1983, pp. 25–7)

Faruqee and Gulhati (1983, p. 29) continue by arguing that population pressure is a significant restraining force on growth, but less directly than is commonly supposed:

> the population problem in Sub-Sahara Africa is manifest not in the form of land unavailability and visible overcrowding but in much more subtle ways. Accommodation of rapid population growth requires massive improvements in the food and larger agricultural sector involving not only substantial public investment outlays in developing land and improving its productivity but also in building transport networks and other infrastructure.

The World Bank's World Development Report for 1984 was the first to focus on less aggregative notions of food availability than global or national stocks and, in doing so, introduced a third element to the population–food producing capacity debate: 'the main issue is not the worldwide availability of food, but the capacity of nations, groups within nations, and individuals to obtain enough food for a healthy diet' (quoted in ICIHI, 1985, pp. 75–6).

The World Bank's 1986 report, *Poverty and Hunger*, maintains this shift of emphasis. It stresses the importance of purchasing power in preference to the notion of population growth outstripping food supplies as a causal mechanism of poverty, malnutrition and risk of famine:

> The world has ample food. The growth of global food production has been faster than the unprecedented population growth of the past forty years. Prices of cereals on world markets have even been falling. Enough food is available so that countries that do not produce all the food they want can import it if they can afford to. Yet many poor countries and hundreds of millions of poor people do not share in this abundance. They suffer from a lack of food security, caused mainly by a lack of purchasing power. (World Bank, 1986, p. 1)

5.6   Conclusion

At the global level, crude Malthusian predictions must be rejected as disproven by history. There is no aggregate shortage of food supplies, nor is there likely to be (barring catastrophes) within the foreseeable future. Unless and until zero net population growth is achieved throughout the world, however, the view that demographic dynamics have no impact on economic growth or per capita food consumption cannot be accepted either.

Demographic arguments become more penetrating if the population issue is separated into its component parts: density and rate of growth. High population *density* in rural areas promotes infrastructural development (the 'Boserup effect'), and is therefore beneficial, at least to the point where competition over arable land and other natural resources degrades the environment and threatens a community's subsistence. Conversely, rapid population *growth* rates undermine household food security by perpetuating high dependency ratios and the subdivision of farmland to the point of unviability. Curbing population growth in these circumstances may reverse both the Malthusian process of declining food output per capita and the Marxist arguments attributing the persistence of rural poverty to the reproduction of a 'reserve army of surplus labour'. (But note that migration and economic diversification offer preferable alternative routes out of a 'crisis of overpopulation' to coercive fertility controls.)

The distinction between density and growth can be applied to the contrasting fortunes (in terms of famine vulnerability) of Africa and Asia. In China, for example, high population density has facilitated the development of rural infrastructure, market integration and the diversification of the rural economy.

Low growth rates, encouraged by the 'one child family' policy (the morality of which is a separate argument), have contributed to the production of adequate per capita food supplies since the 1960s. Unfortunately, in famine-prone regions of Africa, exactly the reverse conditions exist: low population density and rapid population growth. High growth rates effectively reproduce the conditions of poverty and vulnerability across generations, while low densities make it uneconomic to develop the infrastructure, markets and income diversity required to improve living conditions and reduce rural vulnerability to famine.

The key point seems to be that rapid population growth and famine are linked more closely to their common causes, poverty and vulnerability, than to each other. These are the real problems, and attempts to control or prevent famine by controlling (or preventing) population growth only address another symptom of the same disease. Any serious effort to reduce a community's vulnerability to famine requires a more fundamental attack on the social, economic and political mechanisms which generate poverty and inequality than is acknowledged by those who arrive holding food aid in one hand and sterilization kits in the other.

Appendix 5.1 A graphical representation of Malthus's model

Ghatak and Ingersent (1984, p. 254) provide a graphical formalization of the assumptions and predictions of the classical Malthusian model. In their diagram, reproduced below, population acts as a proxy for agricultural labour input, and wages (or average consumption) are determined by average labour productivity. The TC_s line shows total consumption needs as population rises, given a per capita subsistence requirement of OM. An agricultural surplus exists as long as total production (TP) exceeds total consumption needs. (The argument assumes a Cobb–Douglas type of production function.)

However, average product per worker (AP) falls as soon as total production levels off, which it must do eventually, because agricultural output is constrained by diminishing returns at both the intensive and extensive margins of cultivation. When the population reaches OP_m, therefore, the agricultural surplus is zero, and this is the 'Malthusian equilibrium' point. If population exceeds OP_m, such that average product falls below the minimum subsistence level (OM), people will starve.

In the long run, assuming no change in fertility rates or the production system, the 'natural check' of starvation on unconstrained population growth will restrict population to the maximum level (OP_m) compatible with survival, in a tenuous, zero-surplus, subsistence equilibrium.

Watkins and Van de Walle (1983, pp. 8–10) find this kind of graphical representation 'too schematic' to convey Malthus's ideas satisfactorily, for several reasons:

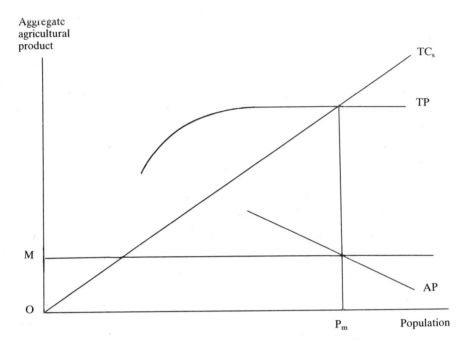

Figure 5.1   A graphical representation of Malthus's model.

First, real income per head is an average notion; very few people actually consume at the average level. Second, it is difficult to determine a recognisable minimum of subsistence. Third, there is a need to distinguish between endogenous and exogenous mortality. . . . Most pre-industrial economies were particularly vulnerable to crises. But how much was that vulnerability the result of population pressure, and how much was it linked to modes of production that accumulated few surpluses, were not very diversified, and were not covered by systems of insurance and solidarity as have been developed by the modern state?

The most fundamental critique, of course, relates to the production function, which in reality is neither uniquely determined nor permanently fixed. There is no reason to believe that the production possibilities available to a society will remain unchanged as population grows. A more realistic modification of the graph above would add a series of discrete production functions above the single TP curve, each intersecting the TC_s line at a higher point, showing that steadily increasing quantities of food were available to a steadily increasing population.

Notes

1. Quoted in Spitz (1978, p. 883).
2. Following Ghatak and Ingersent (1984, p. 185), whose graphical representation of the argument is appended to this chapter (see p. 63).
3. The near-hysteria with which respected academics like Borlaug ('the father of the Green Revolution') treat the population issue is perplexing. 'Looking ahead twenty to twenty-five years, I am very gravely concerned about our capacity to produce food for an additional 2 to 3 billion people. These numbers are frightening. . . . Yet most political leaders are still reluctant to face up to and try to tame the population monster before it destroys world civilisation' (Borlaug, 1975, p. 19).
4. Figures calculated from the World Development Report (1985).
5. The 'prisoners' dilemma' is a simulation game for two players in which co-operation would yield mutual benefits, but the incentive for each to 'defect' is so strong that both do, to mutual disadvantage. The game illuminates real-world situations (such as the nuclear arms race) in which conflicts between individual and collective rationality can lead to negative consequences for all concerned.
6. Another factor is that men often do not allow women to control their own fertility (see Hartmann, 1987). Hartmann (personal communication) concludes that: 'Not only poverty but patriarchy is a cause of rapid population growth.'
7. Dando (1980, p. 195), discussing Paddock and Paddock (1967). Presumably Robert MacNamara was endorsing this view of the world when he described Bangladesh as 'a basket case'.

6

The entitlement approach

Starvation is the characteristic of some people not *having* enough food to eat. It is not the characteristic of there *being* not enough food to eat. While the latter can be a cause of the former, it is but one of many *possible* causes.

Amartya Sen (1981, p. 1)

The famines of the 1970s brought a growing dissatisfaction with supply-side explanations of famine. Food was being sold in village markets while residents of those same villages were destitute and starving. Many writers recognized that poverty was at least as important as food scarcity in causing famine. However, a comprehensive alternative theory was not on offer until Sen described his 'entitlement approach' to famine analysis. Since 1976, Sen has developed this theory in a number of journal articles and books. The best-known exposition is to be found in *Poverty and Famines*, published in 1981.

6.1 The basic entitlement approach

Sen's essential point of departure from supply-side theories is the distinction he draws between aggregate *availability* or supply of food, and an individual's *access to* or ownership of food. Theoretical precursors of the entitlement approach focused on income and 'effective demand' for food, but the notion of 'entitlement' as defined by Sen (1984, p. 497) incorporates more than just earned income or own production: 'Entitlement refers to the set of alternative commodity bundles that a person can command in a society using the totality of rights and opportunities that he or she faces.' The word 'entitlement' itself suggests notions of moral or legal rights – a point Sen makes only in the context of defining what determines ownership of goods, but which Richards (1983, p. 46) expresses in philosophical terms:

Entitlement systems are beliefs, created in political practice, about who ought to get what under what circumstances, and the embodiment of those beliefs in legal and economic process, e.g. land tenure rules, notions of family obligation, wage rates, rules of market transaction, etc. Such standards are contingent and time-bound (they are specific to particular historical circumstances). Consequently they do not (and cannot be expected to) work according to absolute standards of equity. Nor can they be predicted from an economic model.

Most people enjoy a range of sources of entitlement to food, so the approach is broader than the 'income-based' or 'moral economy' approaches.

A person's ability to command food . . . depends on the entitlement relations that govern possession and use in that society. It depends on what he owns, what exchange possibilities are offered to him, what is given to him free, and what is taken away from him. (Sen, 1981, pp. 154–5)

Sen (1981, p. 2) identifies four main categories or types of entitlement relations in private ownership market economies:

1. *Trade-based entitlement*, which describes ownership transfer through commodity exchanges.
2. *Production-based entitlement*, which describes the right to own what one produces with one's own (or hired) resources.
3. *Own-labour entitlement*, which incorporates all trade-based and production-based entitlements derived from the 'sale' of one's own labour power.
4. *Inheritance and transfer entitlement*, which refers to the right to own what is willingly given by others, including gifts and bequests, as well as transfers by the state such as social security or pensions.

From the above categorization it can be seen that entitlements have two aspects or components – that which is *owned* by a person, or her/his 'endowment'; and that which can be obtained by *exchanging* some of that endowment for other commodities or services.

In a market economy, a person can exchange what he owns for another collection of commodities. He can do this exchange either through trading, or through production, or through a combination of the two. The set of all the alternative bundles of commodities that he can acquire in exchange for what he owns may be called the 'exchange entitlement' of what he owns. (Sen, 1981, p. 3)

While entitlements describes the entire range of commodity bundles available to a person, given each individual's unique endowments and exchange possibilities, it is the relationship between entitlements and food that is particularly pertinent in the analysis of famines:

A person is reduced to starvation if some change either in his endowment (e.g., alienation of land, or loss of labour power due to ill health), or in his exchange entitlement mapping (e.g., fall in wages, rise in food prices, loss of employment, drop in the price of the good he buys and sells), makes it no longer possible for him to acquire any commodity bundle with enough food. (Sen, 1988, p. 8)

Mortality is defined as occurring when an individual's entitlement collapses into the 'starvation set' – the set of exchange entitlements, given endowments, which does not contain any feasible bundle including enough food. There are two distinct ways in which such a collapse might occur: (1) *endowments* contract – crops fail, livestock die; and/or (2) *exchange entitlements* shift unfavourably – food prices rise, wages or asset prices fall, so that individuals experience a decline in their 'terms of trade' with the market for food. In the case of self-provisioning farmers, the second category only comes into effect after a failure of the first – if production is insufficient for some reason, so that normally self-sufficient farming families suddenly become market dependent for their food needs.

When this happens, the two components of entitlement failure typically work in tandem to create famine conditions: endowments collapse, triggering food price rises and 'distress sales' of assets at rapidly falling prices – in short, collapses in exchange entitlements. Raikes (1988, p. 70) draws out the implication: 'those especially vulnerable to famine are often those whose savings are least or are held in forms whose value falls drastically (in terms of food) precisely when most needed.'

It should be emphasized that the concept of entitlement is somewhat broader than is suggested by a focus simply on what is owned and what can be acquired by exchange, since some forms of entitlement only come into operation after a loss in ownership or endowment – unemployment benefit, for instance, is not 'owned' by someone who is employed, but forms part of her entitlement in the event that she loses her job. So redistributive transfers must also be considered in the characterisation of entitlements, as Svedberg (1985, pp. 8–9) points out:

> The essence of the approach is that people starve because (1) they have insufficient real income and wealth *and* (2) because there are no other means of acquiring food. That is, inadequate food purchasing power is only a necessary, not a sufficient, pre-condition for (non-voluntary) starvation. The 'other' means of acquiring entitlements to food essentially comprise transfers (redistribution) of food on the international, national, regional or family level. In developed countries, most people's entitlements to food are not restricted by the effective demand they can exert in the market; the welfare state ensures at least a minimum bundle of food to its citizens.

Finally, it is important to note that Sen's exposition of entitlements in terms of a personal 'starvation set' explains no more than individual starvation. At the aggregate (community or regional) level, famine presumably reflects a *systemic* failure of food entitlements. 'Famine is the result of the collapse of an established entitlement system' (Richards, 1983, p. 46). How individual starvation should be aggregated up to famine is not clear, and Sen does not address the definitional problem of *scale* in distinguishing the two. Famine would seem to occur, in Sen's model, when large numbers of geographically or occupationally related individuals, each with unique endowments and exchange entitlement mappings, are plunged into their personal starvation sets simultaneously.

6.2   Strengths of the entitlement approach

The most important feature of the entitlement approach is that it directs attention away from conventional supply-side analyses of food crises, towards an analysis which treats them instead as symptoms of *demand* failure:

> A major failing of traditional development economics has been its tendency to concentrate on supply of goods rather than on ownership and entitlement. The focus on growth is only one reflection of this. Extreme concentration on the ratio of food supply to population is another example of the same defective vision. (Sen, 1983, p. 499)

The point is simply that generalizations drawn from crude aggregates such as food availability per capita erroneously imply a totally equal distribution of food. The corollary of this observation is that the effects of famine are rarely shared equally among all elements of a population. Even in the case of food blockades, where supplies of food are simply denied to an entire region, the wealthy and well-connected invariably survive longer and more comfortably than the poor, because of inequalities in their respective entitlements. During the Dutch food blockade of 1944, for instance, Stein *et al.* (1975, pp. 47–51) report that a black market existed for those who had the necessary assets and connections (see also Chapter 11.4).

> The more fortunate got sporadic extra supplies from the black market and from forages into the country (*hongertochten*). . . . A successful *hongertocht* required knowledgeable contacts who could supply addresses of farmers who might have and sell food, a bicycle, and valuables to barter for the food. Knowledgeable contacts could come from occupational and family connections . . . estimates suggest that at the height of the famine supplements and particularly extra-legal sources doubled the extremely meagre official ration. The estimates do not reflect the experience of a large segment of the population who could not afford black market food and could not forage. . . . The lower social classes were at a disadvantage. . . .

A second major advantage of the entitlement approach is that it avoids the misleading generalizations of gross aggregation, focusing instead on the access to food of individuals or groups within a society. The unit of analysis in Sen's writings on famines tends to be 'occupation groups', presumably because this provides finer distinctions than 'communities' or 'regions', and has milder political connotations than 'classes', which he occasionally also uses:

> Rather than concentrating on the crude variable of food output per head, which is just one influence among many affecting the entitlement of different groups to food, the focus of analysis has to be on the ownership patterns of different classes and occupation groups and on the exchange possibilities – through production and trade – that these groups face. The forces leading to famines affect different occupation groups differently, and famine analysis has to be sensitive to these differences rather than submerging all this in an allegedly homogeneous story of aggregate food supply per head affecting everyone's food consumption. (Sen, 1982, p. 452)

Yet Sen also refers to individuals ('a person', 'a peasant'), as often as to groups or aggregates of people, sometimes almost interchangeably. As noted above, this can create confusion as to whether he is describing starvation or famine:

> Whether a person is able to establish command over, say, enough food to avoid starvation depends on the nature of the entitlement system operating in the economy in question and on the person's own position in that society. Even when the over-all ratio of food to population is high, particular occupation groups can perish because of their inability to establish command over enough food. (Sen, 1984, p. 517)

A third merit of entitlements is that it permits the analysis of famines which occur in 'boom' periods as well as during 'slumps'. Intuition suggests that famine occurs because of a national or regional economic crisis, but this is not necessarily always true. A 'boom famine' is characterized by failures of exchange or trade entitlements for some people because of food price rises or the marginalization of certain occupational groups:

> Boom famines might seem particularly counter-intuitive; but, as discussed, famines can take place with increased output in general and of food in particular if the command system (e.g. market pull) shifts against some particular group. . . . In the fight for market command over food, one group can suffer precisely from another group's prosperity. (Sen, 1981, p. 165)

In other words, a boom for some means greater vulnerability for others, if it takes the form of an uneven economic expansion. Sen cites the 'Great Bengal Famine' of 1943 as a typical 'boom famine' (though some of his critics disagree).[1] Although there was no food shortage at the time, precautionary and speculative hoarding, together with the inflationary pressures of the wartime boom economy, drove up food demand and prices faster than the real wage increases of agricultural labourers, who were not protected as urbanites were, by food rationing at controlled prices. The result was an essentially rural famine which claimed up to 3 million lives, with the majority of victims being agricultural labourers.

A 'slump famine', by contrast, is typified by direct entitlement failures, the most obvious example of which is crop loss following a drought. Those dependent on others for their income (say, landless labourers on cash crop farms) will also suffer during slump famines, as da Corta (1986) explains:

For instance, a drought could lead to a decline in the income of the cultivating population which in turn can lead to employment/income loss (derived destitution and derived deprivation, in Sen's phraseology) for those dependent on farmers for their income. This reduction in purchasing power (and effective demand) could therefore keep prices low even in times of shortage.

Unlike supply-side approaches, which see famine as resulting from a failure of the market mechanism to provide sufficient food to those who need it, the entitlement approach sees famine as a predictable consequence of normal market processes, given that markets respond to purchasing power rather than to needs. No major disruption of the economy is required. As further evidence for the explanatory power of the entitlement approach, Sen (1982, p. 456) refers to cases where food was actually exported from an area while people starved. This could not be explained by a pure 'FAD' approach:

> private merchants and traders will not move food to famine victims when their needs are not translated into money demands. Indeed, frequently food does move out of famine areas when the loss of entitlement is more powerful than the decline – if any – of food supply, and such food 'counter-movement' has been observed in famines as diverse as the Irish famines of the 1840s, the Ethiopian famine in Wollo of 1973 and the Bangladesh famine of 1974.

Elsewhere, Sen also uses his entitlement approach to refute both what he calls 'Malthusian pessimism' and 'Malthusian optimism'. 'Malthusian pessimism' reflects the still prevalent view that food production cannot match population growth indefinitely, and that famine is an inevitable outcome of 'excessive' population growth rates. The analytical and theoretical defects of this naive 'theory', as discussed in Chapter 5, are often translated into bad policies – mostly concerned with reducing the fertility of the poor by various means – which fail to address the real, underlying causes of famine: poverty and vulnerability.

'Malthusian optimism' is, if anything, even worse. Undue emphasis on per capita food supply figures has contributed to famines not being anticipated, and to delayed responses to famine by governments and aid agencies, with predictable and fatal consequences: 'in focusing attention on the extremely misleading variable of food output per head, "Malthusian optimism" has been indirectly involved in millions of deaths which have resulted from inaction and misdirection of government policy' (Sen, 1986a, p. 3). The problem arises because of the complacency which can result if rising food *supply* per capita is taken as evidence that individual food *consumption* is rising concomitantly. This is never necessarily true, and Sen provides ample evidence that famines have happened while food availability was constant or rising:

> Famines may not be at all anticipated in situations of good or moderate over-all levels of supply, but, notwithstanding that supply situation, acute starvation can hit suddenly and widely because of failures of the entitlement systems, operating through ownership and exchange. For example, in the Bangladesh famine of 1974,

> a very large number died in a year when food availability per head was at a peak –
> higher than in any other year between 1971 and 1975. (Sen, 1983, p. 498)

More precisely, while total food availability was more than adequate for national consumption needs, the distribution of access to that food between different occupation groups suddenly became very skewed (see also Chapter 12.4). Distributional shifts cannot be gleaned from balance sheets summarizing aggregate food stocks and flows. A focus on food supply can at best identify only the *regions* affected by a famine; but a focus on food demand can identify the affected *classes* or occupation groups. An obvious policy implication is that famine relief measures can be targeted on those most needing aid, and delivered in the most appropriate form, if an entitlement analysis is adopted.

To summarize, the outstanding theoretical contribution of Sen's approach is in displacing the previously dominant but dangerously misleading 'FAD' approaches to famine, while at the policy level, entitlements offers an analytical framework for more effective famine anticipation, prevention and relief interventions:

> The most important denial made by the entitlement approach is, therefore, of simple analysis in terms of 'too many people, too little food'. . . . The entitlement approach suggests concentration on such policy variables as social security, employment guarantees, terms of trade between non-food and food (especially between labour power and food), and the totality of rights that govern people's economic life. Policies both of long-run nutritional improvements as well as of short-run famine avoidance and relief have to take note of these different influences on food deprivation. A focus on the ratio of food supply to population hides more than it reveals, and this has persistently deranged public policy over the centuries. (Sen, 1980, pp. 616, 620)

Perhaps the most significant indicator of the extent to which entitlement analysis differs from 'FAD' approaches is the extent to which it points to quite different remedial actions once an actual or potential famine has been identified. Although the debates about food aid and other forms of famine relief are beyond the scope of this study, the fact that different theories suggest different policy implications is a primary justification for this theoretical overview. It is therefore important at this point to invoke Sen's attack on conventional famine relief:

> Moving food into famine areas will not in itself do much to cure starvation, since what needs to be created is food entitlement and not just food availability. Indeed, people have perished in famines in sight of much food in shops. This was widely noted in the Bengal famine of 1943 . . . (Sen, 1982, p. 454)

One way of 'generating entitlements' is to distribute free food to the starving. As Sen notes, the problem here is how to discriminate between the truly needy 'and others who might not be averse to having some free food'. This 'leakage' through mis-targeting can make free food handouts a costly form of relief assistance. A more appropriate method, especially in cases where those needing support have lost employment and incomes (e.g. in the case of retrenched agricultural labourers in south Asian famines), is to set up employment programmes and offer food in exchange for work. The advantage of these food-for-work schemes is that they are self-targeting, so that they are generally more efficient than untargeted handouts. A disadvantage which Sen fails to consider is that the causes of entitlement decline vary across individuals and households, so that providing employment does not directly reach such recognized 'vulnerable groups' as children, the disabled and the elderly.

Relief policies such as food-for-work or free food handouts both follow logically from the FAD diagnosis of 'not enough food' in the afflicted region or community. But entitlements can collapse even when there is no evident food shortage. In such cases, provided the market is functioning adequately, it might be appropriate to offer cash-for-work, or even to hand out free cash instead of free food, thereby restoring 'market-based entitlement' to food:

> the most economical policy option may be to *stimulate* the working of the market mechanism . . . rather than to *supplant* it (which food relief or food for work operations would do). To elaborate, if it can be established that sufficient foodgrains exist but that their purchase and sale is being hampered by the absence of purchasing power on the part of the poor, there is a strong case for generating trade by the creation of the required effective demand through cash hand-outs . . . this will enable a vital need to be translated into effective demand through the creation of 'market-based entitlement'. (Kumar, 1985, p. 7)

However, practice may not be so straightforward. In the first place, the problem may have both supply and demand components. Food aid will address both simultaneously. (Having said this, it is interesting that one of the 'cash relief' communities Kumar examined in Ethiopia appeared at first sight to be isolated from wider markets, therefore 'closed' and in the grip of 'food supply failure'. However, once cash was handed out, the grain traders arrived soon afterwards.) Intriguingly, Seaman and Holt (1980, p. 296) argue a case for *selling* food to the starving, if market 'response' rather than 'pull' failure is the problem: 'under conditions where the market mediates some or all of the starvation, a rational approach to relief is through the sale of food rather than entirely through free distribution.'

Another problem with 'cash relief' is that food aid is typically more readily available than cash, because of the policy biases and resources of donors. Besides, handing out money might prove to be simply inflationary, if markets react sluggishly and supplies of food in the short term are, in fact, limited (McAlpin, 1982). Finally, the problem of who is to be given the money is important where it is not clear that cash aid given to household heads will be used in the best interests of all household members.

Looking beyond immediate famine relief, Sen (1988, p. 13) suggests that policies aimed at *diversifying entitlements*, by expanding the range and sources of personal incomes, might offer more durable solutions to Africa's food problems than the naive preoccupation with growing more food. Many studies from a variety of African contexts have demonstrated the value to poor households of maintaining several potential sources of food rather than depending on only one or two sources (see Christensen, 1989; Heyer, 1991; Dercon, 1992). Policies which promote either income stabilization or income diversification are essential if 'Band-Aid' famine relief is to be replaced by a sustained attack on the conditions which give rise to food insecurity and famine.

6.3   Entitlements versus income

The entitlement approach was not the first expression of dissatisfaction with supply-side famine theory. A number of writers had already pointed to the importance of demand failure as an explanation of famine, and the vulnerability of the poor to food price rises was recognized as long ago as the Indian Famine Codes of the 1880s (McAlpin, 1982). Many still argue that 'entitlements theory' adds little to what was already known. It is therefore worth examining the distinction between 'entitlement failure' and other descriptions of failing access to food. Much of the debate centres on whether or not 'entitlements' are effectively the same as 'income':

> Since food is bought and sold in the market in a straightforward way, and since much of the income of the very poor is expended on food, it may be helpful to see the entitlement to food in terms of *incomes*. . . . This rather simple way of seeing the entitlement problem is a bit incomplete since income has to be earned and the causes of the inability to earn enough income would have to be studied, investigating endowments (including labour power) and exchange possibilities (including employment and wages). Nevertheless the level of income is a crucial variable in understanding the entitlement to food and can be treated as such without losing the essentials of a more complete approach. (Sen, 1984, p. 519)

The real value of income depends, of course, on prices, and it is this link between nominal and real purchasing power, especially in terms of food prices, which concerned writers adopting 'income-based' approaches to famine analysis in the 1970s and 1980s. It might therefore be argued that Sen merely introduced a new array of terminology to define phenomena that were already well understood. For example, someone's entitlement to food can fall because either their nominal or their real (food) income declines, or both – either they *earn* less (drastically less if they lose their job), or they can *purchase* less (because food prices rise). In both cases their entitlement to food (or purchasing power) is reduced, and starvation may follow if it falls too far, and no 'safety net' in the form of family support, social security or food aid compensates. Both the 'entitlement' and the 'income-based' approaches predict this outcome. Note also that neither approach regards a food shortage as the direct cause of starvation. Rather, a general shortage *of* food reduces an individual's access *to* food, through the market mechanism.

However, Sen argues that the entitlement approach is broader than the income-based approaches because of the distinction it draws between *direct* and *trade* entitlement failures. This is particularly relevant in the case of food producers, whose greater vulnerability to famine (over low-paid urban workers, for instance) seems at first paradoxical. A brief examination of the relative positions of urban and rural residents soon resolves the apparent contradiction.

Urban wage-earners generally enjoy more stable incomes than small farmers, whose earnings vary seasonally and year-to-year, according to the climate. Urban dwellers have greater political influence than the dispersed and isolated rural poor. Welfare services, such as social security and food voucher schemes, can shield urban workers from the worst effects of job loss, in sharp contrast to the position of, say, landless labourers. Finally, cities have access to food supplies and incomes from a variety of sources, both locally and abroad, while small farmers depend on their agricultural output for both their food consumption needs and as a source of 'exchange entitlement'. This raises the vulnerability of those who derive their living from agriculture dramatically, since a decline in crop yield simultaneously reduces their exchange possibilities *and* the food they have available for consumption – that is, both their trade-based and their production-based entitlements to food. Neither FAD nor the income-based approaches, which each emphasizes one of these effects, has the complexity to recognize both.

Another reason why the focus on incomes is incomplete is that it fails to consider non-market entitlements – which include not just aid and welfare transfers, but also the complex social relationships which exist between rural households (the 'moral economy' and extended family networks, patron–client bonds, reciprocity and sharing arrangements). Bongaarts and Cain (1982, p. 54) contend that in patriarchal societies, a third kind of entitlement can be identified (apart from 'direct' and 'trade' entitlements), which recognizes the importance of the distribution of entitlements *within* the household – namely, the non-market 'dependent entitlement' of women on men:

> women in rural Bangladesh are denied access to important forms of wage
> employment and are prohibited from engaging in many activities necessary for
> agricultural production. The exclusion of women from such activities places them in
> a position of economic dependence on men. Their food entitlement, therefore, is
> frequently established through men: husband, father, or son.

This entitlement will fail in the event of a husband or father's illness, death or desertion, leaving the woman dependent on finding other means of securing food. Bongaarts and Cain argue that women widowed or abandoned during the Bangladesh famine of 1974 were particularly vulnerable for this reason.

In short, entitlements to food are provided not only by incomes, but also by own production and by transfers. Downing (1986, p. 8) summarizes these three categories of 'food entitlements' as: 'the access to food *produced* on one's own holding, *purchased* in local or distant markets, or *donated* by friends, relatives or agencies' (emphasis added).

Of course, these elements are all explicitly mentioned by Sen – they correspond to his categories of 'production-based', 'trade-based' and 'transfer' entitlements. One reason why the broader dimensions of entitlements are often overlooked (particularly transfers) is that Sen himself uses a much narrower concept in his empirical applications than the theoretical framework allows. Swift (1989, p. 10) accuses Sen of unnecessarily restricting his attention to the same topics as those addressed by 'FAD' and the 'incomes-based' approaches: namely, sudden collapses of food production and of real incomes:

> in his detailed analysis of cases, he deals almost entirely with production and exchange failures, concentrating on the relative role of each in the genesis of particular famines. Under the label of entitlements, he is in fact concerned with wage labour rates and livestock prices relative to grain prices.

Sen's own failure to develop his conceptual framework to its full potential may largely explain why the entitlement approach is frequently caricatured (as seen below) as a banal idea dressed up with fancy jargon.

6.4   Limitations of the entitlement approach

Despite its immediate and widespread acceptance in the early 1980s as the new dominant theoretical approach to famine analysis, several reservations about the entitlement approach were expressed which persisted throughout the decade. Initial academic reaction to *Poverty and Famines* ranged from the ecstatic to the scathingly dismissive. Brett-Crowther (1983, p. 95) questioned the book's 'practical value' and its 'academic validity', and concluded: 'Amartya Sen has produced an essay which will save not one life, and may not even save half a conscience.' Mitra (1982, p. 488) opened his attack in the Indian journal *Economic and Political Weekly* with 'Banality becomes Electra. Or does it?'

These rhetorical objections aside, several valid limitations of the approach have been identified. Sen himself mentions five, none of which, in his view, seriously challenges the basic theory. First, he notes that an individual's entitlements may be ambiguously specified, especially in societies where property rights are not clearly defined. This may make it difficult to apply the theory where, say, communal land ownership or interlocking factor markets significantly affect entitlements (da Corta, 1986). Second, in Sen's (1981, p. 49) words:

while entitlement relations concentrate on rights within the given legal structure in that society, some transfers involve violation of these rights, such as looting or brigandage. When such extra-entitlement transfers are important, the entitlement approach to famines will be defective.

As will be seen in Chapter 12, the disruptive effects of war can overturn established entitlement systems, undermining the theory's explanatory power completely. Even without war, Appadurai (1984, p. 483) describes entitlements as 'excessively legalistic' – severe famines especially are characterized by 'the breakdown of morality' (for example, the abandoning by men of their families), so that normal sources of entitlements are eroded or collapse.

Third, since the entitlement approach sees famine mortality as resulting from an inability to obtain sufficient food, it cannot explain excess deaths which are *not* related to starvation – such as epidemics caused by concentrations of displaced people in unsanitary refugee camps. Again, this factor may be more important than Sen allows. If famine mortality is not inversely correlated to individual incomes or entitlements, but is mostly caused by 'a changed disease environment' (de Waal, 1990, p. 481) which strikes more or less indiscriminately, what explanatory role is left for entitlements?[2]

Fourth, the approach implicitly assumes that people facing starvation will consume as much food as they can. But this does not necessarily follow. 'A person starves *either* because he cannot acquire enough food, *or* because he can but does not (e.g., because of inflexible food habits, or laziness, or ignorance). The entitlement approach concentrates on the former' (Sen, 1980, p. 616). While recognizing this bias, Sen did not treat it as significant until 1986, when he acknowledged Svedberg's contribution to the analysis of 'starvation by choice' (Sen, 1986a, p. 10). Svedberg (1985, p. 12) suggested that: 'It is not altogether implausible that some people find the utility of consuming non-food higher than that of food (at the margin), even though they may starve in some sense.'[3] He reasons that, for the poor, other basic needs (clothes, shelter, medicine or fuel) may sometimes take precedence over food, so that 'their maximisation of survival or welfare may imply that some starvation is the "best" possible solution.'

Studies of poor households' responses to famine, or 'coping strategies',[4] confirm that *rationing* of consumption is a universal and almost immediate response to food shortage. Jodha (1975, p. 1619) observed that Indian farmers hit by drought preferred hunger to selling their assets: 'the objective of the farmers' adjustment mechanisms is to protect the assets and the sources of future income of the farmers, rather than current consumption.' Similarly, in western Sudan, in 1984–5, de Waal (1989, p. 7) found that: 'Satisfying the pangs of hunger is not a major concern for famine-stricken families. . . . Their priority was instead to preserve their way of life, to avoid destitution.' This suggests that the entitlement approach concentrates too narrowly on food consumption during famines – as do the 'food availability decline' theories which entitlements set out to depose. In reply, Sen would argue that 'voluntary rationing' applies only to *non*-famine situations:

> if the focus of attention is shifted from famines as such to less acute but possible persistent hunger, then the role of choice from the entitlement set becomes particularly important, especially in determining future entitlement. For example, a peasant may choose to go somewhat hungry now to make a productive investment for the future, enhancing the entitlement of the following years and reducing the danger of starvation then. For entitlement analysis in a multi-period setting the initial formulation of the problem would require serious modification and extension. (Sen, 1986a, pp. 9–10)

The evident disagreement between the theoretical entitlement approach and the empirical coping strategies literature may reflect different perceptions of the nature of famine. Whereas Sen talks of people being 'plunged into starvation' (see Appendix 6.1, p. 82), studies of household responses support the view that famine is a process rather than an event, during which a number of sequential adjustments (such as rationing) are made to minimize the twin threats of destitution *and* starvation.

As a result of his subsequent work on intra-household distribution issues, Sen (1986a, p. 9) later added a fifth limitation of entitlements theory to the list:

> in order to capture an important part of the acquirement problem, to wit, distribution of food within a family, the entitlement approach would have to be extended. In particular, notions of perceived 'legitimacy' of intrafamily distributional patterns have to be brought into the analysis, and its causal determinants analysed.

This deficiency may be one of focus rather than substance. Sen does mention 'inheritance and transfer entitlement' as one possible source of access to food, but analytical attention has concentrated on 'endowments' and 'exchange entitlements', reflecting Sen's concern to describe famines in self-provisioning communities and/or market-based economies. On the other hand, it is obviously vital to explore further how entitlements at the household level translate into entitlements for individual household members. An infant, for example, has no labour power with which to produce food; it has no assets to exchange for food. How does it survive? In Sen's original terminology, on 'transfer entitlements'; more recently, he has referred to '"extended entitlements" influencing intra-household divisions' (Sen, 1988, p. 13); but neither term is very satisfactory. Nor is Downing's reference to 'donations' (1986, p. 8).

Bongaarts and Cain (1982) coined the phrase 'dependency entitlement' to cover intra-household transfers, as discussed above, but this is a passive term which does not reflect the complexity of relationships between husbands and wives, or parents and children. The implication – that households consist of discrete producers and consumers, the second group being totally dependent on the first for its survival – is no more valid empirically than the assumption that all incomes entering a household are pooled, or that resources are distributed equally among household members, or according to need. There is much scope for recent (and ongoing) theoretical and empirical research on 'household economics' to develop this neglected aspect of entitlement theory.

Perhaps Sen glossed over the problem of dependants because of measurement or specification difficulties. The value of someone's assets can be accurately estimated and converted to their food equivalents. But to what level of food is an infant 'entitled'? And how can a collapse in 'dependency entitlements' be predicted, analyzed and quantified? As Field (1989, p. 14) has observed, entitlement is an empirical, not a normative concept, but dependency introduces a certain nebulousness to an otherwise neat and elegant analytical framework.

Stewart (1982), reviewing *Poverty and Famines*, suggests four 'aspects of a famine-prone system' which receive, in her view, inadequate attention in Sen's book. First, famines typically occur when 'normal' entitlement arrangements change suddenly. The theory as it stands says little about how and why such changes come about. Second, since famine invariably affects the poorest most, it requires only minor changes in the entitlement arrangements of groups already on the edge of starvation to push them into famine. Conversely, in societies where average incomes are significantly above the starvation level, and where the incidence of poverty is low, the risk of famine is much less. This suggests that the causes of poverty and of famine are fairly closely related, but Sen only refers to these connections; he does not explore them in any depth. Third, adjustment lags are neglected:

> Famines are about lags in adjustment as well as about entitlement failures – or rather the entitlement failures are largely a matter of time-lags: rice prices rise dramatically; agricultural wages do not follow immediately – in the meantime, during what economists call 'time-lags', people starve. . . . These critical time-lags would not cause starvation if people could use past savings to live on in the meantime, or borrow. But because they are poor they have no past savings and little access to loans. Again poverty and famine-proneness are related. (Stewart, 1982, pp. 145–6)

Extending this thought, it might be relevant to examine the extent to which entitlements generate further entitlements. For instance, wealthier people have preferential access to credit and insurance markets, more political influence over the control and ownership of resources than the poor, and so on. So people with a range of entitlements are better insulated against both the likelihood (*ex ante*) and effects (*ex post*) of adverse shocks to their entitlements. Famines also tend to have polarizing effects, as assets are transferred from poorer to richer people at 'distress' prices.

Fourth, apart from *economic* time-lags, Stewart (1982, p. 146) identifies *political* delays as being significant contributory factors in most famines:

> Food distribution centres are often set up, but they can be too late for some. . . .

The political lags can only occur where there is no ongoing institutional scheme for poverty relief. In developed countries, there are systematic and ongoing relief schemes, which automatically deal with changes in the system. Hence this type of political lag is avoided.

This point echoes the idea mentioned earlier that famines are also caused or prolonged by the non-arrival of food aid – what might be called a failure of 'relief entitlements'. Stewart (p. 146) concludes her review with the observation that *Poverty and Famines* is more descriptive than prescriptive, partly because it lacks a political dimension:

> This book offers a framework, not a cure. . . . we need to get behind the elegant framework to the political economy of reality: what is the politico/economic system that lies behind these entitlement collapses? How can they be avoided? Who will benefit or lose? . . . The framework provides the scaffolding with which to build an analysis of the political economy of poverty and of famine. But more is needed for an effective attack on either.

Other critics have also commented on the static and apolitical nature of the entitlement approach. Mitra (1982, p. 488) criticizes Sen's 'bashfulness' in deliberately not relating 'the problem of poverty and famines to the phenomenon of asset and income inequities'. If wealth is unequally distributed, then so is vulnerability and mortality during famines. But the theory comments only elliptically on the political and socioeconomic processes which precede a collapse of entitlements (such a collapse being a necessary precondition for famine). Bush (1985a, pp. 61–2) implies that it is Sen's focus on famine as an *event* which allows him to ignore the *historical* allocation of differential entitlements and vulnerabilities:

> The emphasis in Sen's account though is too much on the *conjunctural*, immediate cause and outcome of famine: on issues directly linked to the distribution and circulation of food rather than on the interrelationship between the short term changes in peoples' entitlements to food – for whatever reasons – and the longer term social and economic underdevelopment of Africa and elsewhere. It is only by recognising the[se] connections . . . that a more meaningful and adequate analysis of ways to prevent future famine can be made.

Sen's approach effectively treats entitlements as given, or exogenous to the analysis; it cannot explain how entitlements are determined. According to Swift (1989, p. 10), entitlements is 'ahistorical' – 'unable to cope with changing vulnerability over time except by pointing to changing exchange or terms of trade risk. In fact, Sen's analysis treats each crisis as a new event, unrelated to earlier or later crises.' Appadurai (1984, p. 481) offers a solution to this omission, one which would insert a political context behind Sen's socio-economic concept:

> To Sen's conception of entitlement, we need to add another concept that I shall call 'enfranchisement', by which I mean the degree to which an individual or group can legitimately participate in the decisions of a given society *about* entitlement.

Famines raise questions about the relationship between entitlement and enfranchisement in any society, at any moment in history.

Da Corta and Devereux (1991) draw on Appadurai's concept to argue that the conquest of famine requires the effective enfranchisement of vulnerable groups – which is a political as much as an economic process. Elsewhere, da Corta (1986) has argued that the entitlement framework might usefully be combined with social anthropology approaches – in particular, with peasant mobility studies – to add a dynamic dimension to the analysis of the vulnerability of specific groups:

> I contend that for the analysis of famine causation there are two main elements which must not be neglected, both of which are related to the social structure and mobility of individual households and groups:
>
> (1) *a dynamic approach* to place the complete process of entitlement change in a historical perspective and thereby examine the antecedent and sequel processes to the rise and decline of entitlements, as well as changes in the very nature of entitlement systems;
> (2) *a vulnerability analysis* to examine how changes in entitlements over time influence the nature and persistence of vulnerability. This involves a separate examination of long and short term changes in the determinants of:
>   a. individual vulnerability to starvation (defined as susceptibility to an entitlement decline); and
>   b. aggregate vulnerability to famine.

Sen (1986a, p. 4) would defend himself against some of these criticisms by saying that the entitlement approach does not offer a general theory of famine causation, but aims only to provide a coherent framework for famine analysis. 'The entitlement approach provides a particular focus for the analysis of famines. It does not specify one particular causation of famine – only the general one that a famine reflects widespread failure of entitlements on the part of substantial sections of the population.' However, he admits that he is concerned mainly 'with *characterisation* rather than *determination* of exchange entitlements'. He further believes that this is all the approach can do or should do: 'there is clearly little point in trying to develop a general theory of exchange entitlement determination' (Sen, 1981, p. 174). Many of his critics are not so sure.

6.5   Conclusion

There is no doubting that Sen's entitlement approach revolutionized famine analysis during the 1980s. The famous quote at the start of this chapter asserts that famine can occur without a shortage of food. Equally important is Sen's argument that, when a food shortage does occur, its effects will be mediated through the *distribution* of available food among the affected population. 'In essence, Sen's approach has moved the presumption of famine causation from production to distribution, and has, specifically, placed household purchasing power at the centre of investigation' (Crow, 1986, p. 4).

None the less, Sen's theory has also been heavily criticized. Entitlements has been accused of being ahistorical, apolitical, economistic and static. It is regarded by some as too broad for practical application, and by others as so limited that it is tautologous – an elegant, academic way of saying nothing more than 'people starve because they can't buy enough food'.

It is notable that few critics have dismissed entitlements as irrelevant or wrong (though some do hold the view that supply failure has been excessively denigrated as a causal variable, particularly in explaining recent African famines). Rather, they complain that the approach has often been applied too narrowly, and have suggested important ways in which it might be extended. Urgently needed at this stage are the development and incorporation of various non-market or 'transfer' entitlements, including:

- *Dependency entitlements* (between individuals within households);
- What might be called *latent entitlements* (sources of food or income which become operative only when normal sources of entitlements fail); notably:
- *Social entitlements* (claims on or donations from other households); and
- *Relief entitlements* (food aid and other crisis-triggered transfers).

Finally, a better understanding of the historical generation and evolution of individual, household or group entitlements is essential if the persistence of vulnerability to famine is also to be understood. Without a political context and a dynamic dimension, entitlement theory will remain focused on proximate causes; will continue to view famine as a unique, extreme event; and will retain its bias towards food consumption protection as the predominant objective of famine victims – even though all these biases are almost certainly incorrect.

Appendix 6.1   Entitlements and starvation: a graphical approach

On pp. 47–8 of *Poverty and Famines*, Sen (1981) provides an 'Illustration of Endowment and Entitlement', which usefully summarises the key elements of his theory, and also highlights some of its underlying assumptions and limitations.

The first assumption is that there exists a well-specified 'set of commodity bundles, each of which satisfies' an individual's 'minimum food requirement'. In fact, there is a large and growing literature challenging the definition, even the existence, of a 'biological subsistence' in nutritional terms. But this is beyond the scope of Sen's concerns, and may not be a fundamental obstacle.

In Sen's diagram (reproduced as Figure 6.1 below), only two commodities are produced and exchanged – food and non-food. The minimum food requirement is OA. If an individual has a food endowment (through production, say) in excess of OA, that is, in the region DAE, that person is food secure. (Note that the time-period is not specified, and this is a second limitation of the graphical depiction. Changes can only be analyzed in terms of comparative statics. This is not very helpful if the subject under consideration is, say, the management of grain stocks through the dry season in a self-provisioning agricultural system.)

On the vertical axis of Figure 6.1 is the value in *food* terms of a person's *non-food* endowments (cash income and savings, consumer durables, livestock – any asset which can be sold or otherwise exchanged for food). This illustrates the concept of 'exchange entitlements'. The relative prices of food and non-food assets (the 'food exchange rate') determine the amount of food that a person can acquire through exchange or trade. When the price ratio is **p**, the area under OAB is the person's 'starvation set', and the line AB shows all combinations of food and non-food endowment which together satisfy his 'minimum food requirement'.

A numerical example might clarify this idea. Say a male farmer needs 500 kg of grain per annum to survive. If he produces 500 kg (OA) or more, he is self-sufficient and 'food secure' for the coming year. Alternatively, he might own 10 goats (OB), each of which can be sold for 50 kg of grain. This means he is 'food secure' even if he harvests no grain at all. Several combinations of goats owned and grain produced will achieve this same minimum level of food security: 100 kg of production plus 8 goats, 250 kg plus 5 goats, 400 kg plus 2 goats, and so on.

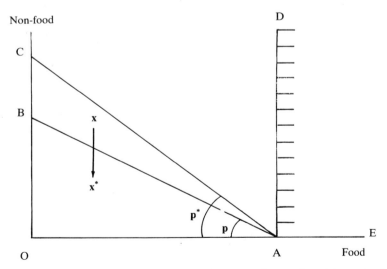

Figure 6.1 Illustration of endowment and entitlement. (Reproduced from A. Sen, *Poverty and Famines* (Oxford: Clarendon Press, 1981) by permission of Oxford University Press.)

Conversely, 200 kg plus 3 goats gives a total food entitlement of only 350 kg, and anyone in this position faces starvation unless he can make up the balance somehow. In Sen's terminology, the 'starvation set' (the region OAB in the diagram) 'consists of those endowment bundles such that the exchange entitlement sets corresponding to them contain no bundles satisfying his minimum food requirements'. (The idea of a 'starvation set' implies that famine is defined by, or results in, death by starvation – itself a controversial assumption.)

A person who is initially in the seemingly secure position of **x** in the diagram (say, 10 goats plus 150 kg of grain harvested) can be 'plunged into starvation' in one of two ways. First, 'if his endowment collapses into the starvation set' (a move from **x** to **x***, or from 10 goats to 5, perhaps because of animal disease or theft). An alternative not shown in the figure is if a farmer moves from producing enough food for self-sufficiency to not producing enough food – say, following a drought. Sen calls this a 'direct entitlement failure'. Second, 'through an unfavourable shift in the exchange entitlement mapping'. In our example, this occurs if the value of goats falls or the price of food rises, so that the price ratio **p** moves out to **p***, and 10 goats are no longer sufficient to buy 500 kg of grain (the 'starvation set' expands from OAB to OAC). Sen stresses the importance of this possibility, which he calls a 'trade entitlement failure', in which starvation can develop simply because market prices move adversely, with *no change* in either asset ownership or food production. In real famines, it is typical for food prices to rise rapidly while asset prices fall, such that the value of individual exchange entitlements dwindle dramatically in the way Sen describes.

However, the notion that someone can be 'plunged into starvation' is deeply questionable. In Figure 6.1, even if entitlements decline or collapse suddenly, they do not *disappear* completely. A harvest may not be adequate to last a full year, but it might last 5 months easily, and 6 or 7 months with careful rationing. In the meantime, alternative sources of income and food (including wild foods, or food aid) can be sought. In short, the idea that a decline in entitlements to below 'subsistence' immediately or automatically produces starvation has to be modified by the realization that there is usually enough time for alternatives to be found which will make good the difference. As we have seen, the literature on 'coping strategies', which blossomed during the 1980s, has shown that famine victims are extremely resilient to threats to their survival, and that they retain multiple objectives during food crises, avoiding hunger being just one of many.

Notes

1. See Sen (1981), Chapter 6. Bowbrick (1986; 1987) has disputed Sen's calculations about food availability per person during the Great Bengal Famine. This rather

heated argument, continued by Sen (1986b; 1987a) and by Allen (1986), seems to have been resolved more or less in Sen's favour.

2. See Chapter 11 for an elaboration of de Waal's (1989) 'health model' argument.

3. Here Svedberg criticizes Sen for not discussing 'voluntary' starvation at all. 'Sen thus seems to rule out the possibility that poor people deliberately choose some degree of starvation (given their constraints) without being ignorant or apathetic.' This is unfair, since Sen (1980, p. 616) does discuss choice at some length, but it is intriguing that in *Poverty and Famines* (1981) the issue is relegated to a footnote (footnote 11, p. 50).

4. See Corbett (1988) and Devereux (1992) for overviews of the 'coping strategies' literature.

7

Famine and food markets

When the sack of millet costs 6000 francs, isn't that a famine?
Nigerien pastoralist (in Laya, 1975, p. 88)

Markets and market agents, especially grain traders, have been blamed for causing famine both by those subscribing to supply-side theories and by those who believe that famine is primarily a problem of poverty, or 'demand failure'. For example, considerable attention has been paid to food price rises, both as an 'early warning' signal of possible shortages, on the supply side, and as a cause of 'exchange entitlement failure', on the demand side. The analysis of the role of markets also has important implications for policy, as relief measures are typically designed to replace market arbitrage or to provide alternative channels for distributing food.

This chapter is not concerned with the international grains trade, nor with the impact on vulnerability of 'commoditization' (the transition from a subsistence-based to a market-based economy) over time. Those debates will be addressed in Chapters 9 and 12 respectively. The purpose here is to examine the relationship between famine victims and their local markets when food is scarce. What *immediate* role do markets and traders play in either exacerbating or alleviating a localized subsistence crisis?

7.1 Basic propositions

In a well-functioning market for goods, demand by consumers and supply from the market must operate effectively and simultaneously. That is, a real demand for the good must exist before traders will be willing to sell to consumers; and traders must respond rapidly and accurately to changing demand signals

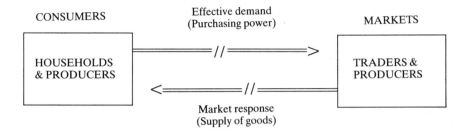

Figure 7.1 Demand failure and market failure.

from consumers. Figure 7.1 illustrates these links. If the commodity being traded is food, a break in either one of these links represents the two distinct ways in which markets might contribute to or create the conditions for famine.

The first of these, 'effective demand' failure, is not due to *market* failure, but is related to the inability of certain groups of people to secure adequate food because they lack purchasing power, despite the existence of functioning markets for food and other commodities. The second category of problem occurs when the market is unable to meet the effective demand for food of a region, even though the necessary demand exists. Only this failure to respond to existing effective demand is 'market failure' in the strict technical sense. Sen (1985a) labels these effects 'pull failure' and 'response failure', respectively.

The entitlement approach is concerned mainly with famines caused by 'pull failure'. This category of problems arises because markets do not and cannot respond to *needs*, but only to *purchasing power* – a factor which may contribute to famines, if poor people lose their ability to buy adequate food. As Sen (1985a, p. 1) emphasizes, starvation resulting from this kind of 'pull failure' can be seen as the outcome of normal market processes:

> 'Pull failure' is not, strictly speaking, a 'market failure' at all, since the market has no preassigned role of giving everyone 'pull' to get what they need. (Those who think of this as a market failure are much too respectful of the market; it is not that kind of institution – with any commitment to equality or justice.) In contrast, 'response failure' *is* a failure of the market in its institutional role.

The distinction between 'pull failure' and 'response failure' mirrors the debate discussed in previous chapters, concerning whether famine occurs because of a failure of demand or of supply. In practice, though, it may be difficult to separate the two. An exceptional rise in food prices devalues the 'exchange entitlements' of food purchasers, precipitating a 'demand failure' as well as signalling that markets are not operating efficiently. Analytical confusion arises here because of the 'natural antagonism' of the marketplace, as consumers strive to meet their food needs while traders simultaneously strive to maximize their profits. This chapter focuses first on arguments which suggest that the operation of markets aggravates demand or 'pull' failure, then on arguments related to 'response' failure.

7.2   Market dependence and demand failure

The most direct link from markets to famine is the fact that depending on markets for food exposes poor people to the possibility of starvation induced by sharply adverse price movements. As the entitlement approach demonstrates, assets and incomes are not the only determinants of purchasing power and food security; what is crucial is the *value* of these resources on the market. During famines, people who normally manage to secure adequate food may find themselves unable to do so, despite controlling the same resources as before:

> If the price of food relative to income rises then the net purchasers, the deficit cultivators and the landless, may no longer be able to satisfy their food requirements. . . . A sudden sharp change in relative prices may therefore bring about famine. (Oughton, 1982, p. 172)

The sequence of events which results in the poor being 'priced out of the market' during a food shortage can be sketched as a chain of causality, as shown opposite (Figure 7.2).

Where incomes are high and supplies fairly reliable, as in the West, buying food in grocery stores and supermarkets does not seem terribly risky. But where incomes are low and markets are fickle, as is typical of famine-prone societies, people who depend on markets for their survival are extremely vulnerable. In relation to south Asia, Harriss (1983, p. 16) has asserted that 'an increasing dependence upon markets for income is associated both with poverty and with nutritionally inadequate control over grain'. Desai (1984, pp. 162, 165) contends that vulnerability is a function of *economic distance* from food production:

> the farther away from direct food cultivation a group is, i.e., the more markets it has to go through to convert endowments into actual consumption, the more liable to starvation it is. Thus, cattlemen of Sahel and Ethiopia, the fishermen of Bengal or tradesmen suffer more than agricultural labourers who suffer more than share-croppers and peasant cultivators. . . . Contrary to market intermediation bringing smooth and beneficent outcomes, it is those who do not have to go through a purchase or sale to convert their income into consumption who are least vulnerable to a decline in real grain wage. The direct producer of grain, either as landowner or sharecropper and the worker who receives a grain wage are safer than he who receives money rent or money wage.

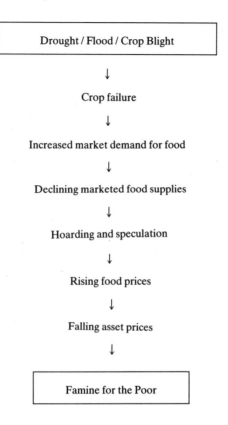

Figure 7.2   Market dependence and famine[1]

Desai's reasoning embodies an assumption that the risks for the poor of market dependence are greater than the risks of agriculture, even in difficult climates – a debatable generalization. But it is certainly true that wage rates and employment opportunities in rural communities are closely correlated with year-to-year agricultural performance. In bad years, farm wage rates fall and workers are laid off or not hired, while farmers are at least assured of whatever food they manage to harvest.

Shepherd (1984, pp. 95–6) uses evidence from the Sudan to argue that serious consequences will ensue if the distribution of food is left to 'free market forces'. He suggests that markets worsen the position of the poor by aggravating demand failure:

> private mercantile control over the distribution of staple food grains has meant that food deficit areas, such as the semi-arid zones, and parts of Southern Sudan, often

do not receive the amounts of grain needed to maintain a reasonable stability of prices. Merchants will sell in areas where there is purchasing power. This means that food deficit areas also tend to be low income areas. The real tragedy is that low income areas are poorly supplied in drought years when livestock mortality is high and savings cannot easily be mobilised. Famine may result, not because of a scarcity of food, but because of poor distribution of available food.

Elsewhere, Shepherd also sees the profit motive as being partly responsible for minor famines in north-eastern Ghana during the 1970s. He describes how land previously used for food production was gradually given over to the production of more profitable cash crops; how the rapid growth of large towns in the region diverted surplus grain from rural consumers towards the satisfying of urban demands; and how changing relative prices discouraged traders from bringing food into the area from other regions, as they had done before in response to local food shortages. These processes steadily undermined the ability of poor farmers in north-east Ghana to withstand drought. The underlying cause of the hunger which resulted was 'the breakdown of the market, on which, it will be remembered, deficit farmers have depended for their survival during lean times' (Shepherd, 1981, p. 20).

Nothing exposes the differences conveyed by wealth inequalities so clearly as the market for food during a crisis, when food prices rise so drastically that the poor often lack the purchasing power to meet subsistence needs. The reason why prices double or quadruple at times of scarcity is simply that food is a basic necessity, so that its demand is highly inelastic around the subsistence level. A small shortfall in production allows traders to increase prices disproportionately, since the same quantity of food will still be needed by consumers, and traders are well aware of the profits to be made if they can control food supplies while the shortage lasts. The problem for market-dependent consumers is that the inelasticity of their demand for food confers a monopoly power on its suppliers – there is simply no substitute for food, whatever its price. Those who can afford the higher prices will maintain their levels of food intake, while those who cannot must necessarily reduce their consumption, and go hungry.

Moreover, the crisis of famine presents opportunities for the rich and powerful to increase their power and wealth, through the market mechanism. As Hartmann and Boyce (1983, p. 189) observe: 'while to most people scarcity means suffering, to others it means profit.' This applies not only to grain merchants. The obverse of impoverishment is accumulation, and famines accelerate polarization within communities, as the poor are forced to transfer their assets to the rich at unusually low prices. Such 'distress sales' are a common feature of most, if not all, famines:

> under famine conditions prices of assets such as livestock and utensils will decline as desperate people rush to sell animals, farm goods and household goods to get money for food. This has been a generally observed feature of famines, and has been particularly remarked upon in a South Asian context. (Cutler, 1984, p. 48)

The same pressures operate in the markets for labour and for land. During food crises, local labour markets arc flooded with poor people looking for work, even at very low wages. These people might even be forced to sell or mortgage their land (or land rights, where land is not privately owned). Again, 'distress sales' of land have been noted more frequently in south Asia than in Africa, where it is often communally owned. During the 1974 famine in Bangladesh, for example:

> The grain merchants were not the only people to benefit from the famine. Moneylenders did a brisk business, and large landowners were able to buy land cheaply from their hard-pressed neighbours. The government's land registry offices had to stay open late into the night to handle the record sales. (Hartmann and Boyce, 1983, p. 189)

The general point is that famine benefits those who already control sizeable resources, such as grain merchants, moneylenders and landowners, while it deprives the poor of their limited resources at unfairly low prices (or through extortionate interest charges on loans). In the case of productive assets such as land or ploughs, especially, 'distress sales' are very serious for the poor, since they entail the conversion of a potential stream of future income into a single cash payment which, when consumed in the form of food, is lost for ever. Once stripped of their assets in this way, the poor lose any possibility for accumulation, and will be doubly vulnerable when the next crisis strikes. And all of this happens through the market mechanism, distorted as it is during famines by simultaneously overpricing restricted supplies of food and underpricing assets sold to realize entitlements to that food.

7.3 Expectations, speculation and hoarding

A considerable literature is devoted to the topic of hoarding (or grain storage for profit) and speculation in relation to famine causation. Some regard these phenomena as examples of market failure or breakdown, while others see them as the normal market function of intertemporal arbitrage. These contrasting views about hoarding – one negative, the other broadly positive – will now be examined in turn.

In virtually every recorded famine, precautionary and speculative withholding of stocks has been blamed for magnifying food supply problems. Spitz (1985, p. 306) quotes Kuang Chung, First Minister to the Duke Huan of the Feudatory of Ch'i, who said in 650 BC: 'That people are starving for lack of food is because there is grain hoarded in storehouses of the rich instead of in government granaries.' The case for the prosecution argues that hoarding is unequivocally bad because it results in artificial scarcities and raises prices excessively:

> If traders and large producers decide to sell stored grain, that selling can ease

prices. If, on the other hand, they decide that prices may continue rising, then they may delay selling their stocks, or even decide to increase their stocks. Such activity would tend to exacerbate any price rise originating in expectations of climatically-reduced output. (Crow, 1986, p. 6)

Countering this view, some neoclassical economists would contend that hoarding can successfuly ameliorate a food supply crisis, by accurately anticipating it. The case for the defence begins with the assertion that speculation in foodgrains should be seen as a rational and desirable response to demand and supply signals. Assuming that traders and producers have full information about market conditions for both the present and the foreseeable future, then even a fairly steep rise in food prices can be said to reflect a justified expectation of higher prices to come. The price rise is not 'excessive', it simply occurs sooner (and less severely) rather than later.

An immediate objection is that rationing of consumption through the price mechanism tends to occur not over time, but between rich and poor, as will be argued below. However, if the theory were true, then a partial withholding of stocks would effectively spread the impact of a food shortage over an extended period. As Oscar Wilde might have said: 'There is only one thing worse than hoarding, and that is not hoarding.'

> If a famine is prolonged, then hoarding at the early stages will improve foodgrain availability later on. . . . Indeed, if there is a complete set of markets, and each one clears at each point in time under Arrow–Debreu assumptions, then one could do no better (at least from a Paretian point of view) than give profit maximizing hoarders a free rein in determining the allocation of consumption over time. Although these are strong assumptions, one can reasonably argue that future scarcity makes at least some storage desirable, even in a famine. (Ravallion, 1987a, p. 59)

This view requires good information on which to base decisions. Inaccurate information – in the form of unrealized expectations of future scarcities, for instance – can cause agents to overreact to demand and supply signals. This has the unfortunate effect of exacerbating the actual problem – a minor production shortfall becomes a major reduction in marketed supplies, and a fairly small price rise is magnified out of all proportion. By reducing dramatically the amount of food that the poor can afford to buy, such a price rise contributes directly to turning a general food shortage into a famine for the poor. 'By this reasoning, famine is attributed to the expectation on the part of foodgrain stockholders of a substantial future price increase or future rationing' (Ravallion, 1985, p. 15)

Ravallion has tested the hypothesis that excessive hoarding due to biased information contributed to the severity of the Bangladesh famine of 1974. Ravallion's econometric modelling of Bangladeshi rice markets during the 1972–5 period took as its starting point the assertion that spot prices for food should reflect agents' 'rational expectations' of future price and supply conditions, if markets are performing well and information is adequate. Conversely,

> if there is convincing evidence that readily available information on likely future scarcity affected current prices independently of realised future prices then it is reasonable to conclude that either market prices do not adjust to eliminate excess demands or that the information on future scarcity is leading to biased price forecasts. In either case, markets are not performing well. (Ravallion, 1985, p. 16)[2]

Ravallion did in fact find evidence of a systematic bias in rice prices before and during the famine, caused by overly pessimistic predictions in the press of expected crop damage due to flood. He concludes that agents were misled by inaccurate information, but were behaving as rationally as could be expected, given this constraint:

> The results indicate that newspaper reports of future crop damage resulted in higher rice prices during the period and that this effect existed independently of future prices. . . . Thus, rice hoarding prior to anticipated production losses was excessive when compared to the likely outcome under competitive conditions with informationally efficient expectations. (Ravallion, 1985, p. 28)

Expectations of food scarcity following the floods were heightened by a US embargo on food aid and by the government's difficulties in buying grain on the world market (see Chapter 12.4). Even so, Sobhan (1979, pp. 1976–7) agrees with Ravallion that food producers and traders over-reacted to expected cutbacks in the government's public food distribution as imports were squeezed during 1974:

> by March, cutback in deliveries of grain began to have a disproportionate effect on grain prices which are acutely sensitive to even small changes in the marketable surplus. Prices almost doubled between February and June 1974. Rising prices and anticipation of shortages fed the tendency to hold grain both by panicky producers and grain traders waiting for a big killing on the market. . . . The famine as it emerged was thus largely man-made rather than one of absolute shortages. Its immediate cause was due to the hoarding and speculation of grain producers and traders. . . . As a result, entire segments of the rural poor were priced out of the market and faced with starvation.

This case study provides strong evidence against the belief that hoarding smooths out food shortages. According to Sen (1981, p. 76), this factor also contributed to the Great Bengal Famine of 1943:

> demand forces were reinforced by the 'indifferent' winter crop and by vigorous speculation and panic hoardings. The hoarding was financially profitable on the basis of even 'static expectations': rice prices had more than doubled in the preceding year. . . . There was an abnormally higher withholding of rice stock by farmers and traders from the winter harvest of 1942–3; the normal release following the harvest did not take place. A moderate short-fall in *production* had by then been translated into an exceptional short-fall in *market release*.

Because speculation and storage behaviour reflect expectations about future price or supply movements, they tend, unfortunately, to be self-reinforcing. If, for instance, a large farmer withholds his crop from the market in anticipation of a price rise, this fall in supply may be sufficient in itself to push up local prices, fulfilling the farmer's expectations. The problem is exacerbated in smallholder communities, where the fact that peasant producers consume much of their own production can create major problems for purchasers. As Seaman and Holt (1980, p. 289) point out, a barely noticeable decline in production can halve the marketed surplus of food and raise its price dramatically: 'all other factors being equal, if 10% of a crop is sold as surplus, a 5% fall in yield would cause a 50% fall in surplus sold, after subsistence needs are met.'

Withholding food from the market is likely to increase as the price of food (or other commodities) rises, for many reasons. Large farmers will withhold their surpluses for speculative purposes, hoping for further price increases; small farmers will store food as a precautionary measure against spiralling market prices; and general inflation might reduce the willingness of farmers to convert their produce into cash. Finally, if farmers are aiming to meet fixed financial commitments (such as rent or taxes) rather than to maximize profits, the proportion of a crop which needs to be sold, as prices rise, will fall. The special feature of food which produces this vicious spiral of falling supply and rising prices stems from food's dual role as a source both of income and of necessary consumption to the producer.

Demand factors add to the problem. A price rise initiated by a supply failure implies reduced production by farmers, who may be unable to meet their subsistence needs from their own harvests, and therefore add their demand for food to that for the reduced marketed supplies. If this demand is supported by 'distress sales' of assets such as livestock, farm implements or land, prices are likely to be pushed up still further. Grain traders and large farmers stand to profit from these transfers of assets from the poor to the wealthy. If a crop failure is widespread, or markets are imperfect, there might be a further increase in the demand for speculative stocks of grain by traders who expect further price rises (provided that prices are expected to rise in excess of grain storage costs).

7.4 Imperfect or fragmented markets

Whereas hoarding modifies the *temporal* allocation of foodgrains during food crises, market fragmentation affects the *'spatial* performance of foodgrain markets in eliminating localized scarcities' (Ravallion, 1987b, p. 13). A single poor harvest can transform a rural economy, as farmers switch overnight from being self-provisioning or surplus *producers* to market-dependent *consumers*. If markets were fully integrated and functioned perfectly, supplies of food could simply be brought in from other markets in surplus areas, with little effect on prices or consumption in either area. Yet dramatic rises in local food prices (which reflect market fragmentation), are symptomatic of food shortages, and have been incorporated as crisis indicators in many famine 'Early Warning Systems' (EWS) for this reason.

The notions of a fully integrated and a totally isolated 'island' economy should be regarded as two extremes on the spectrum of actual possibilities. In reality, the extent to which regional food shortages are translated into local food price rises will depend not on *whether* markets are integrated or fragmented, but on their *degree* of integration:

> the paradox of hunger without severe loss of production depends on the level of aggregation. If Bangladesh is regarded as a fully integrated production system with smooth inter-district flows of commodities, then there is no production problem. But to the extent that there are frictions and difficulties in moving commodities between districts, regionalised losses of production can have severe effects on food prices, intensifying the effects of loss of production, income and employment. (Clay, 1985, p. 203)

Bangladeshi villages are not totally 'integrated' in market terms, nor are rural Ethiopian villages totally 'isolated', but the two situations incline to those respective ends of the 'closed-to-open-economy' spectrum, so it is probable that transport and communications difficulties will play more of a role in explaining Ethiopian than Bangladeshi famines. If traders in Bangladesh can be said to 'over-react' to food shortages (by hoarding), then Ethiopian traders might be accused of 'under-reacting'.

Two issues are relevant in this discussion – transport and communications problems, and spatial price differentials in excess of transport costs. Only the second can truly be said to represent a failure of the market, though both may contribute to the occurrence of famine. Each will be discussed in turn.

It is widely believed that the incidence and severity of famines may be directly related to the level of development of transport networks – particularly roads and railways. It is almost certainly true, as Dando (1980, pp. 101–2) asserts, that 'advances in modern transportation assisted in reducing the numbers of famine deaths in the past one hundred years. International trade has removed spatial restrictions on food supplies to isolated areas.' Drèze (1988, pp. 15–21) argues this for the case of British India:

> Before the large-scale development of the railways from the 1870s onwards, private trade in foodgrains within India notably lacked in dynamism, and local scarcities precipitated very damaging price hikes. . . . Entitlement failures were exacerbated by the sluggishness of trade and the large price disparities obtaining between adjacent regions. . . . Of the fact that the expansion of the railways resulted in a greater tendency towards a uniformity of prices there can be little doubt. One may also generally expect a reduction of price disparities to reflect greater food

movements towards famine-affected areas, and to result in an improvement of the food entitlements of vulnerable sections of the population in these regions.

So the construction of railways in India had a beneficial effect in terms of reducing regional price and food supply disparities, though it did not in itself eliminate famines. Drèze notes that it is not enough for the means to supply a region with food to exist. Traders still need to be attracted into the region, and what attracts them is purchasing power.

Although infrastructure of all kinds has improved dramatically throughout the world during this century, this improvement has been patchy and uneven, to such an extent that many neglected people and regions have possibly been made *worse off* as a result. (As, for example, where food is taken out of rural areas by traders and sold in urban areas, raising rural food prices to the detriment of poor consumers.) Even where good quality transport systems do exist, they are not always appropriate to the needs of the rural population, and do not solve the problems of fragmented markets. This was particularly true in colonial Africa, where administrators supervised the building of numerous sophisticated road and rail networks – primarily to facilitate the extraction of cash crops and minerals from the interior to sea ports. Household food security and foodcrop production were secondary to colonial greed for quick profits, and 'cash crop famines' occurred routinely in several colonies.

The argument that infrastructural imperfections can exacerbate famine is often supported by reference to the problems of famine relief in Africa, where the victims of drought or crop failure often live in isolated and inaccessible communities. As discussed in Chapter 5, low population densities in much of rural Africa mean that there is limited scope for economies of scale in the provision of infrastructure.

Ethiopia is frequently cited as an example of poor infrastructure plus fragmented markets contributing to the general vulnerability of local people. Kumar (1985, pp. 4–5) describes the problems in relation to famine relief policies:

> Donor shipments take longer than expected, increasing the time taken to deliver assistance; breakdowns in the transport network, already overstretched, are to be expected, particularly in the light of the unavailability of spare parts locally. Relief work is made all the more difficult by the terrain of the country: roads are often impassable or cannot handle the heavy lorries required to carry food; the widely dispersed nature of many village communities makes airlifting supplies problematic.

Griffin and Hay (1985, pp. 46–9) identify grain price variability, both over time and between villages which are fairly close together, as evidence of fragmented markets in Ethiopia, and they differentiate between the effects of patchy infrastructural development and market imperfections:

> The evidence thus points to a highly fragmented market with very imperfect flows of grain and information. . . . The most obvious reason for the limited movement of

grain is the nature of the roads and the limited access they provide to rural areas. Grain may have to be packed by mule for days to reach a market where merchants are buying. Furthermore the road system has been developed to serve Addis Ababa. Direct inter-regional links are non-existent. . . . a combination of demand pattern, the political imperative to feed the urban population and poorly distributed transport infrastructure determines the pattern of grain flows, leaving much of the rural areas isolated and without access to the national market. . . . Often the market, such as it is, breaks down entirely and there is little or no trading in areas where production has been disrupted by drought.

An argument which lends support to the 'market fragmentation' theory of famines has been advanced by Seaman and Holt (1980). They suggest that prices rise in a series of 'ripples' around a food shortage region as those afflicted migrate to neighbouring markets where food is more readily available. Seaman and Holt (1980, p. 291) have provided evidence of just such a price wave during the Bangladesh famine of 1974, the speed of the wave 'roughly corresponding to the speed of communication between markets', and they believe that a similar pattern was a feature of the 1974 Ethiopian famine. Cutler (1985b) has subsequently produced 'price contour maps' for food markets in Ethiopia during 1983, which reveal the same process at work.

Cutler (1984, p. 50) sees mass migration as 'a terminal indicator of distress' during famine, at least in Ethiopia, and he describes how waves of migration are reflected in waves of rising food prices around the famine region:

As the food crisis deepens and large numbers of people migrate out of the famine zone, food prices begin to rise at the periphery, reacting to the increased aggregate effective demand of the victims (constrained though it is for individual households) and to reduced supplies as the population in the peripheral areas expands.

This observation contradicts the neoclassical economist's belief that the 'invisible hand' of market allocation will ensure that food supplies move in response to price signals, from 'excess supply' to 'excess demand' areas, until a single-price equilibrium is restored. The 'price ripple hypothesis' reflects the reality of the breakdown of markets and market signals which typically accompanies a crop failure in isolated, self-provisioning communities.

If traders do not bring grain into a deficit village, this might be because people there have no money to buy food. But if the 'price ripple hypothesis' – that prices get pushed up in neighbouring markets around a famine epicentre as people move to markets because of the failure of markets to come to them – is correct, this can only be because demand pressure does exist after all. Food prices would not rise unless some purchasing power 'pull' remained among the population. When people with cash or something to sell have to migrate to buy food, the market has clearly broken down. Cutler (1985b, p. 5) outlines an alternative to the 'entitlements collapse' model of peasant behaviour during a drought-induced regional food crisis:

peasants would respond to crop failures by selling off livestock and by seeking work. At the same time prices of foodgrains in local markets would be forced up to unusually high levels by supply constraints, in turn forcing peasants to buy food elsewhere. Far from being subsistence farmers who had entirely lost their 'entitlements' to food through crop failures (as argued by Sen, 1981), drought-hit peasants would be thrown onto the market, where they would manage to get some income through asset sales. The able-bodied would be forced out of the famine zone in search of work and cheaper food. In this way famine conditions would also be exported as migrants put pressure on supplies in other areas, thereby forcing up the price of grain and flooding labour markets.

And yet the paradox remains: *why* do traders not bring grain into markets where people are desperate for food? In a discussion of the Wollo famine of 1972–4, Devereux (1988) suggests two compatible explanations, one reflecting demand or 'pull' factors, the other supply or 'response' factors. The first argument is that inequalities in wealth distribution within famine villages create inflated signals of real effective demand. Following a local production failure, food prices will obviously start to rise. But high prices do not have the identical effect on all consumers. It is the relatively wealthy who exert most of the real upward pressure on food prices, while the poorest will rapidly be forced out of the market. 'Hence the brunt of the reduction in supply inevitably falls on the poor, because of their acute sensitivity to food price rises' (Devereux, 1988, p. 280).

The second point relates to the 'transactions costs' traders would face in supplying famine villages with grain. Traders would not necessarily respond, even to unusually high prices, because they would recognize this signal as illusory. It would require costly reorientation of marketing routes to start supplying remote villages which were normally self-sufficient with grain; there would be only a few wealthy consumers willing to pay very high prices; and the market would not last beyond the next harvest, when prices and demand would fall back to normal levels. All these factors add up to a much smaller profit potential than the high prices initially suggest:

> Traders may well have found it more convenient, and probably more profitable, to continue their established pattern of transporting food from rural to urban areas, rather than setting up new routes at great cost and uncertain reward to supply small, isolated communities with a few bags of grain each for a short period of time. (Devereux, 1988, p. 278)

The combined effect of these two sets of factors is to suggest a disaggregated explanation of the Wollo famine, one that recognizes the role of both 'FAD' and 'FED' ('food entitlement decline') approaches.[3] Both the 'pull' and 'response' failure views have their merits; both supply and demand factors have explanatory power:

> The Wollo famine might be described as a FAD famine for those who retained some wealth but were unable to convert this into food, due to regional food shortage and market failure, and a FED famine for the poor, who were made

destitute by the collapse of their direct and exchange entitlements, which excluded them from what market for food still remained. (Devereux, 1988, pp. 280–1)

7.5 Conclusion

'The dependence of the population of a low income society on market supplies of food, on the exchange of commodities and money has been recognised as a powerful influence on its vulnerability to famine' (Harriss, 1981, p. 4). Market dependence exposes poor consumers to the threats of destitution and starvation induced by sharply adverse price movements. In particular, escalating food prices and collapsing asset prices may transform a modest supply decline into a critical demand collapse for vulnerable groups. These risks emerge from the fact that food, though a basic necessity for human survival, has been commercialized like any other commodity. The distribution and marketing of food is usually undertaken by traders, whose primary objective is the maximization of profits, rather than the survival of the poor.

Market integration redresses this vulnerability by reducing price differentials across markets. Provided that poverty and transactions costs are not a binding deterrent to traders, food should move smoothly from surplus to deficit areas, with prices rising only in proportion to transport costs. Conversely, the more isolated and fragmented markets are, the greater the incentive for traders and producers to hoard food for speculative or precautionary purposes, and the more likely it is that those markets that do exist will become completely distorted during a local food shortage.

An important practical issue is raised by the distinction, repeated throughout this chapter, between 'response failure' and 'demand failure'. These two disruptions between people and food markets (as shown in Figure 7.1, p. 87) call for significantly different policy responses. Where pure 'market failure' rather than 'demand failure' predominates, governments or international agencies must step in to substitute for the market, as Sen (1985a, p. 3) explains:

> the 'response failure' is often truly serious, and the market often does fail for reasons of ignorance, inefficiency, bottlenecks and manipulation. . . . Further, the governmental role in moving food from other countries into the famine-stricken one cannot really be taken over by traders as such, since the level of organisation and authority needed cannot be found elsewhere.

The failure of the Bangladeshi government's food distribution mechanism probably contributed to the famine of 1974, but Clay (1985, p. 206) argues that its success during a flood crisis of similar magnitude helped to *prevent* a comparable tragedy in 1984:

> the well articulated public distribution system through which large quantities of grain are poured into rural areas, and on a considerably larger scale in periods of

stress, dampens any possible effects of reduced food production on prices and helps sustain livelihoods of many of the most vulnerable.

Demand failure, on the other hand, requires a different approach – a transfer of resources to those who are destitute and therefore cannot secure enough food, even if markets are functioning well and are adequately supplied. 'Demand failure' is an entirely separate problem from 'market failure' – one that also contributes to the origin of famine, but for which markets cannot be blamed. In this case, it might be appropriate to deliver cash relief rather than food aid to famine victims (see Kumar, 1985; Sen, 1985a), to stimulate local production and trade, and to encourage grain merchants to perform their spatial arbitrage role between surplus and deficit markets.

Finally, a limitation in most discussions which relate famine causation to market failure is the economists' tendency to ignore or dismiss *non*-economic sources of subsistence. (This criticism applies equally to the entitlement approach – at least in the way it has commonly been applied to famine analysis to date.) In so far as self-provisioning peasant producers are thrown onto the market when their harvests fail, markets certainly do become immensely important in times of shortage. In addition, though, people survive famines by rationing consumption, gathering wild foods, finding new sources of income, calling on remittances from families or redistributive mechanisms within the community, receiving food aid, migrating, and many other means. The market may be the central focus of concern for economists, but it is only one element in the picture for famine victims. The extent to which market failure should be held responsible for famine is a function of the extent to which vulnerable people depend on markets for their survival, no more and no less.

Notes

1. Adapted from Garcia and Escudero (1982, p. 4).
2. In the original (mimeo) version at Queen Elizabeth House, University of Oxford, Ravallion has the phrase 'market prices do not adjust to reflect scarcities' where the *Economic Journal* version has 'market prices do not adjust to eliminate excess demands'. This modification probably reflects an editor's preference for technical jargon, but it also implies two fundamentally different views of the world – one neoclassical, the other perhaps more humane.
3. The working title of Devereux (1988) was 'FAD + FED = Famine: not a refutation of Professor Sen's theory' (cf. Bowbrick, 1986). 'FED' in this context had two possible interpretations, the first reflecting the jargon of 'entitlements' – 'food entitlement decline' – the second the jargon of economic theory – 'failure of effective demand'.

PART 3

The political economy of famine

8

The management of natural resources

Famine is a consequence of the failure to learn from the constant interactions between a society and its physical environment.

Mesfin Woldemariam (1984, p. 178)

The persistence of famine in Africa is closely connected with the fragility of Africa's natural environment. This in turn relates to other themes in the 'supply-side' vein of famine literature: the role of drought and climate generally in famine causation; the neo-Malthusian 'carrying capacity' debate; and (the specific subject of the present chapter) the control and management of natural resources. The difference in emphasis between this chapter and that on climate is that the earlier discussion focused on *events*, especially droughts, whereas here we examine longer-term *processes*, such as soil erosion. (This is not to suggest that climatic events and environmental processes are unrelated, since they clearly are.)

There are three broad strands to arguments which relate the degradation of natural resources to increasing famine vulnerability. The first sees famines as caused by inexorable 'natural processes', such as the encroachment of deserts on previously arable lands. The second blames the 'ignorance' or 'irrationality' of local people, who are seen as victims of their own inefficient agricultural methods, or of conflicts between private and social ownership of resources. The third strand regards ecological degradation as a logical consequence of exploitative colonial or post-colonial relationships between classes of people and hence between people and nature, and suggests that where capitalist penetration disrupts indigenous social and economic practices, famine is a tragic but predictable outcome. All three views reflect the pessimism of inevitability and are open to criticism for this and other reasons.

8.1 'Natural degradation'

An obvious example of environmental deterioration which might appear to be almost entirely due to natural forces is desertification, or 'desert creep'. Desertification has been defined technically as 'a process leading to reduced biological productivity, with consequent reduction in plant biomass, in the land's carrying capacity for livestock, in crop yields and human well-being leading to the intensification or extension of desert conditions'. But soil erosion and even changing rainfall patterns do not happen spontaneously and independently of human populations. Many contemporary deserts were once the sites of fertile lands and flourishing cities. The implication is that intensive use of fragile ecological resources has at least contributed to making arable lands barren. An alternative definition, therefore, sees desertification as 'the spread of desert-like conditions in arid and semi-arid areas due to man's influence or to climatic change' (UNCOD, 1977, and Rapp, 1974, respectively, quoted in Helldén, 1985, p. 78). Others believe that deserts are and always have been arid. 'The African deserts are not man-made dustbowls; they are to be ascribed primarily to the continent's geographical position' (Grove, 1977, p. 54).

If deserts were static, societies could adjust to living on and around them easily enough. Perhaps some arid land could even be 'reclaimed' through irrigation, as has happened in Israel. But just as human populations in Sahelian Africa grow, so the Sahara is growing too. Whether this expansion is natural or man-made is open to debate, but in either case the main issue for famine prevention is whether or not it can be stopped, and if so, whether it can be reversed. Present trends suggest that even slowing down the Sahara's expansion will be impossible without an enormous international commitment of resources and expertise to programmes of sustainable development in the affected regions. A 1985 report, *The Encroaching Desert*, by the Independent Commission on International Humanitarian Issues (ICIHI) spells out the scale of the problem:

> The top soil of Africa is being rapidly lost. The Sahara, particularly, is spreading with alarming rapidity. The United Nations estimates that the Sahara's front line is advancing at 1.5 million hectares (3.7 million acres) a year. For those on the front, for example in Western Sudan, this means a desert advance of some six kilometres a year. (ICIHI, 1985, p. 81)

On an international scale, desertification directly affects nearly a hundred countries, more than a third of the earth's land surface, and 20 per cent of the world's population. An estimated six million hectares of land are irretrievably lost to deserts each year and another twenty million hectares are rendered unproductive (Jacobson, 1988, p. 10). There is also evidence to suggest that rainfall patterns are being disrupted as the desert advances, so that farming communities in semi-arid savannah regions face shorter growing seasons and rising rainfall variability year to year, which threaten their harvests and hence their survival prospects.

In extreme cases, people are forced to abandon their land altogether. 'The effects of desertification on man appear most dramatically in the mass exodus that accompanies a drought crisis' (El-Hinnawi, 1985, p. 26). Jacobson (1988, p. 7) adds that desertification has 'made refugees out of millions of sub-Saharan African farmers in this decade alone. Migration is the signal that land degradation has reached its sorry end.'

Facts and figures such as these used to be presented in support of the view that a deficient and deteriorating physical environment was a sufficient condition in itself for famine, but the question remains: who or what is to blame? It is often difficult to separate out the effects of nature and of people, particularly where the relationship between the two is delicately balanced initially. For example, as Mortimore (1989, pp. 21–2) points out, it is difficult to assess the extent to which environmental degradation in the Sudano–Sahelian zone of Africa 'is attributable to inappropriate management, since mean annual rainfall has fallen by about 25 per cent in the last two decades' alone:

> Desertification or desert encroachment can result from a change in climate or from human action, and it is often difficult to distinguish between the two. This has commonly led to confusion and misconceptions. A temporary or long-continued deterioration of climate may accentuate the harmful consequences of human occupation of the land and *vice versa*. It has often been suggested that man's activities have resulted in climatic deterioration, but this is difficult to substantiate. (Grove, 1977, p. 54)

Grove continues by noting that, on the *margins* of the desert, 'land use practices determine whether they shall be productive or unproductive', and these are certainly areas where farming, grazing and forestation decisions have an enormous impact on soil quality. The tendency now is to regard desertification and related problems (such as soil erosion) as processes which are at least partly explained by the interaction of people with nature, rather than as purely climatic phenomena. As Woldemariam (1984, p. 178) puts it, 'deficiencies in the physical environment are a way of expressing human limitations rather than objective conditions'. Helldén (1985, p. 78) stresses the importance of separating out the human and the 'natural' contributions to declining land productivity, if 'desert creep' is to be reversed. 'Any measures to counteract desertification must be based on the assumption that man plays a major role in land degradation through mismanagement and non-optimal use of the environment.'

These statements typify what is here labelled the 'benign' view of ecology-induced food crises – namely, that famine is a result of human ignorance or limitations – as opposed to the 'malign' view – that famine results from the cynical and callous exploitation of human and natural resources for private profit. These two approaches are now considered in turn.

8.2   'Indigenous ignorance'

Economic development and population growth affect the relationship of people with their environment in several complex ways, most of them negative. In the opinion of Dando (1980, pp. 105–9), the pressure to produce ever more food is creating 'an agro-environment conducive for eco-catastrophes':

> the best arable land in the world is already in agricultural production, productivity potential is being reduced by soil erosion, degraded cropland requires increased energy inputs to counter lost soil productivity and substantial cropland is being lost annually to urbanization and transportation facility construction. . . . Man, provided with a space home with capabilities to support life unlike other known planets, has planted the seeds of his own destruction.

Though this prediction seems excessively alarmist, in many Third World countries it may be coming true, though usually for an array of reasons, related both to the fragility of the natural environment and to agricultural stress:

> environmental deterioration, once set in motion, can become self-reinforcing. . . . The loss of vegetation cover adversely affects the amount of rainfall, and as the former depends on rain its own decline is also speeded up. The natural environment is never a neutral and passive force in the life people make for themselves. People and nature interact. That interaction has become dangerously unhinged in contemporary Africa. Today, methods of agriculture often reinforce the consequences of weather failure rather than providing the means of coping with it. (ICIHI, 1985, pp. 82–3)

The debate about environmental degradation is frequently linked to the Malthusian notion of a regional 'carrying capacity', this being defined as the number of people and animals a specified area can maintain over a period of time. The argument is that when populations exceed this limit, a cycle of over-exploitation of the land is set in motion which ultimately degrades the natural resource base to such an extent that human and animal survival is unsustainable. The effect is of a long-term 'food availability decline', which might result in famine.

Unfortunately, the concept of a regional 'carrying capacity', while seemingly scientific and precise, is empirically elusive. Also, it is defined in relation to 'average rainfall', or 'normal conditions'. A famine precipitated by severe drought does not prove that an area's 'carrying capacity' has been exceeded, any more than a life-threatening earthquake in San Francisco does, because a drought is an extreme event. Furthermore, the concept relies on restrictive Malthusian assumptions, as Mortimore (1989, p. 25) explains:

> the concept of human carrying capacity, or critical population density, is based on the assumptions, as invalid in the Sudano-Sahelian zone as anywhere else, that technology and the productivity of the land are fixed, and that the population entirely depends on primary production. As subsistence household economies diversify, they can escape the Malthusian net.

The fact that human societies evolve and adapt to changing conditions has led some writers to reject altogether the notion of 'carrying capacity':

There is thus no natural limit to an area's carrying capacity. . . . For there are different levels of sustainable combinations under identical ecological circumstances. To put it another way, there is no one answer to the question, how many people a semi-arid or arid tract of land can support. (Hjort af Ornäs, 1990, p. 118)

Whatever the validity of the 'carrying capacity' idea, population pressure in rural areas clearly is dangerous when it alters the relationship between people and their environment in a mutually harmful way – for instance, if population growth is accommodated by reductions in fallowing periods, by excessive subdivision of farming land, and by cutting down trees for fuelwood faster than they can be replaced. Jacobson (1988, p. 9) comments that such practices, 'while they may ensure a meager harvest for tomorrow, make certain famine is inevitable'.

This is, arguably, precisely what has happened in Ethiopia. Hancock (1985, pp. 74–5) asserts that the drought, which triggered the famine of 1984, 'occurred in a country where environmental degradation, in the form of erosion and deforestation, has been going on for centuries'. More than half the land in the highlands was described in 1984 as seriously or moderately eroded, some 4 per cent of it irreparably (Stahl, 1990, p. 140). Despite several environmental rehabilitation initiatives by the government – building terraces on hillsides, closing degraded areas to farming and tree planting programmes (not to mention villagization and forced resettlement of people in less populated areas (see Chapter 10.2)) – the demographic, economic and political constraints seem insurmountable. 'Due to population increase, stagnation in agricultural technology, civil war and insecurity, the pace of degradation is bound to increase' (Stahl, 1990, p. 140).

It is important to recognize that people do not *choose* wantonly to destroy their environments. Commentators who use cases like Ethiopia to condemn famine-prone communities as 'victims of their own backwardness' have usually failed to consider the secular social and economic (as well as demographic) processes which preceded the production crisis, or its differential impact on various groups of people. Nor do they appreciate the sophisticated strategies indigenous people have devised which, far from decimating their physical environments, enable them to survive all but the worst crises in harsh and unstable ecosystems. Instead, outsiders rush in with 'technical fixes' for Africa's ecological problems – interventions which rarely seem to achieve much good.

Richards (1983, p. 54) criticizes this tendency 'for agencies external to African rural life to imagine that they are filling a vacuum of knowledge and technique. Ecological crisis – overpopulation, pollution, desertification – is seen as a crisis of ignorance and incompetence'. Even worse, Richards continues, are cases where an ecological crisis is 'manipulated as a strategy for bringing about the extension of central political control. Some have argued that the Sahel drought was used in this way by state bureaucracies as a way of gaining greater control over difficult nomad populations.'

The problem of 'overgrazing' in Africa apparently constitutes an even clearer case of the human/nature equilibrium being altered, for a variety of reasons, with consequent problems of environmental deterioration. Pastoralists in Africa traditionally built up their herds of livestock in years of good rainfall, but since they have gradually been forced onto more marginal lands, by political hostility and the advance of commercial agriculture, this may have increased the incidence of desertification. At the same time, as human populations increase and grazing land deteriorates, livestock herds start to fall, undermining the asset base of vulnerable households.

In Karamoja, a drought-prone semi-pastoralist region in north-east Uganda, for example, Fitzpatrick (1986, p. 7) estimates that there were nearly 700,000 head of cattle in 1969, but that this had fallen to between 200,000 and 300,000 by 1985. When drought and war hit Karamoja in 1979–81, the traditional strategy of selling off livestock for cereals had been undermined to such an extent that famine ensued.

These problems are often presented as a 'tragedy of the commons' or 'prisoners' dilemma' situation, arising from contradictory patterns of resource ownership when property rights are not clearly delineated in a community. In the case of pastoralists, the contradiction occurs between *individual* ownership of livestock and *communal* ownership of natural resources such as land, trees and water. The result is that each individual's income from adding to his herd is greater than his share of the social loss (in terms of reduced land quality) resulting from overgrazing, so each individual has an incentive to increase his herd beyond the carrying capacity of the land.

Sen (1981, p. 128) sees the vulnerability of the Sahelian herders to drought and famine as arising from this 'conflict of economic rationale'. Because pastures are held communally and animals are owned privately, this conflict becomes critical when pastureland is in short supply, since a vicious circle is then set in motion:

> The problem is further compounded by the fact that the animals, aside from adding to the family's usual income, also serve as insurance . . . so that the tendency to enlarge one's herd, causing overgrazing, tends to be stimulated as uncertainty grows. And the overgrazing, in its turn, adds to the uncertainty, by denuding the grass cover and helping desert formation.

The conflict between private and socially rational behaviour has already been discussed in the context of population growth; a comparable analysis is thus possible for both the 'overpopulation' and 'overgrazing' syndromes in developing countries. Both arguments assume irrational or ignorant behaviour on the part of those supposedly 'guilty' of overgrazing or overpopulation. The way in which the logic of the overgrazing model is frequently applied to the overpopulation issue has been summarized by Richards (1983, p. 3).

> obeying old and inappropriate instincts, parents continue to produce more children than society needs or there are resources to support. Without change in these

attitudes, mounting pressure on available resources will, it is predicted, eventually cause the collapse of ecological systems. Evidence relating to soil erosion, desert creep, deforestation, and increasing levels of environmental pollution is taken to signal the beginnings of such collapse.

However, since the 'tragedy of the commons' only has relevance when natural resources are limited, it is not sufficient to blame famine in Africa on 'overgrazing' and/or 'overpopulation' without examining the reasons for essential resources being limited *with respect to certain groups of people* in the first place. Just as food insecurity creates the vulnerability which might cause poor households to increase the size of their families, so natural resource constraints (such as the encroachment of farmers into pastoral areas) creates the vulnerability which may result in poor pastoralists increasing the size of their herds 'excessively', or overgrazing limited pasturelands.

Contrary to conventional wisdom, a substantial literature now suggests that pastoralists left to their own devices make very effective and sustainable use of their fragile environments, employing a variety of risk-minimizing strategies not only to protect themselves against drought, but also to preserve the longer-term viability of their herds, their environment and hence their way of life.

Watts (1987, p. 178) applauds 'the belated recognition that farmers and herders are expert practitioners of their respective modes of livelihood and are particularly sensitive to reproduction of the ecological systems of which they are part'. African pastoralists, he continues, have developed 'a plethora of adaptive strategies' in response to changing economic and environmental pressures. 'The recent spate of detailed ethnographic work also emphasizes the intense concern of all herders with the possibility of overgrazing and range deterioration . . . in contrast to the view that pastoral systems inevitably lead to overgrazing.' Timberlake (1985, p. 98) echoes this favourable reassessment:

> Pastoral nomads are not, in fact, locked into a destructive land–livestock relationship. Nor are they romantic independents, living in perfect harmony with Nature. The nomads are highly skilled and knowledgeable herdsmen, with a long tradition of making the best of a tough environment. Many are able to adapt quickly to changing circumstances, to take advantage of new opportunities or to save themselves in time of drought.

It is when external constraints impinge on pastoralism – such as attempts by the state to 'sedentarize' pastoralists, and the encroachment of farmers onto grazing land, or when herds are prevented from crossing (ecologically artificial) national boundaries – that environmental sustainability is undermined. Hjort af Ornäs (1990, p. 117) argues that: 'Freedom of movement across boundaries is necessary so long as extensive methods of livestock herding are practised . . . to maintain the ecological balance.' More generally, Bush (1985a, p. 88) asserts that:

> as the informed observer of pastoral systems now increasingly knows, nomadic grazers 'make the *best use* of marginalised arid lands'. . . . It is precisely the

imposition of grazing controls and sedentarisation, and the creation of ranches, thereby reducing the mobility of herds, that reduces pastoralists' traditional strategies for survival.

The debate over the contribution of human societies to ecological degradation, as epitomized by the controversy over pastoralists, has been summarized by Mortimore (1989, pp. 20, 23) in the form of two opposing hypotheses – two contrasting perspectives on the same situation:

> *Hypothesis 4a* In drought-famine associations, long-term and cumulative environmental degradation – resulting from inappropriate cultivation practices, overgrazing, excessive fuelwood cutting, burning and deforestation – reduces primary productivity and thereby accentuates food crises; the process is self-reinforcing in that increased poverty (both in depth and in social extent) drives the poor to over-use natural resources to which they have access, discounting long-term benefits against survival in the short-term.
>
> *Hypothesis 4b* Poor people value the long-term benefits of productive assets, to which they enjoy secure rights of access, and try to manage them in such a way as to realise these benefits, even at high cost in terms of short-term benefits forgone.

Mortimore (1989, p. 24) concludes that: 'The possibility that indigenous systems of land use are compatible with sustainability tends to be under-estimated.' This is supported by the growing evidence that poor people facing subsistence crises strive to preserve their productive assets at all costs (including 'choosing hunger' in the short term). The only doubt remains over the issue of whether communal assets or *public* goods are preserved as fiercely as *private* goods.

Perhaps the most appropriate conclusion to be drawn from this debate is the usual warning that each of Mortimore's hypotheses might be applicable to specific circumstances, but that neither can describe *all* situations where ecological degradation has heightened vulnerability to famine.

8.3   'Malignant exploitation'

External influences have contributed much to the conditions which brought about Africa's current ecological crisis. Several writers argue that famines in Africa are a long-term consequence of the exploitation of subsistence agrarian economies. The polarizing effects of colonialism and capitalist development, it is argued, have further impoverished already poor nomads and peasants and, even worse, have set in motion a lengthy and complex process of ecological deterioration which has made these groups more vulnerable to drought and famine than ever before.

Radical versions of the 'ecological mismanagement' approach to African famines see capitalist exploitation during the colonial period, followed by post-colonial dependency relationships, as the root cause of much of Africa's present ecological, agricultural and broader economic problems. Several writers have developed this theme, both theoretically and empirically. The crux of the argument is summarized by Blaikie (1985, p. 124), in his polemical book, *The Political Economy of Soil Erosion*:

> soil degradation and erosion can be explained in terms of surplus extraction through the social relations of production and in the sphere of exchange. The essential connection is that, under certain circumstances, surpluses are extracted from cultivators who then in turn are forced to extract 'surpluses' (in this case energy) from the environment (stored-up fertility of the soil, forest resources, long-evolved and productive pastures, and so on), and this in time and under certain physical circumstances leads to degradation and/or erosion.

The problem can be generalized by noting the contradiction that arises between *conserving* a resource for the long-term benefit of the local population and *exploiting* that resource for the short-term benefit of a population far away. Repetto and Holmes (1983, p. 613) argue that the conversion of a controlled subsistence demand into an insatiable commercial demand inevitably initiates its overexploitation. 'This commercialisation of the demand for the resource made the demand largely independent of the size of the local population and undermined the cultural adaptations that had effectively conserved the resource.'

The argument insists that, even if Africans themselves are inflicting irreparable damage on their environment, this is in no way their fault. Rather, they are forced into this ruinous behaviour by the processes of capitalist 'surplus extraction'. The very fact that those who suffer most are those doing the damage is evidence that their behaviour is not 'irrational', but *involuntary*:

> Usually the classes and groups most adversely affected by soil erosion are politically weak, disunited and spatially separated. . . . For those, such as the rural semi-proletariat and the absolutely landless with little control over the means of production with which to meet their needs, even individual responses are denied them. In essence their class position often forces them into using the environment destructively and inhibits any adaptive response to its inevitable deterioration. (Blaikie, 1985, pp. 91, 89)

Meillassoux (1974, p. 27) takes an even stronger line, in his analysis of the Sahelian famine of the early 1970s. (This famine receives more detailed treatment as a case study in the following chapter.)

> If the drought can be seen as an act of nature, the same cannot be said for the famine, which is largely the result of a policy of agricultural exploitation carried out for the benefit of the great powers in the Sahel. This famine crudely reveals that what is called famine or aid is nothing more than a policy of exploitation.

The thrust of this Marxist approach is that colonialism not only robs colonized people, it also rapes their land, the primary objective being the maximization of short-term profits. Meillassoux (1974, pp. 28–30) pursues this theme:

> This is achieved by running an economy of despoliation, on the one hand exhausting
> the soil and/or other raw materials, and on the other, over-exploiting the rural
> population. . . . the extraction of surplus from a mode of production with such limited
> means usually results in the exhaustion of the factors of production. The increase in
> labour productivity, necessitated by demand within the capitalist sector, is paid for
> by destructive methods of cultivation and a depletion of the soil resources.

Arguments of this kind are closely related to the 'dependency theory' and 'development of underdevelopment' literatures. The debate revolves around the question of whether monetization and the commoditization of agriculture typically improves or undermines the food security and general welfare of poor rural communities. Reviewing a number of African case studies, Cliffe and Lawrence (1979, pp. 1–2) suggest that there seems to be a clear correlation between the declining ecological potential and reduced food producing capabilility of rural societies on the one hand, and 'the onset of agrarian capitalism' on the other:

> This is not an argument which simple-mindedly translates the blame for such
> tendencies from 'natural causes' to 'capitalism', as though it were some abstract evil
> spirit. Rather it seeks to explain the widespread hunger in Africa, increased
> dependence of agricultural countries on food imports, and the rapid growth of the
> rural poor, in terms of a complex and interrelated array of forces that have changed
> both the *social system* – the mode of production and the whole superstructure built
> on it: property rights, the division of labour, patterns of kinship – and *ecosystem*,
> the interrelationship between society and environment. The consequences add up
> to a reduced ability of societies, still mistakenly thought of as 'subsistence
> producers', to produce their basic requirements and thus to reproduce themselves.

8.4   Conclusion

Within each hypothesis of famine causation a polemical debate is raging, and nowhere fiercer than in the area of ecological degradation. 'Right-wing' writers blame nature ('desert creep') or 'ignorant Africans' (overgrazing); 'left-wing' writers blame colonialism, capitalism and post-colonial dependency relations. The only consensus in the debate seems to be that it is the *relationship* of human societies to their environment which is crucial.

This chapter has summarized three approaches to the issue of environmental deterioration and its effects on the potential for famine. The order in which they were discussed was suggested by their increasing complexity and sophistication. The first view sees only the overt 'natural' processes and the event of famine in fragile environments, and assumes a direct causality. People are depicted as helpless victims of fickle Nature. The second school looks behind 'natural disasters', at the interaction between people and environment, and argues that 'ignorance' (as revealed in misguided demographic, agricultural or pastoral practices) precipitates the ecological crises which produce

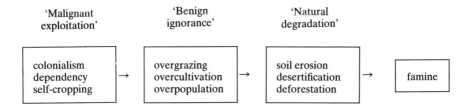

Figure 8.1 Ecological degradation and famine.

famine. The third category examines the interactions between classes and between societies which condition the relationship between particular groups of people and nature, and suggests that those most vulnerable to famine are victims of exploitation or marginalization.

Figure 8.1 illustrates crudely how these schools of thought might be linked – each providing a more fundamental explanation for the final outcome: increased vulnerability to famine. These arguments are not, therefore, mutually exclusive.

Each school of thought proposes quite different policy implications – which again highlights the importance of sound theory in analyzing such complex, vital problems. If vulnerability to famine arises from 'natural degradation', then the problem is a physical one and, given capital and technology, should be solvable by technical interventions such as reforestation and irrigation schemes. If the problem is one of 'benign ignorance', the solution lies in educating vulnerable communities about appropriate management of their herds, better agricultural techniques and methods of soil and water conservation. By contrast, the logical solution to environmental degradation caused by 'malignant exploitation' is social and economic revolution, or at least substantive policy changes involving, say, land reform and income redistribution.

As always, it seems inappropriate to try to arbitrate between the competing explanations discussed above. No single school of thought or hypothesis can provide a complete framework for analyzing the links between ecological degradation and famine. Famines should always be explained as the product of a combination of factors, many of which reinforce each other in the creation of crises. All that can be said with confidence is that the debates aired in this chapter play an important and probably increasing role in explaining food crises in arid and semi-arid areas, particularly those which regularly threaten farmers and herders in Sahelian Africa.

9

Famine and development

Famine is inversely related to development.
John Field (1989, p. 8)

The idea that development may increase vulnerability to famine might seem incompatible with the observation that the risk of famine is lowest, in the contemporary world, in precisely those countries and regions where average incomes and living standards are highest. In theory, development should be about providing communities with their 'basic needs' – better health care, education, employment opportunities, transport and communications, social security services and, of course, secure access to a healthy diet at all times. In practice, policy-makers often equate development with economic growth. Yet there are real reasons to question whether the pursuit of growth is unequivocally beneficial to all segments of a poor and vulnerable population.

Growth generates inequality. While this much is clear, many related questions remain unresolved in the development literature. Is the process of increasing inequality secular or temporary? Is this inequality relative, or does it imply increasing absolute impoverishment for the poor? Under what circumstances is rising aggregate wealth accompanied by rising vulnerability, and how can vulnerable groups be protected?

This chapter examines several strands of the debate which relate 'development' specifically to famine. Most include the proposition that development is associated with increasing inequalities between communities and households, resulting in rising vulnerability for some groups of people. The main ideological and policy divide in the debate is about whether this tendency is irreversible or simply a temporary by-product of development.

9.1   Marginalization and development

An early model of development, Rostow's 'stages of growth', saw all societies as moving smoothly through a similar, linear evolution (albeit at different points in time and at different speeds) – starting out as low income, subsistence economies and ending up as high income, welfare capitalist states. Five stages were identified: 'the traditional society, the preconditions for take-off, the take-off, the drive to maturity, and the age of high mass-consumption' (Rostow, 1960, p. 4). Similarly, many contributions to the 'dual economy' literature saw development in the Third World as being fuelled by the growth of a 'modern', urban industrial sector, which would flourish by absorbing low-productivity rural workers from the 'traditional', subsistence-based agrarian economy, until all this 'surplus labour' is productively employed.

In reality, these projections were extravagantly optimistic, and real-world experience suggests that a more discriminating analysis is required. In most Third World countries, the 'modern sector' has remained small, isolated and capital- or skill-intensive, such that comparatively few people who left the rural areas found permanent wage employment in the cities. Conversely, small farmers who remained on their land were frequently coerced or otherwise induced (by taxes and other needs for cash) to switch out of subsistence food production and into market-oriented cash crop production. Those who could not compete in this brave new world were reduced to sharecroppers or landless labourers, dependent on poorly paid employment on capitalist farms.

The drive for economic growth can leave some people behind – not just 'banished from the mainstream of social and economic progress' (Sahli, 1981, p. 493), but often deprived of their meagre resources too. If this 'marginalization' proceeds too far, they become impoverished and vulnerable to famine. Wisner's (1976, p. 1) definition of 'marginalized' people implies that capitalist development, while causing major disruption in the short run, may or may not be beneficial for the marginalized in the long run: 'A marginal person or household is one whose mode of production has been seriously disturbed or destroyed by its contact with the capitalist mode of production, yet whose productive energies have not yet been absorbed by the latter.'

A more cynical view is that capitalism deliberately marginalizes people in order to exploit them more effectively. Sahli (1981, p. 490) defines marginalization as the formation of harmful dependency links between a poor region or community and some malign external force:

> the phenomenon of 'marginalisation' . . . is an historical process involving the domination of these specific zones by other zones. It is also, and in particular, a phenomenon that has brought socio-economic impoverishment and cultural isolation to a considerable part of the population, in that the undermining of land structures and the pauperisation of the inhabitants of these 'marginalised' zones have led to the dependence of these zones on an external environment, which has a different logic of its own.

In some places, marginalization occurs by literally pushing people into 'marginal areas'. By compounding the pressures on natural resources, this pauperization of people invites calamity. The resilience of both human and natural adaptive mechanisms is tested to the limit as 'marginalized' people are forced to compete among themselves for insufficient and low quality land, trees and water. Sustainable and well-adapted systems of production are undermined, forcing people into patterns of behaviour that unsympathetic observers denigrate as 'ignorant' or 'irrational':

> Once allocated to marginal places, their social relations of production as well as means of production distorted if not virtually destroyed, these marginal people have no alternative but to resort to ecologically unbalanced land use. Thus eco-demographic marginality is caused by socio-political and economic marginality, not the other way round. (Wisner, 1976, pp. 2–3)

This relates back to the arguments in the previous chapter about the use and abuse of natural resources. But Wisner's (1976, p. i) argument here is that this kind of development can increase vulnerability to famine, because it results in 'the destruction of the peasant modes of production and their corresponding sets of adjustments or coping mechanisms to the stress of drought'. Wisner's case study, the Kamba people of Kenya, supports research elsewhere in Africa, which reveals 'that drought vulnerability is a product more of regional growth and income disparities than of physical environmental risk alone; and that famine potential is highest where these regional income and growth disparities coincide with climatic variability and in-migration by landless persons.' In this light, the Kenyan famines of the 1960s and 1970s should be seen as a direct consequence of the marginalization of peasants, following the surge in cotton and coffee cash-cropping during the previous decade:

> Coffee provided an effective modern, external linkage to reduce the famine vulnerability of a few Kamba, while the majority were pushed further into marginality . . . despite the greater spread of newly-generated cash-crop wealth between upland and downland Ukambani, this was not enough to prevent the continuing decline into eco-demographic vulnerability of the majority of Kamba. Serious famines occurred in 1961–62, 1965 and between 1970 and 1974. (Wisner, 1976, pp. 18–19)

It is surely no coincidence that the main recipients of drought relief aid in 1983/4 were these same Kamba people. The process whereby colonialism in Kenya marginalized people and increased their vulnerability to famine is neatly summarized in Wisner's phrase: 'enlarged choice for the few; narrowing options for the many'. While some locals and expatriates were making large profits out of cotton and coffee production, the majority of Kamba were losing their ability to secure adequate food. The result was a series of localized crises, or what Sen would call 'boom' famines – in the midst of a rapidly growing and apparently flourishing economy, thousands of people repeatedly faced destitution and starvation.

9.2 Commoditization and market dependence

A universal feature of capitalist development is the growing significance of markets. This 'commoditization' is associated with broader economic and political 'processes of structural transformation through which previously more self-reliant and smaller-scale societies become incorporated into colonies (now nation-states) and global capitalist economies' (Hansen, 1986, p. 228). It is sometimes argued – with equal passion on both sides – that these twin processes of incorporation and commoditization are the main mechanisms by which 'development' either exacerbates or redresses vulnerability to famine:

> Local food shortages could be determinant earlier in triggering famine in a locality, but incorporation means that alternative supplies of food are available elsewhere. Various authors have interpreted this to have positive or negative consequences, i.e., the change diminished or increased the possibilities of famine occurring. (Hansen, 1986, pp. 241–2)

The immediate contribution of markets to food crises was discussed in Chapter 7. The reasoning here relates to 'commoditization' more generally and over a longer period of time, but the arguments do overlap in some respects:

> As markets spread through and transform rural areas, so individuals come increasingly to depend upon the workings of markets for survival, by selling goods or their own labour to buy food. The net result is an increase in the *vulnerability* of many people, especially those who own few resources bar their labour. Small farmers, pastoralists, labourers, crafts workers become vulnerable not only to drought and pests but also to changes in prices and quantities on volatile markets. Previous payments in kind are transformed into cash: 'more modern perhaps, more vulnerable certainly'. Old methods of insurance against disaster weaken or disappear. As a result, famines can be caused, or more often sharply reinforced, by the normal workings of the market. (Mackintosh, 1990, p. 43)

Similarly, Harriss (1983, p. 1) presents 'an hypothesis about poverty and undernutrition. It is that, among the ultra poor, the incidence and intensity of undernutrition is more often than not associated with the level of dependence of the household upon markets.' This applies not only to the (buyer's) market for food, but also to the (seller's) markets for assets, agricultural inputs and produce. People buy food by selling things – animals, jewellery, labour (for wages) and non-food cash crops. The commercialization of agriculture which frequently accompanied colonialism involved a fundamental transition in rural economic orientation, from one geared primarily to food production for domestic consumption to one directed (at least partly) to raising cash income through producing cash crops (cocoa, coffee, cotton, etc.) for the market. More profitable perhaps; more vulnerable certainly:

> There is almost always some increment of risk in shifting from subsistence production to cash cropping. A successful subsistence crop more or less guarantees the family food supply, while the value of a nonedible cash crop depends on its

> market price and on the price of consumer necessities. Quite apart from the
> frequently higher costs of growing and harvesting cash crops, a bumper cash crop
> does not, by itself, assure a family's food supply. (Scott, 1976, p. 20)

This is not the place to arbitrate on the 'cash crop, foodcrop' debate, only to point out that real and potentially fatal risks are associated with *both* sources of subsistence. Another factor to consider is the change in land tenure systems which often accompanied colonialism. The introduction of private property rights, for instance, 'could result in a group with less powerful representation losing residual entitlements such as hunting rights, thus intensifying difficulties experienced in times of food shortage' (Richards, 1983, p. 43). When forests and other sources of 'secondary crops' get fenced off, access is denied to everybody but the owners – either the state or wealthy individuals whose need for these vital 'famine foods' is negligible.

The case *for* commoditization chooses to overlook these costs and losses in favour of the enhanced opportunities which are provided by linking the local economy to geographically wider markets. The main advantage claimed is in expanding the diversity of incomes and sources of food. In the case of western Sudan, for example, agricultural commoditization is sometimes seen in a broadly beneficial light, as a process which has provided new buffers against disaster:

> It has been argued that the expansion of commercial farming leads to a rural
> population being more vulnerable to famine. In Darfur this did not occur . . . the
> growth of a labour market has in fact made small farmers more secure as there are
> more fall-back opportunities in the case of crop failure. . . . The people of Darfur
> are sceptical of the idea that the growth of what Watts (1983) called
> 'commoditisation' has increased vulnerability to famine. On the contrary, they
> credit their ability to withstand famine to the very same factors. Rather than a
> balance being ruptured in the rural economy, a balance was returning. (de Waal,
> 1989, pp. 69–70)

In Ethiopia, similarly, Dessalegn Rahmato (1987) argues that the contraction in off-farm sources of income – wage labour on coffee plantations and commercial farms, petty trading, credit – after the 1974 Revolution deprived rural people of vital alternative entitlements to food whenever their crops failed during the 1980s.

The argument boils down to this dilemma: deepening dependence or widening diversity? Enhanced vulnerability or expanded opportunity? Which is riskier – dependence on an unreliable climate or dependence on a callous market? While various writers have adopted strong positions on both sides of the debate, these questions can only be answered empirically on a case by case basis. Mortimore (1989, p. 17) cites four examples from Africa where market incorporation resulted in a group of people being 'reduced to dependence on aid'; and one counter-example where farmers 'were able to use their increasing involvement in a national economic system to withstand the adverse effects of drought'. Mortimore's (1989, p. 19) admonition is self-evident yet important:

'the impact of economic change ("development") on the resilience of different societies and social groups under famine stress, and on the processes of pauperisation and accumulation, cannot be generalised.'

The point is not *which* source of food or income is the most risky, but *how many* sources people can draw on. This was the conclusion reached by D'Souza (1988, p. 32), in her analysis of the results of a 1985 survey of drought afflicted Mozambicans:

> Protection from starvation is associated with having a range of options (in the Changara study, animals, cash income, land, remittances, agricultural implements, sufficient manpower, etc.) which in turn is related to having a more diverse source of income. Poverty arises from dependence on a single and uncertain source of income and no means to extend the range of choices.

A bleak example of the latter scenario is suggested by Alamgir's (1980, p. 17) description of the conditions which maintain the economy of rural Bangladesh in a 'low-level poverty equilibrium':

> the situation is compounded by the underlying social structure characterised by a low level of productive forces and exploitative production relations that have generated a set of laws of motion sustaining a very low level of living in which the majority of the population seem trapped.

In Alamgir's (1980, pp. 27–8) depressing vision, this 'famine-prone economy' is hovering precariously just above disaster, acutely vulnerable to the slightest adverse shock:

> Over the years, values of other variables change, but income per capita and foodgrain intake per capita tend to fluctuate between poverty and famine level. In a normal year, social arbitration, patron–client relationships, kinship bonds and occasional intervention from the government and international agencies keep the system from sliding below a crisis point in terms of decline in real income per capita, and consequent fall in foodgrain intake per capita.

In an abnormal year such as 1974, the acute vulnerability of this system is tragically exposed. The above depiction of Bangladesh is strikingly reminiscent of Tawney's (1966, p. 77) metaphor for rural China. 'There are districts in which the position of the rural population is that of a man standing permanently up to the neck in water, so that even a ripple is sufficient to drown him.'

Tawney's analogy hints at an important point: that two connected factors combine to produce maximum vulnerability. Poverty is one element, but equally crucial is the *risk* of either a short-run collapse or a long-term erosion of entitlements to food. Poverty magnifies the danger that 'even a ripple' will induce disaster. The dilemma facing the rural poor is whether choosing 'market dependence' (say, by switching to cash crops out of cereals) will raise their living standards rapidly enough to insulate them against price fluctuations and other 'ripples', or whether the first drop in cash crop prices or rise in food prices will be sufficient to swamp them.

9.3   The moral economy meets colonial capitalism

It is impossible to generalize about whether colonialism, capitalism and agricultural commercialization increased or reduced vulnerability to famine, on balance, without knowing more about pre-colonial societies than we do. It is widely believed, though, that capitalist development typically entails a *disintegration* of the so-called 'moral economy', accompanied or followed by *integration* into the market system, with a corresponding increase in risk. 'The growth of commodity production and market relations has strengthened food security in some aspects, but has also undermined the redistributive guarantees of the pre-colonial economy, replacing them with an uncertain market mechanism' (Swift, 1989, p. 12).

Since rural communities were forced, historically, to rely entirely on their own resources for survival, it is assumed that their energies were directed towards 'simple reproduction' rather than accumulation. The 'moral economy' theorists believe that much stronger non-economic relationships bound community members together in the past than was the case after their incorporation into a wider economy, which promised individual gain at the expense of collective security:

> The fear of food shortages has, in most precapitalist peasant societies, given rise to what might appropriately be termed a 'subsistence ethic'. . . . The precapitalist community was . . . organised to minimise the risk to which its members were exposed by virtue of its limited techniques and the caprice of nature. Traditional forms of patron–client relationships, reciprocity, and redistributive mechanisms may be seen from this perspective. (Scott, 1976, pp. 2, 9)

Scott's (1976, p. 7) description of colonialism in south-east Asia is reminiscent of many interpretations of colonialism in Africa:

> The transformation of land and labour (that is, nature and human work) into commodities for sale had the most profound impact. Control of land increasingly passed out of the hands of villagers; cultivators progressively lost free usufruct rights and became tenants or agrarian wage labourers; the value of what was produced was increasingly gauged by the fluctuations of an impersonal market. [These processes] served to undermine radically the preexisting social insurance patterns and to violate the moral economy of the subsistence ethic.

But Scott (1976, p. 9) is careful not to claim too much for the 'moral economy'. Although some protection was provided against limited or individual threats to subsistence, 'precapitalist society was singularly ill-equipped to provide for its members in the event of collective disaster.' Besides, peasant economies have always been highly differentiated, and are rarely (if ever) as egalitarian as is often surmised.

It would therefore be naive to imply that famines rarely (or never) occurred before the 'invasion of the imperialists', and it is impossible to say whether Africa, had it been left to its own devices, would now be perfectly capable of feeding all its population at all times, despite its uniquely harsh climate and environment. De Waal (1989, p. 61) argues against the view 'that traditional

African systems were well adapted to the threat of drought, and consequently that great famines are a twentieth-century phenomenon', at least for the case of Darfur, Sudan. And Watts (1983, pp. 78–9) accuses some academics of painting 'a mythical "merrie Africa" . . . in their cursory descriptions of pre-colonial subsistence and famine. . . . In a peasant paradise one simply cannot forget about merchants, workers and states even if they are problematic for aspirant anarchists.'

Nor can one forget the fact that famines of the past probably took a much heavier toll, proportionately, on people and animals than they usually do today, simply because there was no possibility of lorry-loads of grain arriving to alleviate food shortages, either in the form of trade or aid. The importance of good transport links to remote communities cannot be over-emphasized as a factor in containing and eliminating famines, and this is surely one of the greatest contributions 'development' has made to reducing vulnerability. As one farmer from Niger commented in an interview: 'The famines of the old times caused much suffering. . . . But people no longer die from famines since there are motor cars now' (Laya, 1975, p. 60). (This is surely one of the most succinctly stated theories of famine ever!)

Returning to the main argument, Mortimore (1981, pp. 16–17) concludes that the replacement of a 'moral economy' with a market economy ultimately 'offers the diversification which is essential' for reduced vulnerability, and he suggests, like Watts, that an ideological romanticism may have biased the debate:

> the disintegration of the precolonial 'moral economy' – with its principles of food storage, social redistribution, reciprocity and group solidarity – by capitalist penetration has been stressed at the expense of the emergence of new opportunities offered within an urbanising and industrialising economy with relatively integrated markets.

9.4 Vulnerability as a 'phase of development'

During the 1970s, social scientists began to focus attention on the increased vulnerability experienced by poor rural households during the *transition* from a peasant or semi-subsistence society to a market economy. The theory is that capitalist penetration of subsistence economies disrupts traditional mechanisms of coping with drought and other crises, and that unless and until alternative sources of income or a social welfare system replaces these mechanisms, large segments of the population will be made more vulnerable to famine than before, even if national incomes and GNP are growing rapidly. The debate about whether the destruction of the pre-capitalist 'moral economy' is 'good or bad' in the long run turns on the phrase 'unless and until'. Burton *et al.* (cited in Hansen, 1986, p. 245) contend that wealthy, 'modern' societies and poor but self-reliant communities may both be less vulnerable to food crises than

[t]hose societies in process of rapid transition or modernization, where
the traditional social mechanisms for absorbing losses and sharing them
among the community have been eroded away and have not yet been replaced
by the accumulated wealth and response capacities of more modern societies.

Sen made an important contribution to this literature when he asserted that the development of (market-based) exchange systems where none previously existed presents both opportunities and 'obstacles' to a society's general development. A pure exchange system, defined as 'one in which all income is derived from some interpersonal exchange' (Sen, 1980, p. 31), is rarely (if ever) observed. Much income in pre-capitalist societies derives from owner cultivation; while 'advanced' capitalist economies are characterized by both market and non-market (social welfare) transfers. But between these two extremes a dangerous tendency toward pure exchange systems is a common feature, albeit temporary, of the development process:

in the process of industrialisation or colonial development a precapitalist economy
typically seems to go through a phase in which its traditional sources of
non-exchange income (cultivation of own land) contract sharply much before the
modern sources of non-exchange income (social security) expand or even come into
existence. There is, then, a much enhanced dependence on the exchange system for
one's survival. (Sen, 1980, p. 31)

This period is associated with new types of risks and vulnerabilities. More succinctly, Sen (1981, p. 173) has written that: 'The phase of economic development *after* the emergence of a large class of wage labourers but *before* the development of social security arrangements is potentially a deeply vulnerable one.' Sen's argument is closely related to the view that the introduction of capitalist values – with resources being allocated through the amoral 'hidden hand' of the market rather than according to needs – undermines the redistributive ethos of the pre-capitalist 'moral economy'. Another way of conceptualizing this phase might be as the period between the moral economy and social welfare; a time when the poor have nowhere to turn at all in times of crisis. As Clay (1986, p. 180) puts it: 'freeing the hidden hand where the basic needs of the *majority* of the people is not assured is potentially a recipe for disaster.'

Sen's awkward label for this awkward period is 'the phase of the pure exchange system transition', or 'PEST' for short. In his view, PEST is significant in terms of 'increasing the vulnerability of large groups of people to economic disasters', and is associated with 'the greater exposure of the economy to the dangers of famines' (Sen, 1980, p. 31). In the Third World, where the unemployed have few sources of protection, one consequence of seasonal or permanent unemployment is malnutrition or 'seasonal hunger'. When entire communities made vulnerable during the PEST phase are further destabilized by climatic variability or adverse processes of development, such as changes in modes of production, the result can be major subsistence crises, or famines.

Sen appears to consider heightened vulnerability during PEST as a temporary problem, affecting the rural poor whose indigenous coping mechanisms and sources of livelihood have typically been disrupted, and have yet to be replaced by satisfactory alternatives. More radical writers than Sen would challenge his perception of development for being too linear and determinist (like Rostow's 'stages of growth'); certainly it seems less applicable to rural Africa, where proletarianization is not very advanced but vulnerability is very high, than to south Asia. In Africa, it is sometimes suggested, the problem is not 'too much' capitalism but 'too little': 'capitalism has failed to "develop" Africa' (Vaughan, 1987, p. 11). Meillassoux (1974, p. 30) believes that it is the partial incorporation of African agriculture into the capitalist system on unfavourable terms which has created the conditions conducive for famine:

> as soon as the domestic subsistence economy, through the use of capital, enters into the sphere of capitalist production, it immediately reveals its low productivity and collapses into bankruptcy. The subsistence economy under a capitalist regime is thus, in effect, unable to withstand any such transition; . . . before the difficult conversion of agriculture is undertaken, capitalism will exhaust the productive capacities of the domestic economy, leading to a shortage of food.

Support for Sen's thesis, not surprisingly, comes from Asia rather than Africa. It is interesting that Scott (1976, p. 10), having criticized colonialism in south-east Asia as a period in which vulnerability increased, suggests that the virtual elimination of famine from that region today is due largely to positive state interventions since independence:

> The colonial period in Southeast Asia, and elsewhere for that matter, was marked by an almost total absence of any provision for the maintenance of a minimal income while, at the same time, the commercialisation of the agrarian economy was steadily stripping away most of the traditional forms of social insurance. . . . In more recent times, of course, the state itself has assumed the role of providing for a minimum income with such devices as countercyclical fiscal policy, unemployment compensation, welfare programs, social medicine, and the negative income tax.

Sen (1990, p. 50) has argued both for general social security programmes and, more specifically, for 'employment guarantee schemes', such as that operating in Maharashtra, India, which functions as a permanent 'wages-for-work' option to whoever chooses to take it up:

> the policy of supplementing people's incomes (e.g., through offering public employment, with wages being paid to the destitute people who seek work) can be one of the most effective ways of preventing famines. This is, in fact, how famines have been systematically prevented in India since independence.

In China, too (the Great Leap Forward famine apart), Sen (1986a) sees the abolition of major food crises as being due to effective state support for the vulnerable. 'The end of starvation reflects a shift in the entitlement system, both in the form of social security and – more importantly – through systems of guaranteed employment at wages that provide adequate exchange entitlement to avoid starvation.'

In fact, the importance of such interventions is economic as much as nutritional. Whereas social security (e.g. unemployment benefit) serves partially to replace lost entitlements following an income collapse (say, redundancy), guaranteed employment schemes have the crucial merit of allowing poor people to preserve their productive assets and limited savings during subsistence crises. This factor makes these schemes a doubly effective form of state intervention. Conventional famine relief has the disadvantage of arriving much too late in the famine process, typically *after* those affected have sold off their assets to buy food. Even if food aid and medical care keep these people alive through the crisis, they will be left extremely vulnerable, forever treading water in Alamgir's 'low-level poverty equilibrium', because of their diminished resources. For instance, emergency asistance to the Sudan continued well into 1986, despite record harvests following several years of drought, because survivors of the famine had been destituted. 'During this famine, their incomes and livelihoods were largely wiped out, leaving the survivors without means to pay for food, even at lower prices' (Raikes, 1988, p. 79). Guaranteed employment schemes, while hardly a perfect solution to poverty and hunger, can keep people alive *and* save them from becoming destitute.

9.5 Case study: the Sahelian famine, 1969–74

The sequence of famines in the West African Sahel have probably provoked more discussion about the links between famine, development and ecological crisis than any other. (Because they raise the specific issue of natural resource management as well as broader development issues, this case study relates to the previous chapter as much as to this one.) But any discussion of the 1970s Sahelian famines must go beyond what Raynaut (1977, p. 19) dismisses as 'the pseudo-evidence of climatic, demographic and cultural determinism'. Raynaut's (1977, p. 18) analysis emphasizes the underlying processes behind the surface explanations of 'climatic uncertainty, excessive population growth, spoliation of the natural environment by man':

> Undeniably in an initial examination invocation of these factors is justified, but very quickly it becomes clear that none among these is a basic determinant, either because it is itself an effect of still deeper causes, or because its own consequences are only brought out by the presence of another factor. It is in this perspective also that we should consider the charge of 'irresponsibility', of so called vandalism, levelled at populations who have, nonetheless, managed to survive in the same environment for centuries without causing irreparable damage to their

surroundings. Their current condition is the result of a weakening of collective control mechanisms as well as being a despairing response to a situation perceived as insoluble.

Before the French colonized much of the West African Sahel early this century, it is generally believed that its inhabitants had developed social, economic, political and land-use systems which allowed them to survive within the harsh constraints of the local environment. Farmers would leave land fallow rather than overexploit it, pastoralists were seasonally mobile and the various groups interacted in mutually beneficial ways. This delicate balance was shattered by colonialism and the 'modernization' and 'internationalization' of the local economy:

> The indigenous economy was distorted as the French developed those sectors most consonant with the imperial power's needs. Stimulation of the export sector not only led to imbalances within the indigenous system but also changed the operational scale of the economy from a regional to a global one. The regional economic organisation involved complex interactions between environment, land use and social systems and the disruptions consequent upon the stimulation of specific sectors of the economy resulted in a breakdown of that complex interaction. While the export sector flourished there was little concern about the social changes and environmental deterioration which were occurring as a result of the distortion of indigenous practices. (Berry *et al.*, 1977, pp. 83–4)

The factor that most increased the vulnerability of the local people to drought and famine was the promotion of groundnut production for export. This induced three major changes, which together produced conditions of economic uncertainty and accelerated processes of ecological decline. First, groundnut cultivation exacerbated both output fluctuations due to climatic disturbances, and the income variability of farmers, because of changing price support policies and generally worsening terms of trade. Falling incomes compelled farmers to expand the area and harvest of groundnuts. This in turn accelerated the destruction of traditional methods of cultivation designed to reduce vulnerability in times of drought. Second, continuous groundnut cultivation soon resulted in declining soil fertility, as fallow periods were shortened and more marginal land was brought into cultivation. Chemical fertilizers, which might have compensated for the decline in fallow periods and fallow lands, were not available at first, and were too expensive for most small cultivators when they were introduced.

These two effects illustrate the way 'development' processes may accelerate ecological degradation and thus erode the capacity of the peasant mode of production to deal with drought. The third relates to marginalization.

Previously, nomads had often brought their herds near farmed areas for part of the year in order to graze their herds, where the soil was fertilized with their manure. But the 'expanding peanut culture' in the Sahel during the 1950s and 1960s drove agriculturalists beyond their previous boundaries and into direct competition for land with the nomads. (This is still happening all along the

Sahel, as the boundary between pastoralists and farmers moves steadily northwards.) As a result, the traditional, symbiotic relationship between the nomads and farmers was severely disrupted.

Acrimonious conflicts over territorial rights resulted in nomads losing much of the pastureland they needed, while the farmers no longer received the fertilizing services of the nomads' animals. The upshot of this marginalization of the nomads was that they were forced into overgrazing their herds by pressures beyond their control, an unavoidable effect for which they are often unfairly criticized. The general point is explained by Dahl and Hjort (1979, p. 8):

> As the land resource base of nomadic pastoralism is diminished, the pattern of pastoral land-use is also altered. The loss of important dry season areas and drought resources means an increased wear on the remaining, more arid, regions. The consequences for the pastoral adaptation of outright losses of landrights are obvious: by restricting pastoral lands to the drier and less productive areas, they are in danger of becoming overgrazed by a more intensive, continuous use of an initially larger number of animals.

Returning to the Sahelian case, Franke and Chasin (1980, pp. 99, 103) defend the accused, arguing strongly that the famine should not be blamed on its victims:

> It would be more accurate to say that the peanut and the profit system were the real 'overgrazers' – not the nomads. . . . The 'overgrazing' of the nomads, such a common phrase in reports on the Sahel famine, can be seen from the example of Niger to be part of a national and international production system that gave them no other alternative and then provided them with the necessary technology for environmental destruction.

Two related issues emerge from this analysis. The first is that there is a 'knock-on effect' in the sequence of rural marginalization being described – first farmers, then pastoralists, were affected. The second is that twin processes of marginalization seem to be operating – the marginalization of land together with the marginalization of people:

> the pastures . . . were victims of cattle and nomads, but only because *these* in turn had been victims of peanut cultivators, politically powerful Africans, and overseas commercial interests. It was in the context of these processes that the drought hit the Sahel, and it was these herders and their animals that suffered the most. It was these processes, from colonial times right up to the eve of the drought that turned drought into famine. (Franke and Chasin, 1980, p. 106)

9.6   Conclusion

This chapter has addressed the assertion that there may be a positive, secular and causal association between 'development' processes generally, and a rising vulnerability to famine of identifiable groups of people. Specifically, various writers have suggested that Africa's experiences of colonialism and capitalism have marginalized poor people, increased their dependence on fickle markets, and undermined 'moral economy' systems which traditionally protected community security. Since all this has happened without the institutionalization of adequate alternatives (at least not yet), whether in the form of secure, well-paid employment or a social security 'safety net', it is alleged that food insecurity and the threat of famine have, if anything, increased during this century.

At the very least, it must be accepted that capitalist forms of development are associated with transitional periods during which the vulnerability of some groups is exacerbated or created. Implicit in Sen's 'PEST' concept is the assumption that such disruption is transitory – a move from one stable equilibrium to another, through a period of increased vulnerability which is regrettable but only temporary. One implication is that if support can be provided to families to 'see them through' this period, then integration into a market economy and rising incomes will eventually reduce the risk of famine. This view is in stark contrast to the 'marginalization' and 'market dependence' approaches, which see processes of increasing vulnerability as secular and not necessarily reversible, except by radical change. The alternative is a permanent dependence on welfare for a substantial and possibly increasing proportion of the population.

The central issue which remains unresolved is whether, on balance, vulnerability to famine is reduced or increased in the long run by the introduction of market relations of exchange to a subsistence-based agrarian economy. On the positive side, it is incontrovertible that certain types of 'modernization' bring important benefits in food security terms:

> famine is a function of underdevelopment in a much broader sense than poverty alone. Famine thrives on poor transport, weak communications, market segmentation, and limited options for alternative employment and protection of income. It also thrives on governments whose operational capabilities do not allow for timely and effective intervention. (Field, 1989, p. 19)

In an article entitled 'Why development eliminates famines', Leibenstein (1982) reasons that (neo-classical) economic development is associated with increases in per capita output; a shift of labour out of the high-risk agricultural sector and into the relative security of manufacturing and services; the integration of regional markets, assisted by improved transportation and communications networks; increased trade with the outside world; and improvements in government services aimed at alleviating or mitigating poverty. Leibenstein (1982, pp. 115–16) concludes confidently: 'Economic development by widening the nature of the economy, and by increasing variety, is likely to decrease the types of discontinuities that cause entitlement famines.'

The limitation of this argument lies in its aggregation. Variety for whom?

Opportunities for whom? Development, in reality, is a very uneven affair, with some people benefiting, but often at the expense of others – and famines choose their victims from the latter category. In the case of sub-Saharan Africa, it is difficult to escape the general conclusion that development strategies pursued by the colonial powers and many post-independent governments have created groups of 'winners' and 'losers', and that one cost of being among the 'losers' is an increased vulnerability to subsistence crises, in the harsh climate and fragile environment of most famine-prone countries. The 'three Cs' – colonialism, capitalism and cash-cropping – may not directly have caused the droughts which precipitated the Sahelian crises, but they certainly contributed to the breakdown of the local population's ability to cope.

Many writers take a position contrary to that of Leibenstein. Seaman and Holt (1980, p. 296) argue 'that the shift from a "communal" to a "market" economy does, in general, as in the Indian experience, mark a shift towards a greater vulnerability to and severity of famine'. Alamgir (1980, p. 47) agrees: 'Substitution of market and exchange economies for a subsistence economy introduces many new factors that may contribute to initiation of foodgrain scarcity or famine.'

Whichever view is the more 'correct' – and both are open to the charge of rhetorical generalization – the policy problems remain acute. An understanding of the origins of famine depends substantially on an understanding of the historical processes which determine vulnerability at the household level. A deeper analysis is needed of how development has conditioned vulnerability in famine-prone communities – including the effects of development between groups within the society; whether new vulnerable groups are created as a by-product of socioeconomic change; what can be done to protect these groups; and how, ultimately, to lift them out of the vulnerability trap. In hunger-prone societies, this surely should be the primary objective of 'development', rather than the myopic pursuit of industrialization and a vague belief that 'trickle-down growth' will eliminate poverty and famines.

10

Famine and government policy

Many famines in the world have actually arisen from and been sustained by inflexible government policies undermining the power of particular sections of the population to command food.

Jean Drèze and Amartya Sen (1989, p. 6)

Whenever a famine occurs in modern times, governments stand accused of sins of commission or omission – either creating the crisis or failing to prevent it. As national and international capacity to respond to disasters steadily improves, so the 'drought equals famine' or 'overpopulation equals famine' equation is increasingly inadequate. The causes of modern famines always include elements which are either directly political – a deliberate act of political will – or indirectly political – a failure to intervene to prevent famine, or famine as an unintended by-product of government policy. Most of the examples found in the literature and in the media, where governments are frequently taken to task, fall into four categories, according to the nature of government's contribution:

1. *Inappropriate policies:* Government policies fail to redress famine vulnerability, or actively marginalize and impoverish specific groups of people, increasing their long-run vulnerability to, say, drought or flood. Included in this category is much of the 'radical' literature on the Sahelian famines.
2. *Failure to intervene:* The inability or refusal of governments to respond to a food crisis (for whatever reason) effectively allows a famine to occur which could have been prevented. The Chinese famine of 1958–61, the Bangladesh famine of 1974, and the Ethiopian famines of 1974 and 1984 are often discussed in this light.
3. *By-product:* A civil war, for example, precipitates famine conditions by

disrupting food production and trade, creating refugees, and preventing aid from reaching affected people. Mozambique and Chad during the 1980s, and Somalia during the early 1990s, are cases in point.

4. *Malign intent:* A government wilfully creates famine conditions, using starvation as a mechanism of repression and subjugation. Examples often cited include the Soviet famine of 1933–4 and the Dutch famine of 1944.

In this chapter, 'urban bias' and agricultural regulation are discussed as examples of inappropriate government policies which can contribute to famine. This is followed by an examination of the reasons why governments fail to respond to food crises. Next, the Soviet famine of 1932–3 is presented as a case study of 'malign intent' of the state towards part of its population – in this case, the Ukraine. Finally, a second case study, the Chinese 'Great Leap Forward' famine, can be interpreted both as a consequence of inappropriate government policies and of government's failure to react because of misinformation about the scale of the problem. The issue of famine as an unintended by-product of military conflict is deferred to the next chapter, which deals specifically with militarization, war and refugees.

10.1   Urban bias

Lipton (1977, pp. 18–19) argues that rural poverty and vulnerability to famine are often a function of government policies which are biased in favour of the interests of urban elites, and which therefore discriminate against the interests of the agricultural sector in general, and of the rural poor in particular:

> So long as the elite's interests, background and sympathies remain predominantly urban, the countryside may get the 'priority' but the city will get the resources. The farm sector will continue to be squeezed, both by transfers of resources from it and by prices that are turning against it. However, urban bias does not rest on a conspiracy, but on convergent interests. Industrialists, urban workers, even big farmers, *all* benefit if agriculture gets squeezed, provided its few resources are steered, heavily subsidised, to the big farmer, to produce cheap food and raw materials for the cities. Nobody conspires; all the powerful are satisfied; the labour-intensive small farmers stay efficient, poor and powerless.

Lipton's view is that urban bias inhibits income and welfare improvements for the poor in Third World countries. This directly contradicts the neo-classical 'trickle-down' theory of growth, which claims that (capitalist) economic development is beneficial to all sections of the population, including the poor: 'urban bias is the root cause of the failure of "development" to remove mass poverty' (Lipton, 1977, p. 89). Similarly, Spitz (1978, p. 868) sees famine as revealing the unequal 'power relations' between town and countryside – relations which are essentially violent in character:

The fact that in times of famine town-dwellers can still get something to eat while country people starve to death is a sign of the power relation between the urban population and the rural population. When a food shortage starts to make itself felt in the towns there is a sharp increase in food prices. . . . The pressure which is then brought to bear on the government by the different social groups in the towns carries all the more weight because the towns are the seat of political power. If the government is to stay in power, it must take effective action to check the rise in food prices. . . . Town-dwellers are therefore relatively well protected against famine, at least in peace-time.

Urban residents are also better able to organize their protests collectively, through trade union demands or civil unrest – demonstrations, strikes, riots, even coups. As Timmer (1989, p. 23) observes: 'Governments are held accountable for provisioning cities at reasonable costs, and citizens have repeatedly demonstrated their capacity to bring down governments that fail in this obligation.' Rural people are by definition physically dispersed, so they tend not to be politically united. The overthrow of Ethiopia's Haile Selassie in 1974 is a case in point:

The cities must be kept tolerably happy because in Ethiopia, as elsewhere, it is the cities not the countryside that present a possible challenge to the Government. If the regime needed a reminder, the course of 1974's 'creeping coup' was clear enough. Haile Selassie's imperial regime might have survived prolonged starvation in the countryside; when food shortages and price rises spread to Addis Ababa and the demonstrations began, his days were numbered. (Gill, 1986, p. 48)

Such leaders see little short-term political gain in paying attention to a rural majority which has no political power – this despite the lesson of the 1968–73 Sahel crisis, during which every government fell, largely because the rural crisis became so severe that it *did* reach the capitals. The policies of nearly all African governments favour the urban elite, by keeping food prices low, or by seeing to it that profits from major cash-cropping schemes go to urban-based companies and individuals. Governments see little economic motive for investing in the rural hinterland. One of Africa's many vicious cycles is at work here: government policies degrade the rural resource base; degraded farmland produces little of economic value. (Timberlake, 1985, p. 12)

Whenever agriculture is neglected or exploited by policy-makers, the consequences are invariably disastrous. In most Third World countries, agriculture is the main source of livelihood for the majority of the population. An agricultural surplus is crucial for two reasons: to earn foreign exchange through primary product exports (especially during early industrialization, when capital imports are essential); and to feed urban residents, so that scarce foreign exchange is not squandered on food imports.

Myopically, instead of being properly supported to achieve these objectives, agriculture has often been 'squeezed' in an attempt to accelerate industrial growth and to provide cheap food for the cities. Agriculture can be squeezed in three ways, apart from purely coercive measures. First, investment in agriculture may be less than private savings generated in rural areas (rural savings are lent to urban borrowers); second, government taxes on agriculture may exceed government spending on agriculture; and third, the internal 'terms of trade' may be turned against agriculture (by holding food prices down as other prices rise). Lack of investment in agriculture causes stagnation and inefficiency, while holding food prices down acts as a disincentive to production and may result in food having to be imported into countries which have the potential to be self-sufficient.

The drive for industrialization in Third World countries often includes low wages policies and 'infant industry' protectionism, policies which artificially raise the returns to industrial investment, as compared with investment in agriculture. Taxing agriculture to support industries which are not yet internationally competitive also removes resources from agriculture and reduces incentives to invest in rural areas. An overvalued currency presents another problem for agriculture, since it encourages imports for urban consumption and possibly investment, but also discourages production of surpluses for export.

In response to all these pressures, farmers may turn their land over to more profitable cash crop production, or they may smuggle their food surpluses into neighbouring countries, undermining national food self-sufficiency objectives in both cases. In adverse circumstances, such as unfavourable international market conditions, the result is rising national and household-level food insecurity. (As will be seen in Chapter 12, Bangladesh's dependence on food aid and food imports resulted directly in the famine of 1974, when those sources of food were cut.) In the African context, peasant producers are constantly undermined by a 'vicious cycle' of dependence on the food surpluses of the North:

> African governments find it easier to stay hooked on the debilitating drugs of free food aid and cheap grain imports than to take the tough decisions necessary to boost domestic production. Farm lobbies in the North find it easier to sustain their over-production when there is such an obvious need for food in the South.
> (*Financial Times*, 4 September 1986)

A 1986 FAO report on African agriculture argued for strong policies by African and Western governments to reverse the trend of growing dependence on food imports and discouragement of local agriculture. The FAO called for more effective incentives for farmers in African countries, in the form of higher prices for domestic food production, an exchange rate policy which discourages food imports, and easier access for small farmers to land and credit. Industrialized countries should help by removing tariff barriers on primary exports from African countries. According to Edouard Saouma, FAO's Director General (quoted in the *Financial Times*, 3 September 1986): 'It makes no sense to offer aid with one hand and to restrict African exports with the other.' If the appropriate steps are not taken soon, the FAO Report predicts

Africa will experience 'repeated and massive famines while food imports could bankrupt even prosperous African countries'.

10.2   Agricultural regulation

A related area of debate relating government policy to famine vulnerability concerns the effects of active government intervention in domestic food markets. Many governments, through their parastatals, control a large proportion of the marketed food supply. Two reasons often given for this intervention are to safeguard farmers against price fluctuations (low and unpredictable prices for produce), and to protect poor consumers from exploitation by merchants (in the form of unreasonably high food prices). In practice, these objectives are rarely achieved. The suppression of private markets can inhibit the production and distribution of surpluses. Where parastatals replace free markets, lack of competition or accountability means that they are often corrupt and inefficient: slow to collect produce and slow to pay farmers. Consequently, parastatals have taken a good deal of blame for recurrent food crises in sub-Saharan Africa. Vaughan (1987, p. 12) has labelled this the 'marketing board' theory of famines. Concisely stated, the argument is that:

> there has been too much inappropriate and damaging intervention in African food production and marketing on the part of overweight bureaucracies. . . .
> Discriminatory pricing policies, inappropriate intervention, and inefficient and corrupt marketing agencies are generally held to blame for declines in food production over much of Africa.

The famine of 1949 in Nyasaland (Malawi) was preceded by the introduction of a Maize Control Ordinance, which was motivated partly by 'intense government hostility to African maize traders' (Vaughan, 1987, p. 97). It suppressed the activities of private traders while extending the control of the government's Maize Control Board. But since the Board was inefficient, 'potential surplus maize producers cut back their acreages so that when a drought occurred in 1949 food stocks in the villages were already dangerously low'. Vaughan concludes: 'If the legislation did inhibit independent traders, and if the Board's own operations were as inefficient as some observers claimed, then it could be argued that this government intervention in food markets was a major cause of the famine.'

Policies designed to regulate or displace food markets are generally directed at prices or distribution mechanisms, or both. Price regulation typically results in low consumer prices as a form of subsidy, ostensibly to protect the poor. However, if the subsidy is not targeted, the wealthy will enjoy the benefits as well as the poor. Worse still, if government price controls create parallel or 'black' markets, or if food prices and supplies on the free market become more volatile as a result, then this policy may be counterproductive. The poorest consumers might secure inadequate food through the official channels, and be unable to afford the high prices demanded on the free or parallel market. A final problem with government-regulated food prices is that they eliminate the signals to which traders in free markets respond (Timmer, Falcon and Pearson, 1983, p. 155), so that a supply or demand problem in a region is less easy to detect and rectify. Severe localized food shortages can develop and remain undetected for some time, as is said to have happened in parts of rural China during the 'Great Leap Forward' famine of 1958–61 (see the case study of this famine later in this chapter, pp. 142–6).

Alternatively, governments sometimes attempt to increase their control over food supplies by regulating food *distribution* – by restricting the movement of food between regions or across borders, for instance. In Ethiopia, private inter-regional trade was prohibited altogether from 1979 to 1988, while in Kenya trade was constrained by heavy taxation of food at regional border posts. The imposition of such barriers on trade can partially or totally insulate a region or a country, turning it effectively into a closed economy, but it is more likely merely to create a 'black market' for traders willing to gamble on the higher profits such legislation offers: 'although market regulation was intended to promote equality and prevent exploitation of farmers through trade, poor regulation, as the Mozambican government found, can create parallel markets and hence reinforce private accumulation and inequality' (Mackintosh, 1990, p. 49). It simply is not possible to ban markets and trade altogether, nor is it necessarily desirable to try to do so. At the very least, trade restrictions will cause traders to add a 'risk premium' to food smuggled between regions. This factor may have contributed to the Great Bengal Famine of 1943.

> The prohibition of export of cereals in general and of rice in particular from each province, which had come into operation during 1942 with the consent of the government of India, prevented the price spiral in Bengal being broken by imports from the other provinces. . . . The price difference between Bengal and its neighbouring provinces had already become substantial by the end of 1942. (Sen, 1981, p. 77)

In Ethiopia during the 1980s, the Agricultural Marketing Corporation controlled a large proportion of marketed foodcrops. In many parts of the country, private traders were banned from trading grain between regions, and hundreds of grain merchants lost their licences. Although some of these restrictions were lifted in 1988, followed by a further round of liberalization during 1990, disincentives to trade (such as transport taxes) remained high. The consequences were negative in several ways;

> Thus the regulations on trade hurt (1) producers from surplus areas, who are unable to sell their grain in deficit areas, (2) consumers in deficit areas, who have to pay higher prices for grain, and (3) the nation, since producers in the deficit areas shift from coffee, which earns foreign exchange and for which the area has a

comparative advantage, to maize, which aggravates soil erosion. (Franzel, Colburn and Degu, 1989, p. 356)

These problems are bad enough in normal times, but they are magnified in famine years. 'A further doubt about the state's restriction of markets is raised by recent research on peasant survival strategies during famine. This work reveals that curtailment of markets increases peasants' vulnerability when their harvests fail' (*ibid.*, p. 357). Since 'distress sales' of assets (animals, farm tools and household goods) to buy grain is a universal response to rural food crises, controls on trade and regulation of markets by the state undermine the ability of famine victims to dispose of their assets *and* to buy grain. Even if these markets continue to exist in a limited form, the chances of getting fair prices for assets sold and food purchased are very low, so that access and entitlements to food are both needlessly reduced. Dessalegn Rahmato (1988, p. 11) reports that some farmers from Wollo walked for several days to sell livestock and buy grain in markets in other regions, where prices were more favourable, during the famine of 1984.

Incidentally, this suggests a potentially effective intervention for government as a buyer/seller of 'last resort', for both food and assets, during famines. One coping strategy observed in 1984 was to sell livestock, which was then taken temporarily out of Wollo, and sold back to farmers after the crisis had passed. Dessalegn (1988, p. 21) finds it curious that 'this simple but effective technique ... has never been considered as a famine response measure by government at the national or local level.'

Given all these undesirable side-effects of government regulation of agriculture, the policy conclusions follow logically from the diagnosis: legalize private trade, raise crop prices to producers (and phase out food subsidies to consumers) and reduce the role of parastatals. These prescriptions have been vigorously promoted since the late 1970s by the World Bank and other institutions, and implemented in the form of 'structural adjustment programmes' by governments throughout Africa, Asia and Latin America.

However, where government intervention in food pricing and marketing is motivated by a genuine and valid concern for the vulnerability of consumers to high prices and food shortages, the effects of the state withdrawing its parastatals and allowing free trade to prevail are potentially very dangerous, at least in the transitional period. Many African governments began to liberalize grain marketing during the 1980s, in the hope that this would stimulate agricultural production and trade, but maintaining a balance between this objective and that of meeting the food security needs of the entire population is proving difficult. On the one hand, where free trade has been effectively suppressed, the private sector may not be ready to fill the vacuum created by the withdrawal of parastatals. On the other hand, the possibility that a few powerful traders will hoard grain to create artificial shortages and high prices (as sometimes happens in south Asia) must be closely monitored.

The tendency for surpluses to be sucked out of rural areas and into the wealthier cities, leaving poor rural consumers unable to pay for grain in village markets, is another problem associated with leaving food distribution to market forces. Since private traders typically do not store quantities of produce for long periods, governments should arguably continue to hold reserve stocks as a contingency measure. Finally, if the state is to maintain a food security role, prices and supplies should be stabilized through buffer-stock operations. Without these and other precautionary measures, the food insecurity problems created or exacerbated by parastatals and government regulation of agriculture will only be replaced by a different set of problems when market forces rule.

All these issues are currently being negotiated throughout sub-Saharan Africa, and it is not yet apparent whether, on balance, famine vulnerability has risen or fallen in 'structurally adjusting' countries, following liberalization. Nor is it clear which groups are gaining and which might lose, in food security terms, as a result of these profound policy changes.

A rather different set of issues is raised by the forced collectivization of agriculture. Where coercion is applied against rural populations by the state, for either economic or ideological reasons, the consequences are invariably counterproductive. Forced collectivization was followed by major famines in the Ukraine, China and Ethiopia. 'Stalin's famine' of 1933–4 in the Ukraine is an extreme case of how a government with sufficient power and political will can exploit agriculture ruthlessly, to the point where the peasantry was literally starved to death. (This famine is discussed as a case study later in this chapter, pp. 140–2.) More recently, Ethiopia's post-1974 collectivization programme has been cited as an example of inappropriate policy which contributed directly to the famine of 1984:

> Famine has resulted primarily from government policies that have been implemented in order to accomplish massive collectivisation of agricultural production and to secure central government control over productive regions of the country where indigenous peoples have developed strong anti-government resistance. (Clay and Holcomb, 1985, p. 194)

'Villagization' was combined with the resettlement of millions of people from northern to southern regions. A few writers (Hancock, 1985; Schwab, 1985) believed that the resettlement policy was voluntary, and that it was motivated by the government's genuine concern for victims of recurrent famine in northern Ethiopia: 'without resettlement, the 1984 emergency will become a permanent condition' (Hancock, 1985, p. 110). But most independent observers detected more cynical motivations. Vallely (1986) argued that the object was to facilitate 'the production of cash crops to earn the regime the hard currency it needs to continue its wars against liberation movements on several fronts.' Interviews with Ethiopian refugees who had fled into eastern Sudan from resettlement camps provide evidence of strong resistance to forced relocation, contrary to Hancock's assertion:

None from either Tigray or Wollo had been resettled voluntarily. They had been deceived or captured when taken. Nearly all with families had been separated from members of their family by the move. . . . Accounts given of the trip south were consistent in reporting conditions of deprivation and life-endangering coercion. (Clay and Holcomb, 1985, p. iv. See also Harrell-Bond, 1986)

Clay and Holcomb identify this policy as a prime contributing factor to famine among both the resettled and host populations:

resettlement is the final blow to a population whose ability to produce has steadily deteriorated over the past decade as a direct result of government policies. . . . The intensification of resettlement, which required indigenous people to supply land, houses, food, equipment and services to arriving settlers, introduced famine where it had not been known recently.

10.3   Response failure

Famines occur because they are not prevented. Famines in Africa in the 1970s (and to a lesser extent in the 1980s) have often been attributed to government negligence. Faced with an impending food crisis, critics argue, governments failed to reallocate public resources in the form of relief, and/or failed to alert the international donor community in time.

There are three reasons why a government might fail to respond appropriately and in good time to a threatened food crisis. Either they have inadequate information on the problem, or they lack the capacity to intervene, or they feel no sense of responsibility to the victims and simply do not care. In short, a famine occurs because of the government's ignorance, incapacity or callousness. It follows from this that two preconditions are needed for effective state intervention, namely, that the government has both the *ability* and the *will* to prevent famine.

In the past, poor transport and communications, together with limited resources, provided an adequate explanation for crop failure leading directly to famine. During the twentieth century, famines have (apparently) been eliminated from one country after another – Russia, China, India, Bangladesh – precisely because of the increasing capacity of governments and international institutions to predict and respond to impending crises. The corollary of this observation is that, where famine still occurs, it almost always could and should have been prevented.

The first reason for government's failing to prevent famine is ignorance caused by lack of information. A well-developed information element is absent from all theories of famine. The literature on famine 'early warning systems' (EWS) is particularly relevant to this issue. Originally, EWS focused on the monitoring and collection of 'objective' variables like rainfall and crop forecasts, together with market prices. In the case of the Indian Famine Codes, for example, if food prices rose more than a predetermined percentage above their seasonal average, this triggered food relief programmes by the state.

As the perception of famine as a social and economic process becomes widely accepted, new variables are being added to the prediction kit (see Walker, 1989). Detailed empirical studies of famine 'coping strategies' are proving particularly useful in identifying what people facing food deficits are likely to do, and in what sequence, so that intervention can come earlier in the process and be directed at preserving people's assets and productive viability, not just their nutritional status and physical survival.

Against the trend towards ever more sophisticated statistical monitoring, the case of Kenya's 'averted famine' of 1984–5 is instructive. Even without what Downing calls a 'centralized, monolithic early warning system', the Kenyan government reacted quickly and fairly effectively to the food crisis precipitated by the failure of the long rains in 1984. Yellow maize, an inferior staple consumed only by the poor and hungry, was imported and mostly sold through the normal market channels. Mass mortality was avoided. Downing (1990, pp. 208, 211), concludes that:

> Elaborate monitoring systems, finely tuned to respond to many levels of food shortage, food poverty and food deprivation are not a government priority. Severe droughts, as in 1984, are easily identified and ad-hoc responses are adequate to avert a major famine. . . . a monolithic famine early warning system is not a prerequisite for effective response.

Kenya 1984–5 is only one of several recent 'averted famines'. (On this case study, see also Cohen and Lewis, 1987; Downing *et al.*, 1989.) It is perhaps appropriate at this point, as an antidote to this chapter's emphasis on governments' negative contributions to famine causation, to mention cases where governments have played a positive interventionist role in famine prevention. Perhaps the earliest example is that of Bihar (India) in 1965–6. Elsewhere in India, institutionalized public works programmes are seen as having reduced the threat of drought-induced food crises in many states – for instance, in Maharashtra in 1970–3 (Drèze and Sen, 1989). Still in south Asia, the Bangladesh famine of 1974 was quickly followed by two further potential food crises, in 1979 and 1984. On both occasions, though, the government's rationing scheme and rapid intervention (through public distribution of imported food on the open market) protected vulnerable groups, restrained food price rises and averted a major tragedy (Clay, 1985; Osmani, 1991).

Returning to Africa, Botswana also successfully prevented famine during the mid-1980s, primarily through maintaining a Drought Relief Programme since 1981 which includes public works programmes and the distribution of free food to specified vulnerable groups (Holm and Morgan, 1985; Hay, Burke and Dako, 1986; Morgan, 1991; Buchanan-Smith, 1992). As the capacity to intervene in incipient food crises continue to improve – and Botswana, for one, has succeeded largely because it is one of the highest per capita food aid recipients in Africa – it is likely that the ratio of averted to actual famines will continue to improve.

The second issue explaining non-response to famine is lack of capacity, where a government is constrained by factors beyond its control – poor roads to affected villages, not enough trucks to move grain in large quantities, no foreign exchange to import food commercially. Even where governments genuinely attempt to channel food to the poor as handouts or at subsidized prices, they often lack the marketing and transport infrastructure required to deliver food to those who need it most. The inaccessibility of some Ethiopian villages was discussed earlier, and is worth reiterating here. A drought-afflicted community which takes days to reach by donkey is inaccessible to conventional relief systems, even with all the good intentions in the world. (In such cases, dropping sacks of grain from planes is sometimes adopted as a last resort.) Similarly, as will be discussed in Chapter 11, war and civil conflict create situations where governments and relief agencies are unable or unwilling to respond to food crises.

Moving on to the third issue in this category – callous disregard – it is difficult to judge, when famines have been deliberately concealed, whether this is due to governments (1) being embarrassed at their failure to prevent a famine, or (2) trying to exclude the possibility of relief being offered, because of their political hostility towards the famine-affected population. The Chinese 'Great Leap Forward' famine provides an example of the first possibility, while the Ethiopian famine of 1974 perhaps illustrates the second case. During the 1980s, too, some governments actively blocked food supplies to 'rebel'-held areas. Government or anti-government forces prevented food aid from reaching famine zones in rural Mozambique, Eritrea and southern Sudan.

The extent to which a government perceives itself to be responsible for its citizens' welfare is a function of its political legitimacy. Governments the world over act in the interests of their most powerful and influential constituents. In much of Africa, these constituencies typically include the military, the bureaucracy and the urban middle class – as noted in the discussion of 'urban bias' (pp. 130–3). The resulting dilemma which faces governments in times of food crisis was summed up by a relief worker in the Sahel in two cynical sentences. 'Starve the city dwellers and they riot; starve the peasants and they die. If you were a politician, which would you choose?' (quoted in Timberlake, 1985, p. 5).

Recently, Sen and others have argued vigorously for the promotion of *democracy* as a solution to famine. Contrasting independent India with China and with much of famine-prone Africa, Sen (1990, p. 50) points out that democratically elected governments are forced to respond to the needs of its citizens, whereas a dictatorial state feels no such responsibility:

With a relatively free press, with periodic elections, and with active opposition parties, no government can escape severe penalty if it delays preventive measures and allows a real famine to occur . . . the diverse political freedoms that are available in a democratic state, including regular elections, free newspapers, and freedom of speech . . . must be seen as the real force behind the elimination of famines.

However, according to Sen's own estimates, 3.3 million Indians still die each year from hunger and hunger-related diseases – the equivalent of a Bengal 1943 famine *every year* (Sen, 1987b). The sub-title of a book on famine and hunger in India refers to 'India's half-won battle' (Etienne, 1988). This suggests that the extent to which democratic rights and a free press can 'enfranchise' the poor and vulnerable is very limited. To put it crudely, famine is newsworthy, endemic hunger is not. Ram (1986, p. 26) prefers to describe the Indian press as 'relatively independent', rather than 'free', and he notes that it has adopted a 'liberal', 'critical watchdog' role rather than a 'destabilizing' or 'adversarial' stance. This means that, while it campaigns strongly on major, visible events such as food crises, it does not pressure the state vigorously enough to address other forms of hunger. Da Corta and Devereux (1991, p. 11) conclude pessimistically that the elimination of famines in India has been achieved only by allowing the persistence of mass poverty, hunger and vulnerability. 'Thus recurrent famines have been replaced by recurrent near famines and recurrent famine relief or, at best, by institutionalised dependence on relief in normal times.'

10.4   Case study: the Soviet famine of 1932–4

Russia was historically prone to repeated and terrible famines. Dando (1980, pp. 144–6) has documented over 100 famines between AD 971 and 1947 – on average, more than one every decade. Traditionally, Russian famines were explained by harsh climatic conditions, rural poverty and the isolation of affected regions.

In this century, four famines occurred in the Soviet Union within thirty years of the 1917 Revolution. The causes of all four were overtly political, a consequence of either state policy or war, so that man-made factors replaced natural causes entirely. The worst of these famines occurred in 1932–4, in which, at 'a conservative estimate', 5–7 million people died (Mace, 1983, p. 34). Two parallel explanations have been advanced, both recognizing the role of the state's callous agricultural policy, but one school arguing that Stalin's motivations were economic, the other claiming that the famine amounted to politically motivated genocide.

The economic arguments focus on the Soviet industrialization debate of the 1920s, and its resolution in favour of agricultural collectivization in order to extract a 'tribute' from the peasantry to finance 'crash industrialization'. The policy originated with Preobrezhansky, who argued for high taxes and low prices on food production. Preobrezhansky believed that investment in agriculture was inefficient, due to the high 'marginal propensity to consume' of poor peasants, so that resources were better invested in urban industry if the goal of rapid economic development was to be achieved (Ellman, 1979, p. 98). This argument, though it neglected the strategic importance of food self-sufficiency, was adopted by Stalin, who introduced mass collectivization, with disastrous effects. Agricultural output fell by 40 per cent in the seven years from 1929 to 1936. Food production per capita never returned to its 1913 level before Stalin's death in 1953. Industry benefited enormously, but only at immense cost to the peasantry.

In the view of Karcz (1979, pp. 414, 424), the famine of 1932–4 was 'a direct consequence of collectivisation.... For 1931–2, grain procurements from collective farms reached the total of 40 percent of collective farm harvest – a factor that contributed gravely to the great Soviet famine of 1932–4.' To make matters worse, compulsory deliveries were introduced in December 1933, at the height of the famine. Despite all this, marketed supplies of grain rose continually between 1928 and 1940, a 'success' which is usually attributed to collectivization. Karcz (1979, p. 455) disagrees:

> this reflects not only the improvement in the functioning of the *kolkhoz* as an instrument of collection or the procurement reforms of 1932–33, but also the death of at least 5 million individuals, largely in the countryside, during the Great Soviet Famine of 1932–34.... The famine reduced the number of mouths to be fed in the countryside, while grain procurements were rising.

Political explanations of the famine see Stalin's policies towards agriculture as motivated by a cynical desire to crush the opposition presented by sections of the rural peasantry. 'Stalin used food as a means of controlling "socially obstinate" peasants within the USSR and induced massive famine in 1933–34 and again in 1946–47' (Dando, 1980, p. 99). This interpretation is given powerful and moving support by the accounts of Ukrainian survivors of the famine, who believe that the famine was engineered by Stalin as an instrument of racial genocide, directed against their nationalist aspirations.

The Ukraine, historically the 'breadbasket' of the Soviet Union, exported 7.7 million tons of grain in 1930. 'In 1932, Stalin again ordered the Ukraine to export 7.7 m tonnes even though the ravages of collectivization had reduced the crop to two-thirds of 1930s level' (*The Economist*, 11 October 1986, p. 100). In the words of *The Ukrainian Weekly*, written fifty years after the event:

> unlike other famines, those caused by drought, pestilence or other natural factors, this one was the desired by-product of a deliberate political policy. In an effort to break the will of a nationally conscious Ukrainian peasantry and to finance rapid industrialisation, the Soviet regime under Stalin ordered the expropriation of all foodstuffs and grain in the hands of the rural population. The result was a holocaust of almost unthinkable dimensions – mass murder by decree. (Hadzewycz *et al.*, 1983, Editors' Note)

Whereas many economists see the famine as one reflecting 'urban bias' directed against the rural agricultural areas in general, the Ukrainian view is that their republic was specifically victimized for narrower political reasons, and they support this with evidence that food was available in neighbouring Russia, while Ukrainians starved. According to Mace (1983, p. 31), police checkpoints were set up along the Ukrainian border 'to prevent the starving from entering Russia and prevent anyone coming from Russia from carrying food with him into Ukraine. This meant a *de facto* "blacklisting", that is, economic blockade, of the entire Soviet Ukrainian Republic.' Oleskiw (1983, p. 11) similarly rejects any explanation of the famine based on national food shortage:

> As millions of Ukrainian peasants were starving, their requisitioned grain was being exported abroad to get the capital needed to finance the industrial development and economic expansion of the Soviet Union. Thus, the famine in Ukraine was a direct result of Russia's socio-political and economic policies towards the non-Russian nations of the Soviet Union, especially Ukraine. The famine was Russia's ultimate economic weapon of mass destruction to subdue the people of Ukraine.

Whether in fact the prime motive was the political subjugation of peasants or economic support of industry remains unclear. Perhaps the two goals simply coincided neatly in Stalin's vision. After Stalin's death in 1953, the coercive model was abandoned, and there have been no famines since. Ellman (1979, p. 97) sees this as a major success:

> Considered historically, the most important achievement of post-Stalin agricultural policy has been to eliminate famines in the USSR. Famines were endemic in Tsarist Russia. . . . As a result of the progress of the Soviet economy since the end of the Great Patriotic War, it seems entirely likely, however, that the famine of 1946–47 will be the last famine ever in Russia/USSR (save only in the wake of nuclear war). This is an achievement of fundamental importance in a country traditionally prone to famines.

10.5   Case study: the Chinese famine of 1958–61

Like Russia, China was traditionally labelled a 'land of famine', and Chinese famines were also attributed mainly to climatic adversity and natural disasters. During the twentieth century, again like Russia, 'acts of God' became superseded by 'acts of man'. 'By the late 1920s and 1930s, the "natural" and political causes of famine were almost indistinguishable' (Li, 1982, p. 688). A famine in Henan province in 1943, for example, 'was due largely to military exigencies: ample grain supplies in neighbouring provinces were not permitted into Henan'.

It has only recently emerged that China was devastated by an enormous famine in the Great Leap Forward period of 1958–61; in its scale certainly the worst anywhere in human history. (Not until the 1980s did China even admit the occurrence of this famine. In 1980, the Chinese economist Sun Yefang referred to 'the high price in blood' paid for the mistaken economic policies pursued during the Great Leap Forward period.) Recently released demographic data indicates that during the period 1958–62 'China suffered a demographic crisis of enormous proportions . . . about 30 million premature deaths and about 33 million lost or postponed births' (Ashton *et al.*, 1984, p. 614). Previous estimates of the number of 'excess deaths' during this period ranged from 16 million (Coale, 1981, p. 89) to 23 million (Aird, 1982, p. 278). Because the data were inconsistent, and perhaps because the figures seemed too incredible, these estimates were in fact conservative.

Apart from its almost inconceivable scale, this famine is unique in that it was due almost entirely to a massive and prolonged decline in food availability – virtually a pure 'FAD' famine, in fact:

> The data on food availability also suggest that, in contrast to many other famines, a root cause of this one was a dramatic decline in grain output, which continued for several years and which in 1960–61 involved a drop in grain output of more than 25 percent. (Ashton *et al.*, 1984, p. 614)

Per capita grain supply fell from 307 kg/year in 1956 to 235 kg/year in 1961. Daily food energy availability fell to an estimated 1,535 calories in 1960, below any figure recorded for 1980 (when the lowest in the world was Ethiopia, at 1,735 calories). A close inverse relationship is observed for China over the 1955–65 decade between total per capita food energy and death rates. Although these are national level statistics, Ashton *et al.* (1984, p. 623) point out that, if anything, a regional analysis would present an even worse picture, given that some provinces (such as Shanghai) seem to have maintained their average consumption levels throughout the period:

> A fuller analysis of the 1958–61 famine would require an investigation of the entitlements of different groups of the population to a share of the aggregate food supply. These differential abilities to obtain food would, in turn, determine the relative suffering of various subgroups from the famine. Regional disparities are likely to be particularly important in this regard, since in the absence of alternative food distribution mechanisms, it is likely that the places suffering from a drop in food output are also those in which incomes and, in most distribution systems, entitlements also fall, tending to localise the famine.

It appears that the worst effects were concentrated in the northern provinces, a predominantly rural area, which was historically prone to food crises resulting from droughts and floods. (Before the famine of 1958–61, the worst famine in recorded history followed a drought in northern China between 1876–9, and it claimed between 9.5 and 13 million lives.) However, Kula (1989, p. 15) has argued that 'during the Great Leap years starvation was most acute in the cities, partly due to the denial of famine by some district authorities and partly due to the poor coordination of transport in shifting supplies from the countryside.'

The failure of the government to import food until 1961 would have added to the difficulties facing urban residents.

It is a tragic irony that Mao's agricultural policy was designed specifically to avoid such disasters, and that Chinese agriculture was seen for some time after the Revolution as a phenomenal success story. One reason for this was that, perhaps because his political support originated in the countryside, Mao gave greater priority to agriculture than did Stalin. Another factor is that the Chinese government was deeply committed to a policy of political autarky and economic self-sufficiency, so that food production had to be supported if imports were to be avoided.

Unlike Stalin's approach, the Maoist model recognized the multi-faceted importance of agriculture: not only in providing food for a growing non-agricultural labour force, but also in supplying capital for industrial investment, generating foreign exchange, and building an internal market for domestically produced goods. This model was also based on collectivization, but it differed fundamentally from Stalinist coercion in that 'whereas Soviet collectivisation was primarily aimed at collecting tribute, Chinese collectivisation was primarily aimed at increasing output' (Ellman, 1979, p. 99). Mao argued that extracting a heavy 'tribute' from agriculture created too much of a disincentive, and that collectivization would succeed only if the real income of the peasantry was allowed to grow rather than made to fall.

The primary objective of the 'balanced growth' strategy was an even development of both agriculture and industry ('walking on two legs'), with neither sector feeding parasitically off the other. It seems fair to conclude that, initially, Chinese development policies, by *encouraging* agriculture, succeeded, whereas Soviet strategies based on *exploiting* agriculture failed. Agrarian reform in China was followed in the early 1950s by collectivization of agriculture. Although this resulted in similar disincentive effects to those observed in the Soviet Union, procurement of grain by the state was less onerous, and in 1958 a record grain crop of over 200 million tons was harvested. The following year, Chou En-lai was able to announce: 'From 1949 to 1958, the average wage of Chinese workers was more than doubled, and the income of peasants was also nearly doubled' (Chou En-lai, 'A great decade', quoted in Wu Ta-k'un (1960, reprinted in 1979), p. 706).

But this apparently satisfactory performance concealed a reality of rising inefficiency, reduced incentives and growing pressure on the collectivized peasantry. Small-scale industrial activities were encouraged on collective farms and communes, to the detriment of agricultural productivity, and procurements were being stepped up. All this was possible, in Sen's view, because of the dictatorial nature of the political system. The famine 'was partly caused by the continuation of disastrous government policies, and that in turn was possible because of the non-democratic nature of the Chinese polity' (Sen, 1990, p. 50).

China also experienced several natural disasters between 1959 and 1961, including droughts, floods, typhoons, plant diseases and insect pests. The 1959 harvest was poor, and despite an explicit change of policy designed to stimulate agriculture, cultivated areas, yields and total grain harvested fell further in both 1960 and 1961. 'Food shortages lowered peasants' incentives as well as their physical capabilities' (Kula, 1989, p. 15).

It seems probable that China's leaders were themselves unaware of the problem until it was too late to prevent a catastrophe. The effects of the production shortfall were magnified by the government's delayed reaction. Mao Zedong's speeches of the 1960s indicate a total ignorance of the scale of the disaster (Sen, 1984, pp. 501–3). The main reason for this was probably not wilful neglect so much as lack of the relevant information.

Output figures were wildly exaggerated, since communes had strong incentives to claim overfulfilment of production targets, and local officials covered up the problems in reporting to their superiors. For example, the official estimate of the 1958 harvest was revised downward several times, from an initial announcement of over 500 million tons to around 200 million tons by 1980. Throughout the 1950s, China was a net grain *exporter*, and it was only in 1961 that international supplies of grain were called on to compensate for food shortages inside the country. A net export of 2.7 million tons in 1960 was reversed to become a net import of 4.5 million tons in 1961, but by then the famine had already been raging for two years. Also during 1961, the state adopted a most unusual strategy to deal with the urban dimension of the famine. 'In order to solve the starvation problem the regime decided to carry out a forced exodus of the population from cities to countryside where food was more easily accessible' (Kula, 1989, p. 15).

Ashton *et al.* (1984, p. 634) conclude that this famine, like so many others, was unnecessary and could easily have been prevented. A combination of factors turned a crop failure into a food crisis, and an inability to respond effectively with aid turned the food crisis into a famine:

> the tragedy of the Chinese famine of 1958–61 is that internal food redistribution
> was obviously limited and major international relief was never even attempted.
> Earlier unwise policies became compounded by ignorance and by the warp of
> international politics. Internally, the destruction of systems of objective reporting
> hid the facts from policy-makers. Externally, the political isolation of China turned
> the requesting and granting of assistance into much more politically charged actions
> than they need have been, and in consequence they never occurred. It would not be
> inaccurate to say that 30 million people died prematurely as a result of errors of
> internal policy and flawed international relations.

In terms of its theoretical implications, Kula (1989, pp. 11, 16) has invoked this famine as a case study:

> to challenge, directly, the entitlement approach. . . . The Chinese famine of 1959–
> 61 offers powerful evidence to contradict Sen's entitlement approach as it took
> most of its toll in areas of high incomes, ie. the cities. Famine was created by the

revolutionary politics of the period which resulted in the failure of agriculture, with devastating results.

Since the proximate cause of the famine was a decline in food availability with no compensating inflows of trade or aid, a supply failure or 'FAD' interpretation might indeed seem adequate for analytical purposes. But Ashton *et al.* (1984, p. 623, as quoted above) provide grounds for challenging Kula's conclusion. Government- and climate-induced 'food availability decline' clearly played a major role in precipitating the Great Leap Forward famine, while the government's failure to respond both exacerbated and prolonged it. But more needs to be known about how food shortages were translated into differential mortality for various groups of people – who died and who survived the famine, and why – before an analytical role for entitlements can be rejected altogether.

10.6   Conclusion

While the *ability* to alleviate or prevent famines has increased dramatically in recent times, the *will* to do so may have lagged behind, as the Soviet and Chinese case studies, and the continuing tragedy of unaverted famines in Africa, confirm. Dando's (1980, p. 155) conclusion reflects a depressing view of human nature and political institutions:

> the failure of a government or a nation to alleviate hunger cannot be divorced from the general attitude of the privileged group a government serves. The problem of hunger and famine is not new in this world and neither is man's inhumanity to his fellow man, at times, to preserve a way of life, group ambitions or national goals.

The enormous power of contemporary governments over the fate of their citizens offers both opportunities and threats. The Chinese and Ukrainian famines were caused almost entirely by domestic government decisions. The difference is expressed in the judgements which are usually made on the two cases. While the Chinese famine is described as a 'tragedy' by most commentators, the word 'genocide' is frequently invoked to describe 'Stalin's famine' in the Ukraine. If the Chinese famine was a tragedy of errors, the Soviet famine was a tragedy of intent. As Watkins and Menken (1985, p. 668) pessimistically conclude, the Chinese case illustrates that the greater power vested in contemporary governments increases both their potential for preventing or alleviating famine, *and* their ability to turn a regional food shortage into a national catastrophe:

> Local food shortages are likely to occur in the future. They may be exacerbated or alleviated by high levels of coordination and control characteristic of the centralised governments of modern states: exacerbated because national policies permit errors of national scope, alleviated because national governments command national

resources. The post-Revolutionary Chinese government developed the ability to implement national policies effectively, making the Great Leap Forward a national rather than a local disaster; the consequences of the widespread subsistence crisis were yet more extreme because of the government's continued insistence on exporting rice.

Despite the generally critical approach adopted towards government policies in this chapter, three reservations should be added: first, that politicians face many competing priorities in reaching policy decisions; second, that there are wide differences within governments, between governments, and over time; and third, that the number of successful cases of famine aversion is rising. Policies shift as governments, priorities and thinking changes, so that it would be unfair to condemn as cynical or ignorant all governments which failed to prevent a famine or eliminate hunger during their terms of office. Nowhere is this more true than in the area of famine prevention and relief, which has been based for so long on erroneous theory, leading to inappropriate actions or inaction which might now be interpreted as callous disregard.

A continuing concern, however, is the failure of governments in famine-prone countries to address the long-term problems which lead up to the short-term crises. In some cases this might be explained by resource constraints – many poor countries seem to lurch from one crisis to another, lacking the reserves to invest in sustained development of either agriculture or industry. If the real, underlying problems are to be adequately addressed, quantities of political will, financial resources, time and international support are required which are simply not available to most Third World governments.

11

War and famine

Famine is the product of war and the transition to the 'heavily armed' state.
Eiichi Shindo (1985, pp. 7–8)

War is the single most significant factor explaining the persistence of famine in Africa today. Not only does war play a major causal role, it is also often the main reason why a famine is not prevented or alleviated. Yet, in contrast to the demographic (Malthusian), economic (entitlement) and other theories already discussed, a complete theory linking war with famine does not yet exist.

Apart from examining the political economy of war and famine, this chapter also considers the effects of an important precursor to war – militarization – and a tragic by-product of war – the creation of refugees or displaced persons. Militarization might have been discussed in the previous chapter, as an example of 'inappropriate government policy'. But since there is a logical progression from military build-up to war itself, it seems reasonable to bracket the two issues together.

Also, since people are displaced by drought and ecological crisis as well as by conflict, the question of refugees and famine could be discussed in a number of contexts. We have chosen to incorporate displacement into this chapter on war because of the remarkable congruence of the 'drought–war–famine trinity' in Ethiopia, Sudan, Chad, Mozambique and Angola during their subsistence crises of the 1980s. The complex interplay of political and environmental factors can rarely be separated out, and in most cases it is impossible even to define people displaced by war and drought as either 'political' or 'economic' refugees.

11.1 Militarization

One strand of government policy which receives a good deal of critical attention in the context of famine vulnerability is that of militarization – the tendency of governments to spend disproportionate amounts of their foreign exchange reserves on arms and 'defence'. According to Speedie (1983, pp. 26–7), two-thirds of all conventional weapons traded are purchased by Third World countries:

> The swollen arsenals of Third World governments don't only provide them with the ability to wage foreign wars, they provide the tools for repressive tactics at home. ... The arms race is a major hindrance to development and the arms trade is feeding on it. Whether they're used or not, weapons have to be paid for, and so the needs of the poor are pushed further down the priority list.

Ethiopia, which had the highest military spending per capita in Black Africa in the mid-1980s, is a case in point. In 1984, a year of major famine, an incredible 46 per cent of the national budget was spent on arms. This led Lemma (1985, pp. 52–3) to complain that 'the Ethiopian government spends most of its budget on "defence" while agricultural and rural developments have regressed to record levels because of lack of finance. ... Spending millions buying arms in such a dire situation is socially unjust.' It is unjust because it can directly increase vulnerability to famine: 'The one early warning system you need of famine is lists of which governments are spending disproportionate amounts of their GNP on military activities: look at Ethiopia, Sudan, Chad, Angola and Mozambique' (O'Keeffe, quoted in Timberlake, 1985, p. 187). Shindo (1985, pp. 10–14) outlines '[t]he logic of heavy weaponisation leading to famine' in three steps. 'First, in that increased military expenditure blocks expenditure on the civilian sector that is more urgently necessary than anything, it is accompanied by huge "opportunity costs". In extreme cases, this takes the form of famine.' ('Opportunity costs' refer to the loss implicit in one area by allocating resources to another.) Even worse, imports of arms drain vital foreign exchange reserves and compound external debt problems. 'Military expansion in Africa is by definition a debt-incurring mechanism, since none of the countries produces its own military hardware' (Raikes, 1988, p. 38).

Second, in so far as spending on weapons increases the power of the military in the country, this lends momentum to further military spending, so that the problem is self-reinforcing. A related point might be made here – that increased military power implies increased repression, one feature of which will be neglect or exploitation of the rural sector.

Third, while military spending in the West is often justified on 'Keynesian' grounds – as a means of generating employment and encouraging scientific innovation – in Third World countries it serves no economic purpose: 'imported weapons and weapons systems, unlike ordinary machines for civilian use, make little contribution to expanding the productive capacity of the developing country and therefore the export capacity.'

The editors of *Review of African Political Economy*'s special issue on 'War and famine' sum up Shindo's argument:

military spending in the developing countries in general is taking up an increasing proportion of state budgets. And it is hardly a coincidence that this should be happening precisely when the world's poor are finding it increasingly difficult to avoid starving to death. Military spending and military rule in much of Africa diverts resources away from the improvement of agricultural productivity. It also diverts resources away from food imports when they become necessary to feed drought-stricken peasantries. (Lawrence, 1985, p. 1)

The point Shindo makes most strongly is that it is the process of militarization itself, regardless of the political ideology or economic policies of the state, which increases famine vulnerability:

The reality of famine as something which affects 'heavily armed' states irrespective of differences of system is in striking contrast with a different reality in the case of those countries, also in Africa, whose military expenditure is relatively low and which have been freed from famine. (Shindo, 1985, pp. 9–10)

Two illustrations of the latter argument are Botswana and Kenya, where famines were successfully averted during the mid-1980s. However, as always when 'monocausal' explanations of famine are offered, it is important to put this hypothesis into context. First, any complete theory of famine must include a variety of problems, so militarization should be seen as one of a number of factors which contribute to the creation of vulnerable communities. Second, it is arguable that the correlation between militarization and famine, though empirically well founded, is spurious. Both may be symptoms of an entirely different problem, rather than one 'causing' the other. (Timberlake (1985), in his book *Africa in Crisis*, argues that *environmental* collapse underlies both the military conflicts and the food insecurity of the 1980s.) Third, the implication that countries are free from famine because they are not 'heavily armed' is not well supported by reality. Shindo's hypothesis fails to explain the case of South Africa, which is the most militarized state in Africa, yet is not susceptible to famine as conventionally defined (though malnutrition is endemic in the Black 'homelands' and 'independent states').

Finally, it does not follow that government spending diverted from armaments and defence would automatically be used for agriculture or for assisting the poor. These objectives are already low on many governments' list of priorities, so the money saved on weapons might well be 'wasted' in some other way. An Oxfam campaign in 1985 called 'Bread not Bombs' assumed that such a trade-off would occur if the international arms trade was simply cut back. But of course, while such a cutback may be *necessary* to release resources for more socially relevant programmes, it is naive to assume that this is a *sufficient* condition, without the political will to do both.

11.2 War

Perhaps the most belligerent expression of government power is a decision to go to war, not necessarily with neighbouring (or distant) countries, but frequently against segments of the population it supposedly represents. Similarly, the most extreme expression of disaffection with a government is to take up arms to try to depose it.

Although drought remains the dominant explanation for African famines in the Western media, a growing number of observers place military conflict at the top of the list. 'War and civil war are probably the most important causes of famine, assisted by the huge amounts spent by some African governments on arms imports and the military' (Raikes, 1988, p. 101). Kula (1989, p. 13) goes so far as to suggest that war constitutes a third category of famine explanation in its own right, after the 'food availability decline' and 'entitlements' approaches:

> As a third dimension to the problem a number of economists . . . draw attention to wars and their complicated politics as one of the major causes of most contemporary famines. Their argument is that wars and the politics of wars suffocate and divert the supply of food which might otherwise have reached the vulnerable sections of the communities.

As already noted, there is no theory that spells out the causal route from war to famine, but a number of consequences of armed conflict are clearly detrimental to food security. The most obvious link is that a war can undermine a subsistence-based food system so dramatically that people are threatened with starvation:

> the central thrust of the thesis is that war (and/or war-time policy by a home government or conquering regime) may badly disrupt normal agricultural, economic and distributive activities and hence promote a food crisis which, it is argued, then tips over into famine. (Leftwich and Harvie, 1986, pp. 29–30)

War as a factor triggering famines is gaining in significance, as the influence of other factors wanes. This century has seen a number of conflicts in which famine induced by food blockades was deliberately used as a weapon, and a number of others in which famine was an unintended by-product of war. A US Presidential Commission on World Hunger concluded that 'widespread starvation due to natural causes has been relatively rare during the past 35 years. . . . Food shortages and famine caused by political conflict have proved harder to overcome' (quoted in Johnson, 1982, p. 98).

Many countries which were previously prone to famines associated with natural disasters are now experiencing famine related to social and economic upheaval, such as that induced by civil unrest or war. In the case of the Kampuchean (or Cambodian) famines of 1975 and 1979, Ea (1984, p. 34) argues that: 'While reasons for a shortage of food in Kampuchea can be attributed historically to natural disasters and over-population, the main causes during the last decade are to be found in political crises and military action.'

As for the African famines of the 1980s, Borton and Clay (1986, p. 1) note that: 'Civil war and externally financed insurgency were primarily responsible for propelling a food crisis into a famine in four out of the six worst affected countries.' Wars in Africa today tend to be civil more often than international, and typically take the form of armed groups inside the country either fighting for their independence (as with the Eritrean People's Liberation Front (EPLF) in Eritrea), or to replace the national government (as with the Mozambique National Resistance (MNR) in Mozambique, National Union for the Total Independence of Angola (UNITA) in Angola and the Sudan People's Liberation Army (SPLA) in southern Sudan). The point which is not always made by famine analysts is that these guerrilla armies are all rural-based, so that peasant communities are sucked in to the battle in various ways.

Having said that 'natural disasters' have less causal significance now than in the past, it is striking that most recent African famines have been characterized by the combination of drought and war. Indeed, it is difficult to think of a famine-prone country which is not afflicted with the drought–war–famine trinity. The obvious relationship between war and drought is that war interferes with both local and external drought responses. For example, the appropriation of surplus grain and animals by an army or guerrilla band in normal years may constitute the appropriation of food and assets needed for the farmer's very survival in a year of drought. And, of course, conflict prevents food from being transported into a drought-affected region. The effects of drought on its own can usually be countered by movements of food from surplus regions, as well as by the adoption of a range of coping strategies (such as selling assets) by the affected population. Similarly, farmers continue producing food during all but the most disruptive of wars (after all, an army marches on its stomach), so war itself rarely explains famine, except where starvation is cynically employed as a weapon of war (see the case study later in this chapter, pp. 159–61).

But any farming community which lies within a conflict zone risks seeing its crops and animals destroyed or requisitioned to feed the soldiers of either or both sides – or simply to deprive the opposition of these valuable resources. Grant (1985, p. 7) of UNICEF describes the profound effects of conflict on people's access to food in poor African villages:

> a squad of troops may come into a village that has already suffered two years of drought, and that squad lives off the village for two or three weeks and then takes a month's supply of food when it leaves – this destroys the established systems for survival. It is therefore no accident that it is the strife-torn areas in Africa which are now suffering most.

In Chad in the mid-1980s, government troops systematically burnt thousands of acres of millet and sorghum during the agricultural season, 'to stop terrorists hiding in the fields', without caring about the hunger this would mean for the farmers concerned. The MNR in Mozambique also destroyed tons of foodcrops just before they were due to be harvested. The famine in Kampuchea in 1975 followed a decline in rice production which was caused by several years of fighting and by heavy American bombing, until 1973, of rural areas – one of many 'deliberate American strategies to disrupt agricultural production' (Ea, 1984, p. 37).

War also threatens crop production by reducing the numbers of men and women actively engaged in agriculture – either they join up with one side or the other (as volunteers or conscripts), or they are taken prisoner, or they are injured or killed. In Mozambique, Angola and Cambodia, the number of amputees caused by farmers stepping on mines has reduced entire communities to economic immobility and permanent dependence on aid. In Ethiopia, tens of thousands of farmers have been forcibly conscripted into the army.

In terms of demographic impact, wars typically raise the ratio of dependants to producers, which magnifies the vulnerability of children, old people and women (especially in areas where farming and fighting are male-dominated). An eye-witness account of the 1960s Biafran War concluded that: 'Of the 1–3 million dead on both sides of the front, probably no more than 10% were killed by direct war action. . . . The majority of the victims are civilians, most of them in the vulnerable groups – children and aged' (Aall, 1970, p. 75). Children were most at risk, and they died 'mostly of starvation', not war.

It is because war is so overwhelming in its multiple impacts that it does not fit neatly into any category or group of famine theories. War not only undermines food production, it interferes with alternatives sources of food too – trade and aid. It is unusual for traders to operate in war zones, even if there is a promise of high profits to be made, and transport routes are always in danger of being destroyed during conflicts anyway. Aid is often ruled out for this same reason. If a famine-prone community stands between a government and a group or rebels or freedom fighters, one of the two parties is bound to have reasons for not wanting supplies of food and medicines to be delivered into the area. (For instance, the government might suspect that relief supplies will be appropriated from famine-afflicted villagers by its enemies, and therefore keep foreign aid agencies away.) Flows of information are also hopelessly inadequate during war, so that identifying a need for assistance and targeting relief interventions are virtually impossible to do with any precision. This problem was encountered during the Biafran famine, as described by Aall (1970, pp. 75–6):

> the emergency has been considerably alleviated through international relief, but it took quite some time before it got off the ground. . . . Particularly in the beginning, the relief was rather chaotic. . . . There were enormous transport and communications difficulties, and it was often impossible to get at the areas where the needs were likely to be the most acute – close to the front.

War undermines traditional coping strategies for dealing with food crises; it increases vulnerability to drought by depriving people of their ability to respond effectively to it. Conflict tends to split countries and communities along ethnic, religious, or 'occupation group' lines. For example, as discussed in Chapter 9.5, the symbiotic relationship between farmers and herders has degenerated into open warfare along much of the Sahel because of competition over land.

It is sometimes said that famine, war and socialism are inextricably related in modern Africa. The argument is that famines are a direct consequence of the 'inefficient' socialist policies of post-colonial African governments (including militarization), and of unrest which develops out of popular opposition to these policies. The implication is that the removal of socialism will mean the end of conflict and, therefore, the abolition of famine.

This is surely an oversimplification at best. In an argument linking the three topics of this chapter, Shindo (1985, pp. 7–8) claims that it is not socialism *per se* which produces famine, but the militarization, wars and refugees associated with achieving and maintaining a socialist system following the often traumatic transition from colonialism to independence:

> May we not then see the famine which engulfs the newly emerging 'socialist' states of Africa as due not so much to the 'inefficiency' inherent in the socialist system as to the large number of refugees produced by war, and to economic crises deriving from insufficiency of national capital being directed to production for the civilian sector as a result of the transition to the 'heavily armed' state? . . . no sooner are the newly emerging states independent (or have their revolution) than, facing war internally and externally, they have to strengthen their military power in order to cope with war and to maintain their power. . . . It could in fact be said of all the newly emerging African 'socialist' countries afflicted by famine that they are states ravaged by civil war, in all of which the degree of militarisation is being intensified.

This assertion, 'that famine is the product of war and the transition to the "heavily armed" state', virtually constitutes a theory of famine for post-independence Africa. In southern Africa, for example, war has been promoted by South Africa as part of its strategy of economic and military destabilization of the 'frontline states'.

The 1982–5 famine in areas of Mozambique was directly attributable to the tragic interaction of drought and civil strife – the confrontation between the Frelimo government and the South African backed MNR (Mozambique National Resistance movement). Tickner (1985, p. 90) describes the build-up to famine:

> In 1983 . . . the MNR launched, with strong South African backing and direction, military offensives in Tete and Zambezia provinces. . . . It was the activity of these MNR bands, particularly in Tete and northern Manica province attacking military convoys from surplus areas going to deficit areas, and from the port of Beira to Tete that contributed so much to the hunger in Tete province. In the north of Inhambane province they similarly cut off the drought-stricken population from food supplies coming from provincial and regional reserves.

The resulting famine was more 'man-made' than 'natural', since the effects of the drought could otherwise have been contained by relief measures. Bush (1985b, p. 10) estimates that South Africa, by supporting the MNR, 'is guilty of more than 100,000 deaths caused through the disruption of famine relief'. The war also contributed to general economic collapse, interference with transport and hence with trade, and the displacement of thousands of people from their homes and farmland. D'Souza (1988, p. 48) summarizes the causes of the famine as 'a combination of greatly reduced agricultural production – itself following from unwise economic policies – drought, and widespread displacement as a result of war'.

Mozambique is far from being the only country where conflict has led to famine. Other cases include countries as diverse as the Netherlands, Ethiopia, Kampuchea and Bangladesh. Although linked by the common factor that each famine was created or fuelled by a war situation, the point at which conflict impinged on household food supplies varied. For example, in the case of the Netherlands (1944) and, arguably, in the Mozambican, Ethiopian and south Sudanese famines of the 1980s, deliberate 'siege' tactics were applied to certain regions. In the Netherlands (see 11.4 below), this tactic was used most overtly and cynically – large non-food producing towns were simply cut off from their only food supply sources.

In Mozambique, food producers and buyers lost their crops because of drought and insurgency, while alternative supplies (imports) were simultaneously reduced because of military and economic pressures. In Ethiopia, subsistence farmers who lost their crops for natural reasons (drought) found the usual alternatives eliminated by military actions and, perhaps, by deliberate government policy. In Bangladesh (1974), conversely, the displacement of farmers and the creation of a refugee population reduced supply of and increased demand for the marketed agricultural surplus – but the surplus was subsequently squeezed further by floods and hoarding. In none of these cases can the famine be ascribed to 'natural' causes alone, whatever the contributory role of droughts or floods.

11.3 Refugees

> In 1985, Africa was a continent in turmoil. Ten million people had fled their homes, some into famine centres, some into cities, many across national boundaries. Most of these were 'environmental refugees', people fleeing land that could no longer support them. Others had fled wars, civil wars and goverment repression. But the connections between the wars of Africa and the 'droughts' of Africa were so tangled that it was impossible to tell who was fleeing what for which reasons.
>
> (Timberlake, 1985, p. 185)

An important reason for the devastating effect of war on food production is that war, like drought, creates refugees. Alienated from their previous sources of income, often having lost all their assets, refugees have no entitlement to food through the normal means, and are totally dependent on aid and handouts –

'dependency syndrome' being a common consequence. The problems are most acute when those affected are farmers. Displaced from their land, they are producing neither for themselves nor for the market. (The same applies to military personnel, especially those conscripted out of civilian life, where they may have been productively employed. The military contributes nothing to GNP, and is a net drain on food and other resources – soldiers, like refugees, need to be fed.)

The other side of the same coin is that those farmers who continue to produce surpluses lose their markets when their customers become refugees. This was noted for the Biafran war and famine of the late 1960s. 'At some places, even in the war-affected areas, some surpluses of, for instance, beans, maize and rice were available, which the farmers otherwise could not sell, in spite of being surrounded by starving refugees who had no money to pay with' (Aall, 1970, p. 79).

The relationship between refugees (or 'displaced persons') and their host population is complex and often – but not inevitably – fraught. A number of scenarios are possible, each having very different implications.

1. Some refugees who move to another region or country go into refugee camps, becoming a net drain on local, national and international resources. How this burden is taken up determines the extent to which the local economy is affected. If the international aid agencies take on the responsibility for maintaining the refugees, then local people should not be adversely affected, and may even profit if they are paid to supply the camps with food and goods.
2. Other refugees become self-settled and have only a nominal impact on the host country. Either they are rapidly assimilated or they live as a self-sufficient enclave which hardly disrupts the local economy at all. A precondition here is that there is no competition over access to land, water supplies and services. (An example is the case of Angolan refugees in north-west Zambia during the late 1970s.)
3. Sometimes refugees enter their host country at the bottom end of the labour market, as agricultural labourers, manual workers, or domestic servants. Here they have a beneficial impact on the host economy, becoming a kind of 'labour reserve', though the refugees' own prospects may not improve much. This scenario requires that the host country has a fairly resilient economy which is not undermined by the sudden entry of thousands of refugees into its labour market. (A case in point is the flight of refugees from civil war in Uganda into southern Sudan during the early 1980s, some of whom at least achieved smooth and rapid integration; see Harrell-Bond, 1986.)
4. In cases where environmental crisis provides the impetus for flight, rather than civil war, the refugees and their unwilling hosts may be equally badly affected. In Africa, the influx of drought refugees frequently imposes

additional burdens on an already strained economy, which can even drag the host region into famine itself. (In eastern Sudan, Ethiopian refugees in the mid-1980s disrupted local economic activities to such an extent that some Sudanese were taken into refugee camps which had been set up for the Ethiopians.)

Regrettably, the fourth scenario above seems to be most typical in contemporary African famines, simply because of the fragility of the host communities. An example is the famine in Dar Masalit, western Sudan in 1984/5, which was exacerbated by an influx of refugees from Chad, causing famine conditions to persist longer than anywhere else in the Sahelian belt from West Africa to Ethiopia. The reasons given by the refugees for fleeing into Darfur related mainly to insecurity in Chad caused by military activity – so they were not drought or famine victims. This is crucial, because famine refugees typically return to their farms as soon as they can, whereas war refugees do not. People who migrate temporarily in search of food are concerned with maintaining their way of life above all else, but war refugees have lost their way of life, and sometimes cannot return home for several years.

It was not the arrival of refugees in Darfur which caused the problems, but their failure to leave. The region had to cope with feeding 120,000 extra people, which it simply could not do indefinitely. A related problem arose from the fact that people classified as refugees received preferential treatment from aid agencies, which caused much resentment among the local Sudanese, who were also under severe food stress at the time. Several Sudanese tried to pass themselves off as Chadian in order to get access to food aid and medical treatment which was being denied to the local population. When relief supplies were inadequate, as was the case in 1985, the local economy collapsed, and the concentration of a large refugee population in a drought-afflicted agricultural area resulted in a further famine (de Waal, 1988).

In a different context, Harrell-Bond (1986, p. 24) has recommended that 'assistance to refugee-affected areas should be determined on the basis of demographic changes and perceived needs, rather than focusing on one group within a community which is itself already impoverished.'

Having been uprooted from their normal environments and crowded together in unsanitary conditions, refugees are highly susceptible to communicable diseases, and it is this unhealthy environment which produces most deaths during famines, rather than starvation. The conventional explanation is that excess mortality in these circumstances is explained by increased *susceptibility* to diseases, because of hunger. De Waal (1989) challenges this 'starvation model' of famine mortality – that 'destitution increases the risk of starvation, and starvation increases the risk of death'. During the Darfur famine of 1984/5, de Waal found that mortality among refugees could not be predicted by wealth differentials or occupation groups. People were killed by an increased *exposure* to infectious diseases, which was explained by a poor public health environment in refugee communities and relief camps. These were factors to which everybody, rich or poor, was equally vulnerable, so that death struck almost indiscriminately.

In terms of famine theory, this argument paints a curiously old-fashioned picture of famine as a 'Malthusian leveller', and therefore challenges the contemporary fashion for seeing famine as selecting its victims from the poor and marginalized elements of society. De Waal's 'health crisis model', which applies particularly to people displaced by drought, states that drought plus social disruption plus economic crisis increases the risks of both a health crisis and a food crisis, but whereas the food crisis increases the risk of destitution, the health crisis increases the risk of death. Given that the Darfur famine was a health crisis as much as a food crisis, Sen's entitlement approach, with its emphasis on identifying who enjoys preferential access to marketed supplies of food, is analytically redundant, and must be silent in all cases where famine mortality is not directly related to starvation.

Of course, not all displaced persons are unlucky enough to go into unhealthy refugee camps (nor are all refugee camps particularly unhealthy). Many move in with relatives far away or make their way to cities, where they survive on minor income-earning activities in the informal sector. To the extent that this competition 'crowds out' those urban residents already scraping their subsistence in petty trading and services, the effect can be to export famine-induced destitution from the countryside to the town. The same argument applies within rural areas, when farmers who lose their harvests through drought or are displaced from their land by war are forced to resort to 'low-status' trades to raise money for food. The rural poor, who depend on these sources of income at all times, will be doubly disadvantaged, as de Waal (1989, p. 164) observed in Darfur:

> These people were hit hardest by the famine. Not only were their markets diminished by the impoverishment of the people who bought their goods and services, but they found themselves competing with huge numbers of extra people trying to follow the same activities.

The worst situation displaced persons can find themselves in is when they lose their usual access to food and are unable to replace this with alternatives – they have no other trade, they cannot find any form of employment, and relief does not reach them. As Aall (1970, p. 75) argues: 'When people who ordinarily live close to the borderline of hunger suddenly have to leave everything and flee into the bush, they are not able to sustain life for long.' In a survey of farming in drought- and war-torn Mozambique, D'Souza (1988, p. 37) discovered that 'the most severe obstacle to subsistence farming, at present, is the widespread insecurity which has caused and continues to cause massive dislocation. The survey results given above show without a doubt that those who are uprooted rapidly fall into destitution.'

11.4   Case study: the Netherlands, 1944

An economic blockade or siege, in which food and supplies are deliberately withheld from a population, constitutes the purest form of a 'food availability decline' ('FAD') famine – one which affects all classes more or less even-handedly. Such a famine occurred in the Netherlands during World War II, resulting in an estimated 10,000 deaths. Although relatively small-scale in mortality terms, it was in many other respects quite remarkable.

For one thing, it was unusual in that climate played no role at all in precipitating the famine. For another, mortality was concentrated in major towns and cities, rather than in rural areas. But perhaps the unique feature of the Dutch famine is that is was, as a chapter title in the book by Stein *et al.* (1975) states, 'Famine in a highly developed society'. Those who suffered during the famine were probably the wealthiest, best educated and most mobile victims of any famine in history. For these reasons, it is difficult to explain the famine in terms of a decline in effective demand or 'exchange entitlements' for food. For once, a pure 'FAD' analysis seems difficult to refute.

The Netherlands today has one of the highest national population densities in the world, mostly urbanized, and has done since at least World War II. Because of this, imports of food were and are essential.[1] This dependence is not unusual – most industrialized areas within countries 'import' their food requirements, either from their own rural sector or on international markets. But concentrations of non-food producing urban people, no matter how wealthy, are always potentially vulnerable to non-economic threats to their food supplies. In 1937, anticipating a war in which the Netherlands might well be isolated or occupied, the Dutch government began reducing its dependence on food imports:

> Immediately on the outbreak of war in September 1939, imports of animal feed stopped and the rationing of animal feed was begun. In May 1940 the Netherlands was occupied by the Germans. Rationing of foods for the Dutch people then began, and measures were taken to adjust agricultural production. . . . In 1944, conditions deteriorated further, and by July 1944 the average daily ration for adults was down to 1350 Calories. The famine came at a time when food supplies were already marginal. (Stein *et al.*, 1975, p. 43)

This exposition reveals that even this famine was not caused by a 'rapid, almost instantaneous decline in food availability from a "satisfactory pre-disaster food state" to a sub-adequate level of food supply' (Mengestu *et al.*, 1978, p. 4). Instead, the famine came at the tail end of a long-term process of increasing vulnerability of the population to food supply shocks, and in this it has much in common with famines in the Third World, which typically afflict those already vulnerable because of their proximity to subsistence.

Vulnerability in the Netherlands developed because of the wilful neglect by the German occupying forces of the food needs of the Dutch population.

Although agricultural production was encouraged and industrial production discouraged, the intention was primarily to serve the food needs of the occupying army, and to boost the supplies of the German population. Aykroyd (1974, p. 98) estimates that about 60 per cent of the Netherlands' agricultural output was 'commandeered' between 1940 and 1944. A large number of working men, including many farmers, were also lost from productive work. Some were rounded up and sent to work in German factories, many were killed, imprisoned or deported, still others went 'underground' for the duration. Hundreds of thousands of hectares of farmland were turned into defensive sea dykes, airfields and military fortifications.

The famine started, ironically, as the war entered its final phase, in September 1944. To support the Allied thrust through the Netherlands and hamper the German defences, Dutch railworkers brought rail traffic to a halt. The Germans responded, as they had threatened they would, by placing an embargo on *all* transport, including food supplies. The intention was cynical and brutal – to starve the Dutch into submission. 'Seyes-Inquart, the Nazi Reichskommissar, prohibited all movement of food from the north and east into western Holland. . . . Seyes-Inquart himself told the Dutch that if the strike were not called off there would be famine. He was right. . . .' (Aykroyd, 1974, p. 100). By November, 'the acute food shortage had become a famine. People were starving' (Stein *et al.*, 1975, p. 44). An open letter sent to Seyes-Inquart and written by Dutch doctors confirms the malevolent role of the Germans in creating the conditions which produced the famine:

> We hold your Administration responsible for the dire shortage of even the most necessary foodstuffs. The want and distress of the Dutch people living in the most densely populated parts of the occupied territory increase day by day. . . . The Occupying Authorities are to blame for these conditions. In the first place, because they broke International Law by transporting to Germany the large reserve supplies available in 1940, and, in the years following 1940, by carrying off a considerable portion of the livestock and food produced in our country.
>
> Secondly because now, in 1944, they are, by confiscation and abduction of nearly all transport material, preventing the Dutch people from distributing the remaining food satisfactorily over the whole country. . . . Ships that were to be used for conveying supplies were seized, and supplies stored in factories, warehouses and in cold storage, were carried off after famine conditions had already been established. . . . There was a time when Germany herself suffered from the terrible effects of a hunger blockade. Then, she condemned the action as being criminal; now, without necessity, she is starving an unarmed people. (Quoted in Aykroyd, 1974, pp. 101–2)

In November, Seyes-Inquart partly lifted the embargo and allowed the use of water transport, but relief measures were aggravated by other problems. 'Winter was both unusually early and unusually severe in 1944. Before much could be done, the canals had frozen and the barges could not move. The freezing of the canals prevented large-scale relief' (Stein *et al.*, 1975, p. 44).

By contrast with famines in poor countries, which generally affect the rural poor more than relatively affluent urbanites, 'the famine was largely a phenomenon of the cities and towns. Rural people produced food for their own subsistence, even at the height of the famine . . . while towns like The Hague and Leiden were starving, villages only two to three miles away were much better off' (Stein *et al.*, 1975, p. 45).

Paradoxically, then, one of the strongest objections to the 'FAD' approach provides the very reason why the Netherlands famine can be analyzed in FAD terms. FAD is usually criticized for its implicit assumption that the region or country affected by famine is a closed economy. No allowance is made in the theory for a decline in local food availability to be offset by imports or relief from outside the region. In this case, it was the German policy of deliberately converting the western part of the Netherlands into a closed economy, by sealing off its transport links with the outside world, which produced the restrictive conditions necessary for a FAD analysis of the consequent famine to hold. Thus it was that the famine lasted as long as the west, in particular, remained isolated and cut off from food supplies – much as a siege laid to a castle or walled town in medieval times would cause starvation of its inhabitants.

11.5   Conclusion

The preceding discussion suggests a framework within which the contribution war makes to famine might be assessed.

First, wars disrupt agricultural production. People in rural areas may be conscripted, disabled, displaced or killed, reducing the numbers actively engaged in farming. Food is often physically destroyed during wars – fields of grain are burnt, granaries pillaged and livestock slaughtered. Farming depends crucially on seasonal inputs applied at the correct time, and people working in the fields are particularly exposed to landmines, crossfire and bombing. If technical and financial support for agriculture and rural development ceases during wars, food production might suffer further.

Second, wars undermine local economies. Food prices rise and markets collapse. Long-distance trade is curtailed. Farmers lose income not only through reduced production, but through loss of demand and markets for, especially, their non-food crops. The access to food of non-farmers may be threatened directly, through reduced food supplies, or indirectly, through lost income. Traders and artisans who depend indirectly on agricultural production or incomes for their livelihood may suffer from 'second-order' effects, or 'derived destitution'. Refugees without cash or assets have no economic claim to food.

Third, wars interrupt flows of food – both trade and aid. In some cases, this is a planned strategy. A trade blockade, a government ban on aid agency intervention, or the shooting down by guerrillas of aid-carrying aeroplanes, is the contemporary equivalent of the medieval siege. The effect is to turn the area into a 'closed economy', with the local population becoming entirely dependent on its own (reduced) resources for survival. *In extremis*, the consequence can be mass starvation – a classical 'FAD famine'. Less cynically, a government's capacity to respond to food crises may be constrained by poor information from affected areas, by logistical problems (roads and bridges blown up, trucks diverted to military uses), and by lack of foreign exchange to buy food, because these funds have been allocated to militarization and the pursuit of the war.

Fourth, wars create new patterns of demand for food, both geographically and across social groupings. In general, the ratio of food producers to consumers falls during conflicts. Soldiers consume food which they do nothing to produce. Formerly self-provisioning farmers also become net consumers, either as members of the armed forces or as displaced refugees. When households and families split up, dependants (children and the aged) lose their conventional source of food, and often require substantial relief assistance if they are to survive.

Fifth, wars undermine people's ability to cope with adversity. Medical and social services become overstretched, immunization programmes stop, health clinics close. Not just food, but animals and other assets which might be sold for food are requisitioned or destroyed by soldiers. Land which is essential for farming or grazing becomes out of bounds because of the military presence. Traditional coping strategies of farmers and pastoralists are undermined as communities are divided, shattering social support networks.

Finally, wars create refugees. Africa, with 10 per cent of the world's population, contained at least 25 per cent of the world's refugees in 1985. In Somalia, one in every seven people was a refugee (Borton and Clay, 1986, pp. 12–13). Some refugees cope with displacement by 'self-settling' and continuing to survive independently. More often, though, they need assistance, at least during a period of adjustment. People displaced by war or drought are extremely vulnerable to communicable diseases, all the more so if they are crowded into unsanitary refugee camps. Occasionally they can drain resources in their new environment to such an extent that they raise the risk of famine for their hosts as well as themselves.

Few catastrophes disrupt access to food so comprehensively as war. A drought may induce crop failure. Market failure or loss of income undermines a person's ability to purchase food. Government callousness or ignorance can prevent food aid from being sent to famine-threatened communities. But war single-handedly threatens production, distribution (through markets, food aid or remittances), and grain stores (which may be confiscated, destroyed or abandoned), thereby undermining all sources of access to food simultaneously.

In summary, war threatens both the production and distribution of food, and therefore threatens food consumption as well. War creates additional demands for food (the army, refugees) while simultaneously constricting food supplies. The relationship between war and famine is direct, lethal and seemingly intractable.

Note

1. This point effectively undermines the supposed link between population density and famine, as posited by some neo-Malthusians, and discussed in Chapter 5 (see also Twose, 1985, p. 9; George, 1976, p. 58). Both point out that population density is higher in Britain and Holland than in Bolivia or even India, yet hunger persists in the latter two countries, and has been eradicated from the former. Food security does not necessarily require food production self-sufficiency.

12

Famine and international relations

Famines do not occur, they are organized by the grains trade.

Bertolt Brecht

The unequal nature of economic and political relationships between countries can heighten famine vulnerability and contribute to the creation of famine conditions. While it is difficult to classify neatly the many points of view which come under this general category, they fall into two broad groups – those that argue that international relationships are generally exploitative and actually generate the conditions which make people vulnerable to famine; and those that argue that international relationships and the institutions which represent them are unresponsive to signals of vulnerability, and therefore allow famines to happen, by neglect rather than design.

Many of the former set of arguments mirror, at an international level, the argument that wealth and power inequalities between groups within countries increase the vulnerability of the poor. The latter set of arguments ranges from the naive view that the poor in poor countries would eat more (and presumably be protected from famine) if the rich in rich countries ate less, to critiques of the performance of the international cereals market, and of the criteria under which food aid is disbursed.

This chapter considers three aspects of this broad and contentious subject: the role of international food markets; the assertion that famines have been caused or exacerbated by international neglect; and the politics of food aid. The literature on each of these topics is enormous in itself, so rather than attempting a comprehensive review, this discussion will select contributions to the literature which illustrate typical themes.

12.1 International food markets

Many writers have elaborated on Brecht's bald statement above, though few have managed to draw a direct connection between the operations of the global grain market and any specific named famine. In an examination of the power of the seven major international grain companies, Morgan (1979, p. vii) demonstrates that the dependence of many countries on American food surpluses has had far-reaching consequences, one of which may well be an increased vulnerability to famine:

> After World War II, dozens of countries that had once fed themselves began to depend on a distant source – the United States – for a substantial part of their food supply. As America became the center of the planetary food system, trade routes were transformed, new economic relationships took shape, and grain became one of the foundations of the postwar American Empire. Food prices, diets, the dollar, politics, and diplomacy all were affected.

Control of this vital trade is far from free and competitive. On the contrary, this is one of the world's most inscrutable oligopolies, and it is hardly regulated or controlled at all, despite the importance of the commodity in which it is dealing. Seven families own the seven major grain merchant houses, which have no public shareholders and therefore little obligation to disclose information. This gives them unprecedented power to manipulate the demand for food on the world market to their own ends. Moreover, because companies favour stability in their trading relations, they tend to deal with regimes which exercise strong control over their populations – that is, with repressive, rightwing 'democracies' or military dictatorships. There is no 'conspiracy theory' at work here; just a coincidence of self-interest between multinational and political elites:

> The interlocking interests of the regime, the grain trade, the locally based multinationals, and the American farm bloc are not difficult to untangle. Agricultural imports are, to begin with, a means of maintaining the status quo. The availability of the imports makes it possible to postpone radical domestic reform, land redistribution, and the redirection of credit to different sectors of the society. The sale of the imported food on the local economy (the government does not give the food away) generates money that can be used to pay the civil servants, police forces, and soldiers who make up the regime's base of political support. And the imported food helps to hold down inflation, which is a primary cause of unrest in the middle class (students, merchants, businessmen). (Morgan, 1979, p. vii)

Morgan offers several examples of abuse by the grain multinationals of their unprecedented power. One case is that of Zaire, which was supplied with grain by Continental Grain Company from 1973. In 1974, when copper prices began to fall, Zaire lost vital foreign exchange and ran up large debts with many overseas creditors, including Continental. The company responded in 1976 by withholding shipments of wheat until a number of demands were met about debt repayment and control of wheat imports. The government was forced to surrender immediately, with the result that Continental 'became Zaire's sole importer of wheat and sole manufacturer of flour, and it received authority to control imports of any competing flour almost as if it were a government agency' (Morgan, 1979, p. 227).

Just as, at the local level inside a country, speculation, hoarding and other distortions in food markets increase the vulnerability of the poor to famine, so the ability of a few multinational corporations simply to cut off grain supplies at any time – even if this power is rarely exercised – constitutes a permanent threat to national food security. Food is power: 'Whoever controls food exports controls the world.'[1]

The multinational grain companies have become central to the national food security of many other countries. The chain of events in Zaire powerfully illustrates the dangers of this dependence. More generally, this case study illuminates the vulnerability of most Third World economies, on two fronts, in international import and export markets. Many African countries derive most of their foreign exchange from exports of one or two primary commodities (cash crops like coffee or cocoa, minerals like copper), for which they receive low, variable and often declining prices on world markets. In the uncertain climate of international commodity markets, the only guarantees are that today's price will change tomorrow, and that volume and price agreements struck with trading partners will not last. Price rises, like the coffee boom of the late 1970s, are often followed by slumps, leaving those producers who switched into the crop expecting quick profits counting their losses instead. In 1986, for example, cotton production in Tanzania was more than double that of the previous year. But in July the price of cotton on the world market halved on a single day. Former President Nyerere likened this to a devastating crop blight or drought:

> The result for our economy – and the income of the peasants – is similar to that of a natural disaster: half our crop, and therefore of our income, is lost. Our peasants – and our nation – have made the effort, but the country is not earning a single extra cent in foreign exchange. That is theft! (Quoted in George, 1988, p. 99)

The problem is compounded by the efforts of institutions such as the World Bank and IMF (as part of 'structural adjustment programs') to encourage cash crop production in debtor countries. When eight or ten poor countries raise their output simultaneously, the only winners are the multinationals who buy up the crop at 'competitive' prices, and consumers in the West who pay less for coffee, chocolate and other commodities because of this induced competition among the exporting economies. If the cash crop exporters simultaneously face rising import bills for such essentials as oil and food, then these countries are trapped in a vice from which there is no obvious means of escape. Not only the amount of foreign exchange they earn, but also its purchasing power, is falling steadily over time. 'Many commodity exporters have suffered a prolonged deterioration in their terms of trade. Over the last ten years, African countries have lost as much as 20 per cent of the purchasing power of their exports' (ICIHI, 1985, p. 30).

Apart from putting the brakes on the development potential of primary exporters, foreign exchange constraints also undermine the country's ability to achieve food security through food imports. This raises the perennial debate over whether governments should be importing cereals like wheat at all, rather than promoting self-sufficiency in indigenous staple foods like millet or cassava. The Ghanaian government ran a campaign for self-sufficiency in 1988 with the slogan: 'We must grow what we eat and eat what we grow.' Like many other food deficit countries, Ghana perceives the international cereals market as unreliable, unresponsive to needs and burdened with political 'overheads'. In fact, the performance of the international cereals market in recent decades seems to refute at least the first of these perceptions. In southern Africa, for example, Koester (1985) shows that variations in international cereals supplies and prices, at least since the early 1970s, have been significantly less than comparable variations within South African Development Coordination Conference (SADCC) countries.

None the less, this Hobson's choice, between pursuing food security objectives through domestic production (dependence on a fickle climate) or through foreign imports (dependence on fickle world commodity markets), must seem as double-edged to African policy-makers as does the 'cash crop or foodcrop?' dilemma facing individual smallholders. Even if self-reliance is more costly economically than dependence on international cereal markets, political uncertainties are such that preferring imports of food over unstable local production merely exchanges one set of vulnerabilities and risks for another.

12.2   International responsibility and response

An obvious rejoinder to arguments that the international grain market is unreliable at best and jeopardizes the food security of the poor at worst, is that no profit-making enterprise can be expected to demonstrate either morality or compassion. Conversely, the 'international community' supposedly has both, and famine prevention is increasingly perceived in the West as at least partly 'our' responsibility. A strong expression of this opinion appeared in the British press at the height of the mid-1980s African famines. 'A civilisation entertained by the media spectacle of millions of Africans starving while consuming the under-priced products of African labour cannot call itself civilised.'[2]

As the capacity of the international community to respond to food crises has steadily gained momentum during the past half century, so has the argument for international moral responsibility. Its strongest form is the assertion that there comes a point where the suffering inflicted by design, neglect or incapacity on citizens of a given country becomes so unjust that international responsibility overrides the sovereignty of the state involved and impels intervention (Green, 1976; Brown and Shue, 1977).

Whatever the validity of the theory, the practice is sadly at variance. The international community has shown itself to be highly selective and morally inconsistent in its decisions about when, where and how to intervene in the domestic affairs of countries in crisis. The depressing and seemingly endless cycle of famines in sub-Saharan Africa since the early 1970s suggests either that something is wrong with international communications or that moral posturing by politicians and international civil servants bears little relation to reality.

Given that the international community has not always been prompt in its mobilization of relief, the obvious question is, why not? There are two main explanations for the fact that famines are still allowed to happen. The first suggests that the problems are technical. Poor information, difficulties in discriminating between a temporary food problem and the 'irreversible decline' into famine conditions, and logistical constraints all have some explanatory power. Also, access is sometimes denied to a famine-stricken area, for instance, where the state is prosecuting a civil war against that segment of the population. On the other hand, the assertion that a lack of information or problems with transport was the overriding determinant of the limited response of the international community to the African famines of the 1980s is clearly inadequate. The FAO predicted famine in many parts of the continent and publicized its predictions for months before the international community made any serious effort to mobilize its resources (Gill, 1986; Hay, 1986). The 'revelation' of the Ethiopian famine in 1984 on BBC television lends powerful support to the contention that information about a critical food situation was being ignored.

This leads on to the second, more cynical argument, that the 1980s African famines occurred as the result of withheld relief – a lack of response to information – on the part of potential recipient governments, food aid donors, or both. In this context, national governments of countries prone to famine are often blamed. For example, Green (1976) analyzes the events leading up to the 1973 Wollo famine in Ethiopia and concludes that there was a 'cover-up' by the Haile Selassie government *and* the donor community in Addis Ababa, but mainly by the former. 'Cover-up' remains a common accusation whenever famine appears to strike unexpectedly, but could seemingly have been prevented – as in Sudan in 1989/90.

Whether signals of impending mass starvation were suppressed by governments during the 1970s or not, governments nowadays generally possess both better information and greater awareness of the damaging political consequences of ignoring a serious food crisis. Although the extent to which blame for a delayed response is apportioned between governments and donors can be debated, governments have recently been all too ready to declare an emergency. The nature of their relationships with the donor community appears to be a far more important determinant of how quickly food aid flows and in what quantities.

It is interesting to note, for example, that in five countries in eastern and southern Africa affected by drought during the early 1980s, the response of the donor community appeared to be unrelated to the severity of the situation, the amount of information available or the resources of the country to deal with the problem on its own. A whistle-stop comparison of the experiences of these five countries reveals some puzzling contrasts.

In Ethiopia the situation was serious, information flows were relatively good, government response mechanisms were in place, foreign exchange reserves were low; but the response was tragically late. Similarly, in Kenya, the drought was worst in a part of the country where information was good and government technical and material resources were well organized. Foreign exchange reserves were under pressure but, compared with Ethiopia, abundant; yet food aid requests were over-subscribed. In Mozambique, by contrast, the situation was serious, formal information was limited and unreliable, but the government appealed early on the basis of qualitative information gathered from many parts of the country, foreign exchange reserves were exceedingly low; the response was late.

In Zimbabwe, the drought mainly affected the southern part of the country, information was good, the donor community responded promptly to limited appeals; and late arrivals of food aid were sufficient to transfer to other countries before they contributed to overflowing food stocks following the first good harvest. In Botswana, the situation was serious, information was excellent, government response mechanisms were in place, the foreign exchange position was excellent and, it has to be said, was used to finance a large part of the relief effort; the World Food Programme and bilateral donors supplied a substantial amount of food aid promptly in response to government appeals.

Clearly, there is more to eliciting a response from food aid donors than a food crisis, good information and the capacity to deliver food aid to people who are starving. The Ethiopian case is such an appalling example of 'late' relief that it is considered here in more detail. However, the situation prevailing in Mozambique between 1982 and 1984 was hardly less shameful.

The main sequence of events in Ethiopia have been reported by Gill (1986), who acknowledges first that the Ethiopian government had been known to ask for aid in excess of its needs in the past, so that when it did so in 1984, donors were understandably sceptical. (A defence of the Ethiopian government's relief 'overestimates' is that it knew very well that it would only receive a proportion of its request. Thus, information becomes seriously undervalued over time.) None the less, as Gill (1986, p. 32) comments: 'The notion that Ethiopia had cried wolf before was a poor substitute for argument. At its most cynical, it allowed donors to justify inaction in 1984 because not quite enough people had died of starvation in 1983.'

Because US public policy at the time was stridently anti-Marxist, the United States has been open to a good deal of criticism over Ethiopia. In fact, European countries and multilateral aid agencies performed no better. Nevertheless, a suspicion remains that if Ethiopia had not proclaimed itself a Marxist state, the famine would have been averted. The official US position was that famine relief aid would be sent to Ethiopia with no political strings attached. Peter McPherson, the head of USAID, reiterated this line in the *Washington Post*, in March 1985:

> The United States' motto has been 'A hungry child knows no politics.' Our emergency aid will go anywhere there is hunger, regardless of our relationship with the Government in question. Ethiopia, where seven million are affected, is the largest recipient of our emergency aid to Africa despite the Marxist character of its Government. (Quoted in Gill, 1986, p. 54)

In reality, however, the situation was quite different. What Gill describes (intriguingly) as 'Ethiopia's relief entitlement' from the United States had been steadily reduced from the late 1970s:

> In 1980, Ethiopia received 43,000 tonnes of American food under the Title II programme; in 1981 that figure had been almost halved to 24,000 tonnes; in 1982 it was quartered again to 6,000 tonnes. . . . According to the following year's budget proposals, running from October 1983, Ethiopia was to be removed entirely as a recipient of American humanitarian aid. USAID's noble maxim 'A hungry child knows no politics' was apparently inoperative. (Gill, 1986, p. 56)

There is no doubting that the motivation for this was political. When additional emergency relief for Ethiopia was requested in 1984, Republican senators tied the vote to a request for funds for military assistance to El Salvador and for the 'Contras' who were fighting the left-wing Sandinista government in Nicaragua:

> The Administration's tactic – justified publicly on the grounds that it was the only way to get Central American military budgets through Congress – provoked outrage. . . . House Speaker 'Tip' O'Neill said that the Administration had 'shown it is ready to starve Africans so that it can kill Central Americans'. (Gill, 1986, pp. 64–5)

As always with 'single-cause' explanations of famine, it is important not to condemn the international community's inadequate response to the point where all other factors are ignored altogether. Carim's (1985, p. 14) description of Ethiopia's 'hungry millions' as 'pawns in the game of superpower ideologies', for instance, conveys the 'helpless victims' image almost as paternalistically as do media stereotypes of Africans with outstretched hands, begging for food. Sender and Smith (1985, pp. 8–9) put such views into perspective:

> Far too frequently . . . no explanation of poverty in developing countries is sought in terms of internal political forces, domestic policy failures, the class character of

particular regimes, or the deficiencies of their economic strategy. The explanations offered are often much too simple: for example, that Reagan, Thatcher, the CIA and EEC bureaucrats conspired to block aid to Ethiopia and starve 900,000 people unfortunate enough to live in an identifiably Marxist state. . . . The point being made here is certainly not a denial of the horrors and brutality that in many parts of the world, most notably and recently in Central America, have stemmed directly and indirectly from US foreign policy, and from foreign military and economic subversion. Rather, the question being raised is to what extent these interventions, by themselves, can explain outcomes.

Similarly, Lemma (1985, pp. 51–2) argues that 'leftist apologists' are unwilling to blame the Ethiopian government at all for the famine, instead blaming 'external forces' exclusively:

The united conspiracy of capitalist and anti-socialist forces from the US, Western and Middle East countries in blocking aid to 'Marxist Ethiopia' is loudly over-stated. Little emphasis is placed on analysing the internal political forces and economic record. . . . To be contemptuous of Western capitalist policies and conspiracies is one thing, but to gloss over the weaknesses of Third World repressive and military governments because they brand themselves 'socialist' or 'Marxist' is another matter.

It is important that this balance be maintained. It is, in any event, naive to expect that altruism will ever dominate national and international politics. The argument that international concern for famine victims bestows an authority to override sovereign rights should be accepted only with great caution, given its implicit assumption that the policies of food aid donors are more objective, more 'caring', and less prone to duplicity or corruption than those of aid recipients. If donors proclaim altruism and compassion, but demonstrate only cynicism and self-interest, this does nothing for any reputation of integrity and moral superiority to which they may aspire.

12.3   The politics of food aid

If a case is to be made for famine being the result of a failure to respond to warning signals, then the politics of aid agencies deserve as close examination as those of governments. In order to do so, it is necessary to say something about the motives of food aid donors. As the 'real' motives are rarely if ever revealed, this exercise must be speculative. (It should also be stated that it is bilateral food aid donors whose motives tend to be the most overtly political.)

Non-altruistic motives for supplying food aid include the following. Agricultural surplus countries look for outlets when the demand for exports does not meet the supply available. Patronage is implicit in any donor–recipient relationship, and food aid is no exception. If nothing else, aid relationships create the basis for closer relationships in other spheres. However, patronage may have more sinister aspects, aspects that are often glossed by the way these issues are presented to Western electorates by the media.

Some critical writers view North-to-South food aid in the same light as Victorian charity – as a palliative designed to assuage the guilt of the affluent and to maintain the docility and dependence of the poor. Hall and Jacques (1986, p. 13) comment on the 1985 'Live Aid' event in Britain, which raised millions of pounds for Ethiopia, in this light:

> Some genuine reservations have been expressed about the limitations of the kind of 'famine consciousness' which has developed in the wake of Live Aid/Sport Aid. It certainly cannot yet be said that the majority of people in Britain . . . have properly grasped the dynamic relationship between 'us' and 'them' across the North/South divide... It has been argued that, although the famine movement is beginning to highlight these deeper aspects of the problem, it has, like the older aid and emergency agencies, portrayed Africa simply as victim linked to the charity of the West in what is essentially a paternalistic relationship.

More generally, Spitz (1978, p. 885) describes food aid programmes as 'a means of forestalling the development of a political consciousness which might degenerate into social disorder. It increases the power of the donor countries which demands all kinds of services in return, and it offers wider opportunities for manoeuvering to people in key positions at the national and local levels.' Spitz's (1978, p. 886) solution to the problem of food aid and famine is both radical and idealistic:

> to refuse the deceptively easy solution offered by a food aid programme that has to be paid for in a thousand different ways means that a country must rely entirely on its own resources; the people must be roused to action so that, disdaining the mentality of recipients of public assistance, they realise that the scourge of famine must be eliminated by taking immediate steps to resist the acceptance of food aid programmes on terms determined by the donors, and by pursuing a long-term policy of transforming internal relations of inequality and external relations of dependence in such a way as to build a society which shall be more just and more firmly in control of its own development.

As Spitz mentions, explicit conditions on the receipt of food aid are often imposed by donors, whether in terms of commercial transactions which follow or in policy changes which the donor finds desirable. The term 'conditionality' has been widely replaced recently by 'policy dialogue', to imply that both sides are willing to adjust. Donors obviously retain most of the negotiating power, however, and most of the criticism arises from the extent to which some donors press 'conditionality' to the point of coercion. At the limit of 'conditionality' is the threat of sanction – the withdrawal of aid with the explicit objective of forcing through a 'recommended' policy change, or even with the aim of bringing down a government (see the Bangladesh case study later in this chapter, pp. 174–6).

US dominance of world trade and aid in cereals, particularly wheat, began with the post-World War II Marshall Plan. Agricultural policies which encouraged the production of surpluses were difficult to reverse, because of the power of the farm lobby in US politics, and food aid became a mechanism for 'dumping' these surpluses while achieving other goals as well. The Third World soon became the major recipient, for both domestic and foreign policy political reasons. '*Food aid* was the combined solution to American surpluses and to further integrating Third World agrarian societies into the capitalist sphere of the world economy' (Friedmann, 1990, p. 16). During the 1950s and 1960s, US food aid to the post-colonial Third World 'undermined local agriculture, creating new proletarians dependent on commercial food, and new nations dependent on imports' (Friedmann, 1990, p. 17).

So one of the primary aims of US PL 480, when it was launched in 1954, was to dispose of US grain surpluses. Humanitarian considerations were of secondary importance (at best) from the outset, as Christensen (1978, p. 188) explains:

> American efforts to dispose of surplus abroad were made primarily through Title I, and as such were often more oriented toward providing general political and economic benefits to governments than they were toward reaching and assisting the undernourished. Local elites could gain revenue through the sale of PL 480 commodities in domestic markets.

This dilemma spills over into the conflict of interests between US marketing interests abroad and the desire of Third World countries for food self-reliance:

> One of the American PL 480 programme's professed principal aims is the expansion of markets for US agricultural products. Another is encouraging development in countries determined to improve their own agricultural production. It is doubtful whether these two aims can ever be compatible.' (Jackson with Eade, 1982, p. 85)

Saylor (1977, p. 205) suggests that the humanitarian motivation of PL 480 food aid ranks below a number of 'traditional objectives' which reflect US self-interest, these being: '(1) surplus disposal, (2) market development, (3) complement to foreign policy, and (4) humanitarian assistance.' The potential for conflicts between the first three of these objectives and the fourth is obvious, as is the reality that, when such contradictions have occurred, the first three have invariably taken precedence. As Dando (1980, pp. 98–9) points out: 'Food is power; it is not a weapon. The denial of food with resultant famine is the weapon . . . many politicians contend food is now one of the principal tools in America's negotiating kit.'

Nau (1978, p. 203) supports this view: 'governments may use food resources in international diplomacy for two purposes: 1) to influence international food markets, and 2) to influence international economic and political relationships going beyond food markets.' The United States is often accused of using its 'food power' in both senses, with the government manipulating its use of food aid, and American grain companies abusing their power in world trade markets:

> North American agricultural wealth holds the key to world famine relief
> operations. Faced with a deficit balance of payment crisis in part related to energy
> problems and cost of imported oil, both the United States and Canada have
> attempted to increase one of their most lucrative gold securing export items – food.
> The use of food as an instrument of foreign policy, to shore up the dollar and to
> influence internal politics of foreign nations, has been wielded by the United
> States. (Dando, 1980, p. 99)

Evidence for the assertion that the United States used food aid in its
(successful) attempt to overthrow the Allende regime in Chile is provided by
the fact that 'less than a month after the coup, the United States approved a
large Title I credit sale of wheat to the new, right-wing junta which was *eight
times* as large as the total food aid credits provided during the entire Allende
period' (Wallerstein, 1980, p. 160).

Shaughnessy (1977, p. 94) defines 'political uses of food aid' by the United
States as 'the provision of food assistance resources in situations where the
primary rationale for assistance is the furtherance of U.S. self-interest to attain
foreign policy, strategic, or economic objectives.' (Shaughnessy might have
inserted 'or denial' after the word 'provision'.) So US food aid can be – and is –
deliberately used to achieve specific foreign policy objectives. A notorious case
in point is the Bangladesh famine of 1974, which is now discussed from the
perspective of the United States' contribution to its causation.

12.4 Case study: the 1974 Bangladesh famine

At the time of writing, the 1974 famine in Bangladesh remains the last 'crisis of
mass starvation' in south Asia. As with all famines, a complex chain of causality
explains this famine better than a single factor. The tragedy was precipitated by
flooding (which destroyed about 12 per cent of the national rice harvest),
fuelled by speculation and hoarding by grain merchants, and sealed by US
foreign policy towards Bangladesh (which delayed vital food aid, fatally
undermining the government's relief effort). The significance of the international dimension is summarized in the title of a paper by Crow (1986), 'US
policies in Bangladesh: the making and the breaking of famine?', where 'the
making' refers to the events of 1974, while 'the breaking' applies to 1984, when
famine was successfully *averted* because of effective intervention.

By 1974, after two decades of a growing 'food gap', illustrated by a rising
absolute and relative share of food imports in total consumption, together with
a growing foreign exchange crisis, Bangladesh was in a highly vulnerable
position. The war of independence had displaced millions of people, and badly
disrupted agricultural production, contributing to six poor harvests in
succession between 1971 and 1973. When floods disrupted rice production in
1974, the worst affected people were not just farmers, but agricultural and

other labourers: 'households dependent on wage labour for their livelihood were "squeezed" between, on the one hand, rising food prices and, on the other, falling wages and falling employment' (Crow, 1986, p. 10).

Prices rose excessively, as was seen in Chapter 7.3, because the minor production shortfall was magnified by merchants hoarding grain and driving prices up to a level which was prohibitive for the poor. The government, short of foreign exchange at a time when world wheat prices were extremely high, was unable to intervene effectively by importing grain. Instead of making good the shortfall through its public distribution channels (which might also have kept private market prices under control), the government selectively *cut back* on these programmes, favouring those groups who had the greatest political influence – and the lowest economic or nutritional need:

> The Statutory Rationing and Priority Group ration (to major urban centres, industrial workers, police, army, state employees) were not curtailed. Instead, the government cut back those food distributions targeted at poor rural populations, Modified Rationing and relief. (Crow, 1986, p. 21)

Repeated requests by the Bangladesh government in 1973 and 1974 for additional US PL 480 food aid were ignored or refused. The United States had apparently decided to manipulate the crisis to achieve political goals of its own. It even withheld its *normal* allocation of food aid – US food aid to Bangladesh in 1973/4 (the famine year) was just 17 per cent of the total for the previous year, and 10 per cent of that delivered in 1974/5. Wallerstein (1980, p. 162) describes this tactic disparagingly as 'the explicit manipulation of food aid by the United States as strategic leverage for political and economic objectives (i.e., food power)'.

Before lifting its aid embargo, the US government insisted that Bangladesh drop charges against '195 Pakistanis who were responsible for the genocide of 1971 in Bangladesh' (Sobhan, 1979, p. 1977). More significantly, though, the United States also objected to sales of jute sacks by Bangladesh to Cuba, on the grounds that this violated 'the terms of the PL 480 legislation which prohibited the allocation of US food aid to any nation trading with Cuba or North Vietnam' (Wallerstein, 1980, p. 161). Dr Nurul Islam, Chairman of the Bangladesh Planning Commission, 'retorted by expressing surprise and shock that the United States would actually insist that a destitute Bangladesh should restrict its exports' (McHenry and Bird, 1977, p. 82).

None the less, by now desperate for food aid, the Bangladesh government agreed to make the necessary concessions. Significant volumes of wheat were, eventually, sent – more than 18 months after the first request. By this time the famine was almost over. Hundreds of thousands of people had died:

> The crucial delay between the surrender of the Bangladesh government to US pressure and the actual signature of the agreement happened while floods were ravaging Bangladesh. Rice prices reached a peak of Tk 263 per maund in October and famine victims were dying in the streets of Dacca. . . . This grim drama was

being transacted in the capital city in the full view of the US embassy as to the nature and gravity of the crisis. (Sobhan, 1979, p. 1979)

Of course, the same might be said of the merchants who hoarded private stocks. As usual, the famine victims were those who had the least control over food, while the beneficiaries were those who manipulated their 'food power' for maximum economic and political profit.

The whole episode has deeply disturbing implications. People had been allowed to die unnecessarily: adequate supplies of food were available as soon as the politicians agreed to release it. Sobhan's (1979, p. 1979) conclusion is scathing:

The US had served a cruel reminder to the South that there could be no collective southern position as long as food deficit countries like Bangladesh remained completely vulnerable to US pressures. It further reminded these dependent countries that their pretensions to national sovereignty lasted as long as it took for the next bad harvest or natural disaster to make its appearance.

12.5   Conclusion

The links from international economic conditions to specific Third World famines are indirect and often difficult to pinpoint. But at the general level there clearly is some connection. If it is true, as Friedmann (1990, p. 15) says of US grain surpluses (at least prior to 1972–3), that they reflect 'a unique combination of farmer strength in national policy and national strength in the world economy', then the corollary must equally be true: that Third World food deficits and rural famine vulnerability reflect farmer weakness in national policy and national weakness in the world economy. Not that there is a direct causal route from US surpluses to African famines, but they are at least a conditioning factor.

The environment of international relationships in which famine-prone countries operate is exceedingly complex. Multiple interests compete for profit, for power, for patronage and for assistance. The poorest countries are generally in the weakest position to secure what they need for their poorest citizens. It is also a fact that the ruling elites in the poorest countries, as elsewhere, do not always have, as a primary concern, the needs of their poorest citizens.

Unravelling these complicated intersections and conflicts of interest is very difficult, and attempts to pin the blame for famines on one group or another are usually simplistic and unfair. But some general conclusions can be drawn from this brief discussion. The first is that altruism is rarely a dominant characteristic of international relationships – either commercial or political. Mutual self-interest is likely to continue to be the main basis for international agreements, including those related to the prevention of famine.

Second, extending this thought, it is equally naive to expect the grains trade to have a 'heart'. Agents in any market operate for only one reason: to make profits. Having said this, it is arguable that private individuals and organizations forced Western governments to respond to Africa's 'food crisis' in 1984. However, this is not an intrinsic quality of the market place; it should not be expected and the market should not be criticized for lacking moral integrity. This is no part of its operation.

Third, the moral position of governments is more debatable. In so far as some assume a stance of moral responsibility, they can be held morally accountable for their actions. In so far as they represent an electorate, they can be asked to account by that electorate. If the market cannot be expected to move food from regions of plenty to feed the starving, and individual charity is inadequate for the task on hand, and if public arbitrage is imperfect, then to whom can the starving look with certainty for relief?

Finally, the relief of famine in the face of global plenty is not an economic problem, but a political and moral one. (Of course, to the extent that famine is a product of poverty, the *abolition* of famine clearly is an economic matter. Here, however, the focus is on the *relief* of famine by, *inter alia*, food aid.) Unfortunately, recent events demonstrate all too clearly that even democratically elected governments are reluctant to acknowledge responsibility, moral or otherwise, for victims of famine in their own or other countries. This is where the moral and practical dilemma lies. If governments are not responsible for famine alleviation, who is?

Notes

1. Jacques Chonchol, former Chilean Minister of Agriculture, quoted in Morgan (1979, p. 226).
2. Derek Bishton, 'Editorial' in *Ten.8*, quoted in *The Guardian*, 30 August 1985.

PART 4

Conclusion

13

A summary of theories

> Famine ends famine.
> Ben Jonson (*Explorata*)

This book has reviewed a number of competing and complementary explanations of famine. This concluding chapter briefly restates the main lines within each debate, describing their essential features and major limitations without, it is hoped, losing too much of their complexity and subtlety.

13.1 Defining famine

Dictionary definitions of famine derive from the Western perception of famines as 'crises of mass starvation'. This has three elements: (1) food shortage, (2) severe hunger, and (3) excess mortality. These (conventional) definitions contain an implicit theory – a theory that is wrong. Famines have occurred: (1) with no food shortage (Bangladesh, 1974), (2) where excess mortality was caused by disease, not starvation (Darfur, 1984), and (3) with perhaps no excess mortality at all (Sahel, 1972–4). One of the best 'outsider' definitions is Walker's (1989):

> famine is a socio-economic process which causes the accelerated destitution of the most vulnerable, marginal and least powerful groups in a community, to a point where they can no longer, as a group, maintain a sustainable livelihood.

Famine victims in Africa and Asia identify various intensities of food crisis, from hunger through destitution to death. Death is not essential to the definition. Thus in Sudan, people talk about 'famine that kills' as only one kind of famine. They see famine as: (1) a problem of destitution, not just starvation, and (2) a continuation of normal processes, not a unique event.

13.2 Theories: background

Droughts, floods, wars, grain hoarding – these and other disruptions to food supplies 'trigger' subsistence crises by threatening a population's access to food. They are the immediate causes of food crises, which the Western media and public see as the main causes of famine. But these precipitating factors or 'triggers' lead to famine only where particular groups of people are vulnerable to famine. Vulnerability is more complex, and usually implies processes rather than events. Underlying processes 'set people up' for natural disasters or economic crises. They cause vulnerability, which is the real problem in the eradication of famine.

Supply-side theories of famine (e.g. 'FAD') typically concentrate on precipitating factors. Demand-side theories (e.g. exchange entitlement collapse) are rather better at explaining processes of impoverishment and vulnerability.

13.3 FAD theories

Explanations of famine based on food supply shortages have been labelled by Sen 'Food Availability Decline' or 'FAD' theories. Two of the most popular 'supply-side' theories – 'drought causes famine' (climate) and 'population growth causes famine' (demography) – are frequently applied to contemporary African famines.

13.3.1 Climate

Drought or flood causes food shortages and can lead to famine in rainfed agricultural areas of Africa and south Asia. Reduced production of food is only one of several problems; secondary effects include reduced rural employment (reduced income for buying food); and higher food prices (reduced purchasing power).

While these are real and serious consequences of climatically induced food shortages, the 'theory' does not stand up under closer scrutiny. Four criticisms reveal its limitations. First, drought, flood or crop blight disrupts food production, not distribution. So FAD assumes a totally closed economy, with no access to sources of food outside the affected area. A robust theory must explain why food does not come in from elsewhere, in the form of either trade or aid. Second, FAD implies that everyone is equally affected, but the rich rarely die during famines. FAD cannot explain why some groups of people have better access to food than others. Third, the idea that a calamitous drought leads directly to famine is too simplistic. People in drought-prone areas have developed a range of insurance mechanisms and coping strategies which help them to survive. Drought develops into famine, in sub-Saharan Africa, if it is especially severe and protracted, if it operates in tandem with other threats to food security (notably war), if coping strategies have been undermined or exhausted, and if interventions designed to prevent famine fail to materialize, are inappropriate, or arrive to late. Finally, since drought does not always lead to famine (e.g. in the United States), the theory fails to distinguish between situations where people are vulnerable to drought and those where they are not. Drought causes crop failure, but *vulnerability* to drought causes famine.

13.3.2 Population

The basic Malthusian argument is that population increases indefinitely, but land is strictly limited. Therefore, the demand for food will eventually outstrip any potential food production. Starvation acts as a 'natural check' on population growth: famine restores the balance between food demand and food supply.

In reality, though, famine is not a 'Malthusian leveller'. Only a tiny percentage of a population affected by food shortage dies as a consequence. Those most likely to survive are young and middle-aged adults, and almost all famines are followed by a post-famine 'baby boom', which rapidly compensates for the excess deaths. Second, Malthus failed to foresee either the *agricultural* revolution (which raised food production); or the *transport* revolution (which improved food distribution). Western Europe is several times more densely populated than Africa, and has only a fraction of its population working in agriculture, yet it produces enormous agricultural surpluses and is not famine-prone (except during war). Nor is Japan famine-prone, despite having to import the bulk of its food needs, being too densely populated to achieve food production self-sufficency. Finally, classical Malthusian theory is challenged by the 'Boserup effect' – population concentration encourages investment in rural infrastructure which reduces vulnerability (roads, irrigation), because of economies of scale, and (less clearly) may stimulate technological innovation.

Although Malthus's original propositions have been convincingly refuted by history, several contemporary 'neo-Malthusian' variants insist that famine can still be explained in terms of 'too many people, too little food'. The concept of 'carrying capacity' relates population numbers in rural areas to the economic viability of their environment (e.g. a 'people:arable land' ratio), and suggests that where the environment is fragile or degraded, famine follows from the fact that the 'regional carrying capacity' has been fatally exceeded. Related to this is the economic argument that high population *growth rates* perpetuate poverty (at the household level) and famine vulnerability (at the regional level) by excessive partition of land among heirs, and high dependency ratios (consumers/producers). Finally, there is the argument that 'death control' is being practised in societies where 'birth control' is needed even more urgently – modern medicine keeps more people alive, but falls in birthrates have lagged behind. The single prescription recommended by neo-Malthusians is birth control, by coercion if necessary – China's 'one child family' policy, for example.

An obvious retort to the 'birth control brigade' is that they have failed to realize the importance of children, especially in poor families, as an insurance against risk. High fertility is a response to poverty and famine vulnerability, not a cause. In the West, a demographic transition to low fertility regimes occurred *after* living standards rose. In parts of Africa, though, there is a real 'population problem' caused by the adverse combination of low population density (no beneficial Boserup effect) together with high growth rates (which perpetuates poverty). This combination, where it exists, clearly has some power in explaining persistent vulnerability to famine.

13.4 Economic theories

Two theories of famine focus on the operation of markets during food crises – Sen's 'entitlement approach' and two variations on 'market failure': speculation and hoarding, and imperfect or fragmented markets.

13.4.1 Entitlements

Although several theorists had recognized the relationship between poverty and vulnerability to famine before the publication of *Poverty and Famines* in 1981, Sen's book decisively shifted the focus of famine analysis from supply-side to demand-side explanations. Sen demonstrated that famine can and does occur with plenty of food in the region or country, because people have differential access to this food, and its distribution can shift unfavourably even if aggregate food availability is adequate and constant or rising. Individual or household vulnerability to starvation depends on their unique 'entitlement to food'. This concept has four components, in Sen's original formulation:

1. Trade-based entitlement ('exchange entitlement').
2. Production-based entitlement ('direct entitlement').
3. Own-labour entitlement (from 'selling' labour power).
4. Inheritance and transfer entitlement (gifts, bequests).

Famine occurs when entitlements collapse into the 'starvation set' – say, when farmers' millet crops are destroyed by locusts or the price of a cash crop (coffee, cotton) falls, landless labourers loses their employment, or traders hoard grain until prices rise too high for market-dependent consumers. In addition, other groups which depend on the incomes of those affected by famine will suffer 'derived destitution' – Sen's famous example is that of rural barbers in Ethiopia during the 1970s famine. The strength of this approach is that it identifies which groups of people will be affected by various threats to availability of or access to food. Entitlements recognizes that famine strikes particular identifiable groups; it does not afflict populations equally nor at random. This is an important contrast to FAD approaches, which focus on the aggregate people:food ratio. For instance, landless labourers in Bangladesh starved in 1974 when rice prices rose – but production and food availability were higher than in 1972 or 1973.

Although entitlements arguably represents the most important conceptual advance in famine theorizing since Malthus, it has been subject to criticisms, the most constructive of which propose ways in which it should be extended. One such area is the intra-household distribution of food, which clearly is not determined on any recognizable 'entitlement' basis. Children have no legal claim over food, so perhaps the notion of 'dependency entitlement' should be introduced (difficult to quantify though this would be). Other 'non-income' sources of food include 'relief entitlement' or 'latent entitlement' – sources that are only mobilized when conventional sources fail.

Another criticism of entitlements is that it concentrates on *proximate* causes of famine – market prices, incomes – rather than addressing underlying causes. How are entitlements generated? Why are some people vulnerable to entitlements collapse and not others? A possible solution to this complaint is to develop a dynamic version of the theory which can account for the historical determination and evolution of different types of entitlements over time. If entitlements was linked up with (say) peasant mobility studies, this would address the point that famine vulnerability is related to the *risk* of entitlements collapse, not just the *level* of household or personal entitlements to food.

Recently, a more fundamental critique of the entitlement approach has developed around the fact that it focuses so heavily on food deprivation, and presumes that famine mortality is induced by starvation. This 'food first' bias leads Sen to write about people being 'plunged into starvation' when their entitlements collapse. Starvation is a long and painful process, not a sudden event like, say, a heart attack. Also, famine coping strategies include 'choosing hunger' in order to avoid destitution – rationing consumption rather than liquidating assets to maintain food intakes, as Sen implies. Finally, in many contemporary African famines, death may be better explained by health crises (in relief camps or among refugee populations) than by starvation.

13.4.2 Market failure

'Pull failure' must be clearly distinguished from 'response failure', when the contribution of markets to famine is discussed. The first is caused by poverty, and can therefore be explained in terms of a lack or collapse of 'exchange entitlements' to food. 'Response failure' occurs when markets fail to meet an effective demand, and this is 'market failure' in the strict sense. A dependence on markets for food is dangerous if markets are unreliable, so that 'response failure' during food crises is possible. Markets can fail to function well either temporally or spatially.

Hoarding food, whether for precautionary or speculative reasons, can magnify food shortages and price rises. The 'temporal arbitrage' argument, that hoarding smooths out future shortages and dampens price rises, does not hold where a minority of traders can withhold food to drive prices up excessively, or where exaggerated fears of future shortages result in panic hoarding beyond what is justified in reality. This was the case in Bangladesh 1974, when pessimistic forecasts translated a minor shortfall in rice production into a major shortfall in marketed supplies.

If most south Asian famines can be analyzed in terms of a 'failure of temporal arbitrage', African famines fall more obviously into the 'failure of spatial arbitrage' category. Markets fail in rural Africa when self-provisioning food *producers* suddenly become market-dependent *consumers*, in bad years. (In south Asia, by contrast, a large landless class exists which is permanently market-dependent.) The fact that African traders fail to meet rural needs for food is not entirely explained by lack of entitlements, as some readings of Sen might suggest, but by the distortion of normal market activities which this dramatic transformation entails.

Village markets in famine-prone Africa are small and isolated. During famines, the demand for food rises, but this is a temporary, localized phenomenon. Recognizing this limited scope for profiteering (even at the high prices prevailing in village markets), traders simply continue supplying their usual customers in towns and cities. This explains the seemingly paradoxical 'price ripple hypothesis': that food prices rise in waves spreading outwards from a famine epicentre, as people migrate to better supplied markets when traders fail to bring food to the villages. Since prices do rise, this suggests that trade fails not because peasants are destitute, but because of various 'transactions costs' – high transport costs, the difficulty of reorienting trading routes, and the limited, temporary demand in villages as compared to the larger, permanent markets in cities.

13.5   Political economy explanations

While the 'FAD' and 'economic' explanations discussed above can be described as 'theories of famine', a number of less well specified hypotheses have been offered which fall loosely under the rubric of 'political economy of famine'. The first two – natural resource (mis)management and development processes – go neatly together, while the next three – government policy, war and international relations – are also closely related.

13.5.1 Natural resources

Large parts of sub-Saharan Africa are facing ecological crisis. The threat to farmers in Sahelian areas, as desertification spreads and rainfall (apparently) becomes more unreliable, is obvious. Writers who relate these environmental problems to famine see different causal processes behind the same phenomenon. Three groups can be identified, each of which places a different emphasis on the respective roles of 'nature' and of 'man'.

One group believes that Sahelian communities are victims of nature – a changing climate results in 'natural degradation' of the soil, so that agricultural production is undermined and food shortages follow. A second group links environmental crisis to 'carrying capacity' – effectively blaming famine victims for 'overpopulation' and 'overgrazing', which put pressure on fragile resources: soil erosion accelerates as fallow periods are reduced, farms are partitioned until unviable, even the climate is affected (e.g. rainfall decreases because of loss of tree cover). Ultimately, in this Malthusian scenario, the land simply cannot support the numbers of people and animals it is supposed to feed.

The third group locates African famine victims between two contradictory forces – their fragile resource base, which should be protected at all costs, and the profit motive, which aims at the extraction of wealth for maximum, short-term gain. The commercialization of African agriculture, encouraged by such factors as the imposition of taxes and the promotion of cash cropping during colonialism, led to sometimes fatal over-exploitation of natural resources for individual profit – resources which once used to be conserved for the community's benefit.

13.5.2 Development

Colonial and post-colonial development processes and programmes have clearly failed to eliminate vulnerability to famine in much of sub-Saharan Africa, even if Asia seems to have famine finally under control. Much of the debate about the effects of socioeconomic change on vulnerability is speculative, since it is impossible to say what would have happened under alternative conditions. Some writers believe that capitalist-style development is the best way to conquer famine, and that it is merely taking longer in Africa than elsewhere, because it is less advanced, because of general poverty, or because of lack of political will by local governments. Other commentators argue that Africa has been 'set up' for continuing famines by inappropriate development strategies, such as the pursuit of economic growth through industrialization and the neglect of agriculture (as discussed below). These writers talk about 'marginalization' – the fact that development creates winners and losers by generating wealth for some and impoverishment for others. While the winners accumulate land, assets and power, the losers (such as peasants and pastoralists) are pushed onto less productive land. During crises, they will be forced to transfer their meagre resources (labour power, land rights, assets) to the wealthy on unfavourable terms, so that polarization increases. If this view is accurate, then inequality is reinforced, not mitigated, by 'normal' development processes.

A complementary argument is that the commoditization of agrarian communities results in the breakdown of their internal support systems or 'moral economy'. Capitalist development entails a disintegation of reciprocity and co-operative insurance networks, and an integration into the market system. Where people used to help each other during subsistence crises, it is argued, now they try to profit from the distress of their neighbours. In Western societies, state-sponsored social security compensates for our limited sense of personal responsibility for the poor and hungry, but this 'safety net' has yet to be introduced into most famine-prone countries. (The guaranteed employment schemes in parts of south Asia offer a good model of an appropriate social security programme for the rural poor.) Sen has coined the term 'PEST' – 'pure exchange system transition' – to describe this period of heightened vulnerability which occurs after the disruption of the 'moral economy' and before the introduction of effective social security programmes.

13.5.3   Government policy

Governments contribute to famine directly, by inappropriate or deliberately harmful policies towards vulnerable groups, and indirectly, by failing to intervene to prevent famines.

'Inappropriate policies' include urban bias (neglecting or squeezing agriculture to support industry, bureaucrats and the military); setting up inefficient or corrupt marketing parastatals; fixing low producer prices; and prohibiting free trade of food.

Institutional 'response failure' can be caused by (1) lack of information (no famine early warning system); (2) lack of resources (no foreign exchange to import food, no trucks to distribute food); (3) logistical constraints (poor roads, inaccessible villages); and (4) callous disregard (embarrassment, political hostility towards famine communities). A good example of the first problem is the Chinese 'Great Leap Forward' famine of 1958–61, during which the central authorities apparently knew very little about the extent of the food crisis because quotas were still being delivered and local Party officials had an incentive to report favourable production results even when harvests were very poor. Lack of resources and logistical constraints are common problems facing institutional attempts to deliver food aid to famine-stricken communities in rural Africa, even today. Finally, an example of political callousness and hostility is the Ukrainian famine of 1933–4, which has been interpreted as a deliberate exercise in political repression through the weapon of mass starvation.

13.5.4 War

Conflict, military rule, militarization, political refugees displaced by war – this nexus of problems combines to create famine vulnerability throughout sub-Saharan Africa today. Military rulers feel little sense of accountability to the general public, particularly those who are doubly disenfranchised by the absence of democracy and by poverty. Rather they are concerned with retaining power, if necessary by acquiring high-tech armaments and fighting extremely destructive wars against internal opposition groups. In Ethiopia in the famine year of 1984, 46 per cent of government spending was on 'defence'.

Conflict in contemporary Africa involves direct disruption of food production systems to an unusual extent. This is because most wars are waged in rural areas, where there are few obvious military targets (no aircraft hangars or munitions factories). Government or rebel forces appropriate men, food and animals; burn crops and destroy granaries; plant mines in fields which disable farmers; and create food blockades by disrupting trade and preventing food aid from getting through. Starvation is either deliberately inflicted as a weapon of war, or follows when the population is left with few reserves and no alternative sources of food.

When people suffering from war and/or drought flee their land, often to neighbouring countries, they might face hostility as they compete for scarce resources with the host population. Even if relief camps are set up for them, they are vulnerable to epidemics (diseases being the main killers during famines, *not* starvation) because of the concentration of displaced people in often unsanitary conditions.

The list of countries in sub-Saharan Africa afflicted by the 'twin horsemen of the apocalypse' – war and famine – during the past ten years alone makes depressing reading: Ethiopia, Sudan, Somalia, Mozambique, Angola, Chad, Liberia. ... Regrettably, this list of war-induced famines seems destined to grow even longer, given the proliferation of armaments and the absence of democratic accountability in a large number of African states.

13.5.5 International relations

The influence of international institutions (grain multinationals, food aid donors, development agencies) on famine is less direct than that of 'trigger events' such as drought and market failure.

Where production self-sufficiency is unrealistic, dependence on the world market is unavoidable. But the ability of large grain companies to control food prices and supplies is obviously a matter of concern. The profit motive and food security objectives are often in conflict with each other, notably where a poor country lacks foreign exchange to make good a production deficit.

The humanitarian response of the international community to famine has improved dramatically since World War II. None the less, famine relief programmes have invariably been criticized for arriving too late (being activated only once the terminal stages of crisis are visible), being inappropriate (imported food aid rather than locally purchased food or cash relief, emphasizing food more than medical supplies), and too narrowly focused (treating famine as a crisis independent of longer-term processes). Non-emergency food aid is also intricately related to international political relationships and alliances, as Bangladesh in 1974, and Marxist Ethiopia ten years later, discovered to their cost.

13.6 Policy implications

The stereotypical image of African famines in the West remains that of malnourished children receiving food aid in relief camps. Recent theoretical and empirical developments in famine analysis suggest, however, that a number of important changes in famine relief policies need at least to be considered.

If famine is a process, one possible consequence of which is death, rather than an event which is defined by 'excess mortality', then relief should come much earlier in the process than the 'terminal indicators of distress' (mass migration, surges in child malnutrition statistics) which usually trigger external interventions.

Since famine is characterized by its victims as a crisis of accelerated impoverishment and destitution, as well as one of hunger and starvation, donor interventions should attempt to preserve assets and incomes, rather than focusing simply on nutrition status and feeding schemes. This will also protect famine victims against future crises, since their economic viability will be maintained and their coping strategies will not have been exhausted in responding to the immediate problem.

Given that a food shortage is usually localized rather than nationwide, more efforts should be made to procure food from surplus regions in the area (e.g. through 'triangular food aid' arrangements) instead of automatically shipping in tons of wheat and other produce from Western Europe or North America. This will stimulate local production and trade (avoiding disincentive and dependency effects), as well as offering aid recipients more appropriate types of food than Western cereals and dairy products.

When famine follows a collapse of entitlement to food, rather than a collapse in food availability, interventions should aim at restoring entitlements, rather than adding to already adequate food supplies. This could take the form of cash-for-work (as opposed to food-for-work), or cash aid (as opposed to food aid). A prerequisite is that local markets are functioning well and are responsive to signals of effective demand.

Finally, if famine mortality is caused more by a 'changed disease environment' than by starvation and hunger-related diseases, then the providers of emergency food aid should pay much greater attention to 'health aid', in the form of immunization, water purifiers, sanitary conditions in refugee camps, and so on.

13.7   Conclusion: determinants of vulnerability

Famine today appears to be concentrated in a single sub-continent. While there are dozens of reasons for the persistence of rural vulnerability in sub-Saharan Africa, five bear reiteration as this review of explanations for famine comes to an end:

1. *Risk* of fluctuations in income or sources of food – the (un)reliability of harvests in semi-arid, drought-prone areas, for example, is more significant than average *levels* of food production or cash crop income. As environmental stress deepens in Sahelian areas and elsewhere, crop production is likely to become increasingly insecure.
2. *Dependence* on a single source of income or food (either the market or self-provisioning). The solution is diversification – cash-cropping *plus* food crops; or, even better, off-farm income or remittances, which provide a major protection against crop failure, since they are not closely correlated with climatic variability.
3. Absence of *latent* entitlements – the 'moral economy', social security, employment guarantee schemes – each of which provides a 'safety net' against entitlement collapse. Particularly vulnerable are societies where 'traditional' systems of mutual support have been disrupted and have not (yet) been replaced with institutionalized relief or welfare systems.
4. *Disenfranchisement* – people can be excluded from political processes and economic growth in many ways, not only by being denied a vote. A powerful, undemocratic government may lack the political will to assist the powerless; repress the media so that the poor have no voice; and discourage development projects or even food aid during famines.
5. *War* – in rural Africa, conflict can undermine all aspects of a food system simultaneously – production, storage and distribution (trade and aid). As the institutional capacity to deal with drought and food crises continues to improve, war will probably remain as the last major proximate cause of famine in Africa.

At the time of writing, millions of rural Africans appear to be as vulnerable to famine as ever – perhaps more than ever. Local institutions and Western donor agencies may or may not have 'learnt the lessons' of the 1970s and 1980s crises, but all they can do is improve the timing and effectiveness of their interventions; they cannot prevent the droughts, stop the wars, or even 'develop' Africa out of its poverty and vulnerability. Famine recurs, again and again, long after the capacity to eradicate it has been achieved. It seems that Jonson was wrong. Famine does not end famine. Famine begets famine.

Bibliography

Aall, C. 'Relief, nutrition and health problems in the Nigerian/Biafran war'. *Journal of Tropical Pediatrics*, **16**(2), June 1970.

Ahmad, E., Drèze, J., Hills, J. and Sen, A. (eds.) *Social Security in Developing Countries*. Clarendon Press, Oxford, 1991.

Aird, J. 'Population studies and population policy in China.' *Population and Development Review*, June 1982.

Alamgir, M. *Famine in South Asia*. Oelgeschlager, Gunn and Hain, Cambridge, Mass., 1980.

Alamgir, M. 'An approach towards a theory of famine'. In J. Robson (ed.) *Famine: Its Causes, Effects and Management*. Gordon and Breach, New York, 1981.

Allen, G. 'Famines: the Bowbrick–Sen dispute and some related issues'. *Food Policy*, August 1986.

Appadurai, A. 'How moral is South Asia's economy? – A review article'. *Journal of South Asian Studies*, May 1984.

Ashton, B., Hill, K., Piazza, A. and Zeitz, R. 'Famine in China, 1958–61'. *Population and Development Review*, December 1984.

Aykroyd, W. *The Conquest of Famine*. Chatto and Windus, London, 1974.

Aziz, S. (ed.) *Hunger, Politics and Markets*. New York University Press, New York, 1975.

Bernstein, H., Crow, B., Mackintosh, M. and Martin, C. (eds.) *The Food Question: Profits Versus People?* Earthscan, London, 1990.

Berry, L., Campbell, D. and Emker, I. 'Trends in man–land interaction in the West African Sahel'. In O. Dalby *et al.* (eds.), *Drought in Africa*. International African Institute, London, 1977.

Blaikie, P. *The Political Economy of Soil Erosion in Developing Countries*. Longman, London, 1985.

Bongaarts, J. and Cain, M. 'Demographic responses to famine'. In K. Cahill (ed.), *Famine*. Orbis Books, New York, 1982.

Borlaug, N. 'Food and fertilizer are needed now'. In S. Aziz (ed.), *Hunger, Politics and Markets*. New York University Press, New York, 1975.

Borton, J. and Clay, E. 'The African food crisis of 1986'. *Disasters*, December 1986.

Boserup, E. 'The impact of scarcity and plenty on development.' In R. Rotberg and T. Rabb (eds.), *Hunger and History*. Cambridge University Press, Cambridge, 1983.

Bowbrick, P. 'The causes of famine: a refutation of Professor Sen's theory'. *Food Policy*, May 1986.

Bowbrick, P. 'Rejoinder: an untenable hypothesis on the causes of famine'. *Food Policy*, February 1987.

Brett-Crowther, M. 'Malnourished database'. *Food Policy*, February 1983.

Brown, L. 'The complexity of the food problem'. In S. Aziz (ed.), *Hunger, Politics and Markets*. New York University Press, New York, 1975.

Brown, P. and Shue, H. (eds.). *Food Policy: The Responsibility of the United States in the Life and Death Choices*. The Free Press, New York, 1977.

Bryceson, D. 'Colonial famine responses: The Bagamoyo district of Tanganyika, 1920–61.' *Food Policy*, May 1981.

Buchanan-Smith, M. *Drought and the Rural Economy in Botswana: An Evaluation of the Drought Programme, 1982–1990: Drought Income Transfers and the Rural Household Economy*. Food Studies Group, Oxford, 1990.

Bush, R. 'Briefings: "Drought and Famines"'. *Review of African Political Economy*, **33**, August 1985a.

Bush, R. 'Unnatural disaster – the politics of famine'. *Marxism Today*, December 1985b.

Cahill, K. (ed.). *Famine*. Orbis Books, New York, 1982.

Campbell, D. and Trechter, D. 'Strategies for coping with food consumption shortage in the Mandara Mountains region of north Cameroon'. *Social Science and Medicine*, **16**, 1982.

Carim, E. 'Don't use aid as a weapon. Pawns in the game'. *New Internationalist*, **151**, September 1985.

Chambers, R., Longhurst, R. and Pacey, A. (eds.) *Seasonal Dimensions to Rural Poverty*. Frances Pinter, London, 1981.

Christensen, C. 'World hunger: a structural approach'. In R. Hopkins and D. Puchala (eds.) *The Global Political Economy of Food*. University of Wisconsin Press, Madison, 1978.

Christensen, G. *Determinants of Private Investment in Rural Burkina Faso*. PhD Thesis, Cornell University, 1989.

Clay, E. 'The 1974 and 1984 floods in Bangladesh: From famine to food crisis management'. *Food Policy*, August 1985.

Clay, E. 'Releasing the hidden hand'. *Food Policy*, May 1986.

Clay, J. and Holcomb, B. *Politics and the Ethiopian Famine 1984–85*. Cultural Survival, Cambridge, Mass., December 1985.

Cliffe, L. and Lawrence, P. 'Editorial: agrarian capitalism and hunger'. *Review of African Political Economy*, **15/16**, May–December 1979.

Coale, A. 'Population trends, population policy, and population studies in China'. *Population and Development Review*, March 1981.

Cohen, J. and Lewis, D. 'Role of government in combatting food shortages: Lessons from Kenya 1984–85'. In M. Glantz (ed.) *Drought and Hunger in Africa: Denying Famine a Future*. Cambridge University Press, Cambridge, 1987.

Corbett, J. 'Famine and household coping strategies'. *World Development*, **16**(9), 1988.

Cox, G. 'The ecology of famine: an overview'. In J. Robson (ed.) *Famine: Its Causes, Effects and Management*. Gordon and Breach, New York, 1981.

Crow, B. 'US policies in Bangladesh: the making and the breaking of famine?' *Development Policy and Practice: Working Paper No. 4*. The Open University, Milton Keynes, 1986.

Currey, B. 'The famine syndrome: its definition for relief and rehabilitation in Bangladesh'. In J. Robson (ed.) *Famine: Its Causes, Effects and Management*. Gordon and Breach, New York, 1981.

Currey, B. and Hugo, G. (eds.) *Famine as a Geographical Phenomenon*. Reidel, Dordrecht, 1984.

Cutler, P. 'Famine forecasting: prices and peasant behaviour in northern Ethiopia'.

Disasters, **8**(1), 1984.

Cutler, P. 'Detecting food emergencies: lessons from the 1979 Bangladesh crisis'. *Food Policy*, August 1985a.

Cutler, P. 'The use of economic and social indicators for famine prediction and response: summary of findings of ESCOR research scheme R3779'. Overseas Development Association, London, 1985b.

da Corta, L. *The Persistence of Famine: A Dynamic Approach Combining Entitlement and Peasant Mobility Theories in the Analysis of Vulnerability to Famine*. Preliminary draft of a DPhil thesis, St Antony's College, University of Oxford, 1986.

da Corta, L. and Devereux, S. 'True generosity or false charity? A note on the ideological foundations of famine relief policies'. *Development Studies Working Paper No. 40*, Centro Studi Luca d'Agliano, Turin and Queen Elizabeth House, Oxford, 1991.

Dahl, G. and Hjort, A. *Pastoral Change and the Role of Drought*. Swedish Agency for Research Cooperation with Developing Countries, Stockholm, 1979.

Dalby, D., Church, R. and Bezzaz, F. (eds.) *Drought in Africa 2*. International African Institute, London, 1977.

Dando, W. *The Geography of Famine*. Edward Arnold, London, 1980.

Dando, W. 'Man-made famines: some geographical insights from an exploratory study of a millennium of Russian famines'. In J. Robson (ed.) *Famine: Its Causes, Effects and Management*. Gordon and Breach, New York, 1981.

de Janvry, A. *The Agrarian Question and Reformism in Latin America*. Johns Hopkins University Press, Baltimore, Md., 1981.

de Waal, A. 'The perception of poverty and famines'. *International Journal of Moral and Social Studies*, **2**(3), Autumn 1987.

de Waal, A. 'Refugees and the creation of famine: the case of Dar Masalit, Sudan'. *Journal of Refugee Studies*, **1**(2), Oxford, 1988.

de Waal, A. *Famine that Kills: Darfur, Sudan, 1984–1985*. Clarendon Press, Oxford, 1989.

de Waal, A. 'A re-assessment of entitlement theory in the light of the recent famines in Africa'. *Development and Change*, **21**, 1990.

Dercon, S. *Household Strategies to Cope with Income Fluctuations: An Analysis of the Effects of Producer Price and Asset Market Interventions on Cotton Producers in Tanzania*. DPhil Thesis, University of Oxford, 1992.

Dernberger, R. (ed.) *China's Development Experience in Comparative Perspective*. Harvard University Press, Cambridge, Mass., 1980.

Desai, M. 'A general theory of poverty?' *Indian Economic Review*, July–December 1984.

Dessalegn Rahmato *Famine and Survival Strategies: A Case Study from Northern Ethiopia*. Food and Famine Monograph Series No. 1. Institute of Development Research, Addis Ababa University, 1987.

Dessalegn Rahmato 'Peasant survival strategies'. *Beyond the Famine: An Examination of the Issues Behind Famine in Ethiopia*. International Institute for Relief and Development, January 1988.

Devereux, S. 'Entitlements, availability and famine: a revisionist view of Wollo, 1972–74'. *Food Policy*, August 1988.

Devereux, S. *Household Responses to Food Insecurity in Northeastern Ghana*. DPhil Thesis, Balliol College, University of Oxford, 1992.

Downing, T. *Climate Impact Assessment in Central and Eastern Kenya: Notes on Methodology*. CENTED. Clark University, Worcester, Mass., July 1986.

Downing, T. 'Monitoring and responding to famine: lessons from the 1984–85 food crisis in Kenya'. *Disasters*, **14**(3), 1990.

Downing, T., Gitu, K. and Kamau, C. (eds.) *Coping with Drought in Kenya: Local and*

National Strategies. Lynne Rienner, Boulder, Col., 1989.

Drèze, J. *Famine Prevention in India*. Development Economics Paper No. 3. London School of Economics, January 1988.

Drèze, J. and Sen, A. *Hunger and Public Action*. Clarendon Press, Oxford, 1989.

D'Souza, F. 'Famine: social security and an analysis of vulnerability'. In G. Harrison (ed.), *Famine*, 1988.

Dumont, R. and Cohen, N. *The Growth of Hunger*. Marion Boyars, London, 1980.

Dupaquier, J. and Grebenik, E. (eds.) *Malthus Past and Present*. Academic Press, London, 1983.

Ea, M. 'War and famine: the example of Kampuchea'. In B. Currey and G. Hugo (eds.) *Famine as a Geographical Phenomenon*. Reidel, Dordrecht, 1984.

Economist, The 'Genocide in the Ukraine', 11 October 1986.

El-Hinnawi, E. *Environmental Refugees*. United Nations Environment Programme, Nairobi, 1985.

Ellman, M. *Socialist Planning*. Cambridge University Press, Cambridge, 1979.

Etienne, G. *Food and Poverty: India's Half Won Battle*. Sage Publications, 1988.

Faruqee, R. and Gulhati, R. *Rapid Population Growth in Sub-Saharan Africa: Issues and Policies*. World Bank Staff Working Papers No. 559. World Bank, Washington DC, 1983.

Fenton, J. 'Ethiopia: victors and victims'. *New York Review*, 7 November 1985.

Ferris, B. and Toyne, P. *World Problems*, Hulton Ed. publications, Amersham, 1970.

Field, J. 'Beyond relief: a developmental perspective on famine'. Paper presented at the *14th International Congress of Nutrition*. Seoul, Korea, 20–25 August 1989.

Fitzpatrick, J. *Karamoja, Uganda: A Case Study*. Paper for WFP–ADB Seminar on Food Aid for Development in Sub Saharan Africa, Abidjan, 8–11 September 1986.

Foege, W. 'Famine, infection, epidemics'. In G. Blix, Y. Hofvander and B . Vahlquist. *Famine, Nutrition and Relief Operations in Times of Disaster*. Almquist & Wirsells, Uppsala, 1971.

Food and Agricultural Organization *Land, Food and People*. FAO, Rome, 1984.

Franke, R. and Chasin, B. *Seeds of Famine*. Allanheld and Osmun, Montclair, 1980.

Franzel, S., Colburn, F. and Degu, G. 'Grain marketing regulations: impact on peasant production in Ethiopia'. *Food Policy*, **14**(4), November 1989.

Friedmann, H. 'The origins of Third World food dependence'. In H. Bernstein *et al.* (eds.) *The Food Question*. Earthscan, London, 1990.

Garcia, R. and Escudero, J. *Drought and Man: The 1972 Case History. Volume 2: The Constant Catastrophe: Malnutrition, Famines and Drought*. Pergamon Press, Oxford, 1982.

Gartrell, B. 'Debates: "Searching for 'the roots of famine': the case of Karamoja"'. *Review of African Political Economy*, **33**, August 1985.

George, S. *How the Other Half Dies*. Penguin, Harmondsworth, 1976.

George, S. *A Fate Worse than Debt*. Penguin, Harmondsworth, 1988.

Ghatak, S. and Ingersent, K. *Agriculture and Economic Development*. Harvester Press, Brighton, 1984.

Gill, P. *A Year in the Death of Africa*. Paladin, London, 1986.

Glantz, M. (ed.). *Drought and Hunger in Africa: Denying Famine a Future*. Cambridge University Press, Cambridge, 1987.

Glantz, M. 'Drought, famine, and the seasons in sub-Saharan Africa'. In R. Huss-Ashmore and S. Katz (eds.) *Anthropological Perspectives on the African Famine*. Gordon and Breach, New York, 1987.

Grant, J. 'Famine today – hope for tomorrow'. *The Alan Shawn Feinstein World Hunger Program*. Working Paper No. 1. Brown University, Providence, February 1985.

Green, S. *The Politics of Famine*. 1976.

Griffin, K. *Land Concentration and Rural Poverty*. Macmillan, London, 1981.

Griffin, K. and Hay, R. 'Problems of agricultural development in socialist Ethiopia: an overview and a suggested survey'. *Journal of Peasant Studies* **13**(1), October 1985.

Grigg, D. *The World Food Problem*. Basil Blackwell, Oxford, 1985.

Grove, A. 'Desertification in the African environment'. In D. Dalby *et al.* (eds.) *Drought in Africa*. International African Institute, London, 1977.

Hadzewycz, R., Zarycky, G. and Kolomayets, M. (eds.) *The Great Famine in Ukraine: The Unknown Holocaust*. The Ukrainian National Association for the National Committee to Commemorate Genocide Victims in Ukraine 1932–33. Jersey City, New Jersey, 1983.

Hall, S. and Jacques, M. 'People aid: a new politics sweeps the land'. *Marxism Today*, July 1986.

Hallett, G. *The Economics of Agricultural Policy* (2nd edition). Basil Blackwell, Oxford, 1981.

Hancock, G. *Ethiopia: The Challenge of Hunger*. Gollancz, London, 1985.

Hansen, A. 'Coping with famine, drought, and war in sub-Saharan Africa'. *Studies in Third World Societies, No. 36: Natural Disasters and Cultural Responses*. College of William and Mary, Williamsburg, Virginia, June 1986.

Hardin, G. 'Lifeboat ethics: the case against helping the poor'. *Psychology Today* **8**, 1974.

Harrell-Bond, B. *Imposing Aid: Emergency Assistance to Refugees*. Oxford University Press, Oxford, 1986.

Harrison, G. (ed.) *Famine*. Oxford University Press, Oxford, 1988.

Harriss, B. *Marketing, Moneylending, Food and Famine*. Institute of Social Studies, The Hague, October 1981.

Harriss, B. *Markets and Rural Undernutrition*. Mimeo. Nutrition Policy Unit, London School of Hygiene and Tropical Medicine, June 1983.

Hartmann, B. *Reproductive Rights and Wrongs: The Global Politics of Population Control and Contraceptive Choice*. Harper & Row, New York/London, 1987.

Hartmann, B. and Boyce, J. *A Quiet Violence: View from a Bangladesh Village*. Zed Press, London, 1983.

Hartmann, B. and Standing, H. *Food, Saris and Sterilisation: Population Control in Bangladesh*. Bangladesh International Action Group, London, September 1985.

Hay, R. 'The political economy of famine'. *Nutrition and Health*, **4**(2), 1986.

Hay, R., Burke, S. and Dako, D. *A Socio-economic Assessment of Drought Relief in Botswana*. Report prepared for the Inter-Ministerial Drought Committee, Government of Botswana. UNICEF/UNDP/WHO, Gabarone, 1986.

Helldén, U. 'Land degradation and land productivity monitoring – needs for an integrated approach'. In A. Hjort (ed.) *Land Management and Survival*. Scandinavian Institute of African Studies, Uppsala, 1985.

Heyer, J. 'Poverty and food deprivation in Kenya's smallholder agricultural areas'. In J. Drèze and A. Sen (eds.) *The Political Economy of Hunger, Vol. III: Endemic Hunger*. Oxford University Press, Oxford, 1991.

Heyer, J., Roberts, P. and Williams, G. (eds.) *Rural Development in Tropical Africa*. Macmillan, London, 1981.

Hjort, A. (ed.). *Land Management and Survival*. Scandinavian Institute of African Studies, Uppsala, 1985.

Hjort af Ornäs, A. 'Pastoral and environmental security in East Africa'. *Disasters*, **14**(2), 1990.

Holm, J. and Morgan, R. 'Coping with drought in Botswana: an African success story'. *Journal of Modern African Studies*, **23**(3), 1985.

Hopkins, R. and Puchala, D. (eds.) *The Global Political Economy of Food*. University of Wisconsin Press, Madison, 1978.

Huss-Ashmore, R. and Katz, S. (eds.) *Anthropological Perspectives on the African Famine*. Gordon and Breach, New York, 1987.

ICIHI (Independent Commission on International Humanitarian Issues) *Famine: A Man-Made Disaster?* Pan Books, London, 1985.

Jackson, T. with Eade, D. *Against the Grain: The Dilemma of Project Food Aid.* Oxfam, Oxford, 1982.

Jacobson, J. 'Environmental refugees: a yardstick of habitability'. *Worldwatch Paper 86.* Worldwatch Institute, Washington DC, November 1988.

Jodha, N. 'Famine and famine policies: some empirical evidence'. *Economic and Political Weekly*, 11 October 1975.

Johnson, D. 'Increasing availability of food for the world's poor'. In K. Cahill (ed.) *Famine*. Orbis Books, New York, 1982.

Karcz, J. *The Economics of Communist Agriculture: Selected Papers*, ed. A. Wright, Purdue University, International Development Institute, Bloomington, Ind., 1979.

Kocher, J. 'Socio-economic development and fertility changes in rural Africa'. *Harvard Institute for International Development*. Discussion Paper No. 16. Harvard, 1976.

Koester, A. *The Scope for Regional Cooperation in the Food Economy among Southern and Eastern African Countries*. IFPRI, Washington DC, 1985.

Kula, E. 'Politics, economics, agriculture and famines: The Chinese case'. *Food Policy*, **14**(1), February 1989.

Kumar, G. *The Ethiopian Famine and Relief Measures: An Analysis and Evaluation*. UNICEF, Addis Ababa, January 1985.

Kumar, G. *Ethiopian Famines 1973–1985: A Case Study*. Paper presented at the WIDER Conference on Food Strategies, Helsinki, July 1986.

Lawrence, P. (ed.) *World Recession and the Food Crisis in Africa*. Review of African Political Economy, James Currey, 1986.

Laya, D. 'Interviews with farmers and livestock-owners in the Sahel'. *African Environment*, **1**(2), Dakar, April 1975.

Leftwich, A. and Harvie, D. *The Political Economy of Famine*. Institute for Research in the Social Sciences. Discussion Paper 116. University of York, York, 1986.

Leibenstein, H. 'Famine and economic development'. In K. Cahill (ed.) *Famine*. Orbis Books, New York, 1982.

Lemma, H. 'The politics of famine in Ethiopia'. *Review of African Political Economy*, **33**, August 1985.

Li, L. 'Food, famine, and the Chinese state'. *Journal of Asian Studies*, August 1982.

Lipton, M. *Why Poor People Stay Poor*. Temple Smith, London, 1977.

Lowenberg, M. *et al. Food and Man*, John Wiley, New York, 1974.

Mace, J. 'The man-made famine of 1932–33: what happened and why'. In R. Hadzewycz *et al.* (eds.) *The Great Famine in Ukraine: The Unknown Holocaust*. Ukrainian National Association, Jersey City, New Jersey, 1983.

Mackintosh, M. 'Abstract markets and real needs'. In H. Bernstein *et al.* (eds.) *The Food Question*. Earthscan, London, 1990.

Mamdani, M. 'Disaster prevention: defining the problem'. *Review of African Political Economy*, **33**, August 1985.

McAlpin, M. 'From famine to food crisis: Bombay presidency 1871–1921'. Mimeo. Tufts University, September 1982.

McHenry, D. and Bird, K. 'Food bungle in Bangladesh'. *Foreign Policy*, **27**, 1977.

McIntire, J. *Food Security in the Sahel: Variable Import Levy, Grain Reserves and Foreign Exchange Assistance*. IFPRI, 1981.

Meadows, D. H., Meadows, D. L., Randers, J. and Behrens, W. W. *The Limits to Growth*. A report for the Club of Rome's project on the predicament of mankind, Earth Island, London, 1972.

Meillassoux C. 'Development or exploitation: is the Sahel famine good business?' *Review of African Political Economy*, **1**, 1974.

Mellor, J. and Gavian, S. 'Famine: causes, prevention, and relief'. *Science*, **235**, January 1987.

Mengestu, A., Asrat, D., Mawaee, A. and Hay, R. *A Theory of Famine Assessment.* UNICEF Food and Nutrition Surveillance Programme, Addis Ababa, November 1978.

Mitra, A. 'The meaning of meaning'. *Economic and Political Weekly*, 1982.

Moore, F. and Collins, J. *Food First.* Houghton Mifflin, Boston, 1977.

Morgan, D. *Merchants of Grain.* Penguin, Harmondsworth, 1979.

Morgan, R. 'Social security in the SADCC states of southern Africa: social welfare programmes and the reduction of household vulnerability'. In E. Ahmad *et al.* (eds.) *Social Security in Developing Countries.* Clarendon Press, Oxford, 1991.

Mortimore, M. 'Five faces of famine: the autonomous sector in the famine process'. *International Geographical Union: Study Group on Famine Research and Food Production Systems.* Freiburg University, 10–14 November 1989.

Nabarro, D. 'Teaching programme staff to identify food shortages and to tackle their consequences'. *Proceedings of the Nutrition Society*, **46**(2). Cambridge University Press, Cambridge, July 1987.

Nau, H. 'The diplomacy of world food'. In R. Hopkins and D. Puchala (eds.) *The Global Political Economy of Food.* University of Wisconsin Press, Madison, 1978.

New Internationalist. Oxford, September 1985.

Nnoli, O. 'Desertification, refugees and regional conflict in West Africa'. *Disasters*, **14**(2), 1990.

O'Brien, J. 'Sowing the seeds of famine: the political economy of food deficits in Sudan'. *Review of African Political Economy, ***33**, August 1985.

Oleskiw, S. *The Agony of a Nation: The Great Man-Made Famine in Ukraine 1932–33.* The National Committee to Commemorate the 50th Anniversary of the Artificial Famine in Ukraine 1932–1933, London, 1983.

Osmani, S. R. 'Nutrition and the Economy of Food: Implications of some recent controversies'. In Drèze, J. and Sen, A. *The Political Economy of Hunger, Vol. III: Endemic Hunger.* Oxford, Clarendon Press, 1991.

Oughton, E. 'The Maharashtra droughts of 1970–73: an analysis of scarcity'. *Oxford Bulletin of Economics and Statistics*, **44**(3), August 1982.

Paddock, W. and Paddock, P. *Famine – 1975!* Weidenfeld and Nicolson, London, 1967.

Parrack. In J. Robson (ed.) *Famine: Its Causes, Effects and Management.* Gordon and Breach, New York, 1981.

Perlman, M. 'Opportunity in the face of disaster – review of the economic literature on famine'. In K. Cahill (ed.) *Famine.* Orbis Books, New York, 1982.

Rahaman, M. 'The causes and effects of famine in the rural population: a report from Bangladesh'. In J. Robson (ed.) *Famine: Its Causes, Effects and Management.* Gordon and Breach, New York, 1981.

Raikes, P. 'Seasonality in the rural economy (of tropical Africa)'. In R. Chambers *et al.* (eds.) *Seasonal Dimensions to Rural Poverty.* Frances Pinter, London, 1981.

Raikes, P. *Modernising Hunger: Famine, Food Surplus and Farm Policy in the EEC and Africa.* Catholic Institute for International Relations, London, 1988.

Ram, N. 'An independent press and anti-hunger strategies'. Paper presented at the WIDER Conference on Food Strategies, Helsinki, July 1986.

Rangasami, A. ' "Failure of exchange entitlements" theory of famine: a response'. *Economic and Political Weekly*, **XX** (**20, 21**), 12 and 19 October 1985.

Rapp, A. *A Review of Desertization in Africa. Water, vegetation and man.* SIES Report No. 1. Lunds Universitats Naturgeografiska Institute, 1974.

Rasmusson, E. 'Global climate change and variability: effects on drought and desertification in Africa'. In M. Glantz (ed.) *Drought and Hunger in Africa: Denying Famine a Future.* Cambridge University Press, Cambridge, 1987.

Ravallion, M. 'The performance of rice markets in Bangladesh during the 1974 famine'. *Economic Journal*, March 1985.

Ravallion, M. 'The economics of famine: an overview of recent research'. *Working Papers in Trade and Development*, **87/13**, Australia National University Research School of Pacific Studies, June 1987a.

Ravallion, M. *Markets and Famines*. Clarendon Press, Oxford, 1987b.

Raynaut, C. 'Lessons of a crisis'. In D. Dalby *et al.* (eds.) *Drought in Africa 2*. International African Institute, London, 1977.

Repetto, R. and Holmes, T. 'The role of population in resource depletion in developing countries'. *Population and Development Review*, December 1983.

Review of African Political Economy, **15/16**. 'The roots of famine', May–December 1979.

Review of African Political Economy, **33**. 'War and Famine', August 1985.

Richards, P. 'Ecological change and the politics of African land use'. *African Studies Review*, **26**(2), June 1983.

Rivers, J., Holt, J., Seaman, J. and Bowden, M. 'Lessons for epidemiology from the Ethiopian famines'. *Annales Société Belge de Médecine Tropicale*, **56**, 1976.

Robson, J. (ed.) *Famine: Its Causes, Effects and Management*. Gordon and Breach, New York, 1981.

Rostow, W. *The Stages of Economic Growth*. Cambridge University Press, Cambridge, 1960.

Rotberg, R. and Rabb, T. (eds.) *Hunger and History*. Cambridge University Press, Cambridge, 1983.

Sahli, Z. 'The phenomenon of marginalisation in underdeveloped rural communities'. *Third World Quarterly*, **3**(3), July 1981.

Saylor, T. 'A new legislative mandate for American food aid'. In P. Brown and H. Shue (eds.) *Food Policy*. Free Press, New York, 1977.

Schoepf, B. 'Food crisis and class formation in Shaba'. *Review of African Political Economy*, **33**, August 1985.

Schwab, P. *Ethiopia: Politics, Economics and Society*. Frances Pinter, London, 1985.

Scott, E. (ed.) *Life Before the Drought*. Allen and Unwin, Boston, Mass., 1984.

Scott, J. *The Moral Economy of the Peasant: Rebellion and Subsistence in Southeast Asia*. Yale University Press, New Haven, Conn., 1976.

Seaman, J. and Holt, J. 'Markets and famines in the Third World'. *Disasters*, **4**(3), 1980.

Sen, A. 'Ingredients of famine analysis: availability and entitlement'. Working Paper No. 210. Cornell University, Ithaca, NY, 1979.

Sen, A. 'Economic development: objectives and obstacles'. In R. Dernberger (ed.) *China's Development Experience in Comparative Perspective*. Harvard University Press, Cambridge, Mass., 1980.

Sen, A. *Poverty and Famines*. Clarendon Press, Oxford, 1981.

Sen, A. 'The food problem: theory and policy'. *Third World Quarterly*, **4**(3), July 1982.

Sen, A. 'Development: which way now?' *Economic Journal*, 1983.

Sen, A. *Resources, Values and Development*. Basil Blackwell, Oxford, 1984.

Sen, A. *Points on Food, Cash and Entitlements*. Mimeo. University of Oxford, 1985a.

Sen, A. *Commodities and Capabilities*. North-Holland, Amsterdam, 1985b.

Sen, A. 'Food, economics and entitlements'. *Lloyds Bank Review*, April 1986a.

Sen, A. 'The causes of famine: a reply'. *Food Policy*, May 1986b.

Sen, A. 'Reply: famine and Mr Bowbrick'. *Food Policy*, February 1987a.

Sen, A. 'The political economy of hunger'. Lionel Robbins Memorial Lectures. London School of Economics, London, 12–14 May 1987b.

Sen, A. 'Hunger and entitlements: research for action'. Workshop on Famine and Famine Policy. Tufts University, 25 February 1988.

Sen, A. 'Individual freedom as a social commitment'. *New York Review*, 14 June 1990.

Sender, J. and Smith, S. 'Famine: what can the Left give?' *Marxism Today*, January 1985.

Shaughnessy, D. 'The political uses of food aid: are criteria necessary?' In P. Brown and H. Shue (eds.) *Food Policy*. Free Press, New York, 1977.

Shenton, R. and Watts, M. 'Capitalism and hunger in northern Nigeria'. *Review of African Political Economy*, **15/16**, May–December 1979.

Shepherd, A. 'Agrarian change in northern Ghana: public investment, capitalist farming and famine'. In J. Heyer *et al.* (eds.) *Rural Development in Tropical Africa*. Macmillan, London, 1981.

Shepherd, A. 'Nomads, farmers, and merchants: old strategies in a changing Sudan'. In J. Scott (ed.) *Life Before the Drought*. Yale University Press, New Haven, Conn., 1984.

Shindo, E. 'Hunger and weapons: the entropy of militarisation'. *Review of African Political Economy*, **33**, August 1985.

Singer, P. 'Reconsidering the famine relief argument'. In P. Brown and H. Shue (eds.) *Food Policy*. Free Press, New York, 1977.

Sobhan, R. 'Politics of food and famine in Bangladesh'. *Economic and Political Weekly*, 1 December 1979.

Speedie, A. 'How the arms race kills'. *Sanity*, August 1983.

Spitz, P. 'Silent violence: famine and inequality'. *International Social Sciences Journal*, **XXX (4)**, 1978.

Spitz, P. *Drought and Self-Provisioning*. UNRISD, Geneva, June 1980.

Spitz, P. *Economic Consequences of Food/Climate Variability*. UNRISD, Geneva, 1981.

Spitz, P. 'The right to food in historical perspective'. *Food Policy*, November 1985.

Stahl, M. 'Environmental degradation and political constraints in Ethiopia'. *Disasters*, **14**(2), 1990.

Stein, Z., Susser, M., Saenger, G. and Marolla, F. *Famine and Human Development*. Oxford University Press, Oxford, 1975.

Stewart, F. 'Poverty and famines: book review'. *Disasters* **6**(2), 1982.

Stewart, F. 'Food aid: pitfalls and potential.' In UNICEF/WFP, *Food Aid and the Well-Being of Children in the Developing World*. UNICEF, New York, 1986.

Svedberg, P. *Food Insecurity in Developing Countries: Causes, Trends and Policy Options*. UNCTAD, Geneva, 1984.

Svedberg, P. *The Economics of Food Insecurity in Developing Countries*. Institute for International Economic Studies, University of Stockholm, January 1985.

Swift, J. 'Why are rural people vulnerable to famine?' *IDS Bulletin*, **20**(2). Institute of Development Studies, University of Sussex, Brighton, April 1989.

Tawney, R. *Land and Labour in China*. Cambridge University Press, Cambridge, 1966.

Tickell, C. 'Environmental refugees: the human impact of global climate change'. *Natural Environment Research Council Annual Lecture*. London, 5 June 1989.

Tickner, V. 'Military attacks, drought and hunger in Mozambique'. *Review of African Political Economy*, **33**, August 1985.

Tilly, L. 'Food, entitlement, famine, and conflict'. In R. Rotberg and T. Rabb (eds.) *Hunger and History*. Cambridge University Press, Cambridge, 1983.

Timberlake, L. *Africa in Crisis*. Earthscan, London, 1985.

Timmer, C., Falcon, W. and Pearson, S. *Food Policy Analysis*. Johns Hopkins University Press, Baltimore, Md., 1983.

Timmer, C. 'Food price policy: The rationale for government intervention'. *Food Policy*, **14**(1), February 1989.

Torry, W. 'Social science research on famine: a critical evaluation'. *Human Ecology*, **12**(3), 1984.

Torry, W. 'Drought and desertification as constraints on the agricultural development of the western Sudan'. *Studies in Third World Societies, Number 36: Natural Disasters and Cultural Responses*. College of William and Mary, Williamsburg, Virginia, June 1986.

Twose, N. *Why the Poor Suffer Most: Drought and the Sahel*. Oxfam, Oxford, 1984.

Twose, N. *Cultivating Hunger*. Oxfam, Oxford, 1985.

UNCOD A/CONF 74/36 '*Plan of action to stop desertification*'. Report of UN Conference on Desertification. Nairobi, 1977.

UNICEF *The State of the World's Children 1985*. UNICEF, New York, 1985.

UNICEF/WFP *Food Aid and the Well-Being of Children in the Developing World*. UNICEF, New York, 1986.

UNRISD 'Famine risk and famine prevention in the modern world'. UNRISD, Geneva, June 1976.

Vallely, P. 'Land blighted by ideology'. *The Times*, 30 October 1986.

Van Schendel, W. *Peasant Mobility*. Van Gorcum, Assen, 1981.

Vaughan, M. *The Story of an African Famine: Gender and Famine in Twentieth-century Malawi*. Cambridge University Press, Cambridge, 1987.

Walker, P. *Famine Early Warning Systems: Victims and Destitution*. Earthscan, London, 1989.

Wallerstein, M. *Food for War – Food for Peace*. Massachusetts Institute of Technology, Cambridge, Mass., 1980.

Watkins, S. and Menken, J. 'Famines in historical perspective'. *Population and Development Review*, December 1985.

Watkins, S. and Van de Walle, E. 'Nutrition, mortality, and population size: Malthus' court of last resort'. In R. Rotberg and T. Rabb (eds.) *Hunger and History*. Cambridge University Press, Cambridge, 1983.

Watts, M. 'The sociology of seasonal food shortage in Hausaland'. In R. Chambers *et al.* (eds.) *Seasonal Dimensions to Rural Poverty*. Frances Pinter, London, 1981.

Watts, M. *Silent Violence: Food, Famine and Peasantry in Northern Nigeria*. University of California Press, Berkeley, 1983.

Watts, M. 'Drought, environment and food security: some reflections on peasants, pastoralists and commoditization in dryland West Africa'. In M. Glantz (ed.) *Drought and Hunger in Africa: Denying Famine a Future*. Cambridge University Press, Cambridge, 1987.

Wisner, B. 'Man-made famine in eastern Kenya: the interrelationship of environment and development'. IDS Discussion Paper No. 96, July 1976.

Woldemariam, M. *Rural Vulnerability to Famine in Ethiopia: 1958–1977*. Vikas, Addis Ababa, 1984.

World Bank *Accelerated Development in Sub-Saharan Africa: An Agenda for Action*. World Bank, Washington DC, 1981.

World Bank *World Development Report 1984*. Oxford University Press, New York, 1984.

World Bank *World Development Report 1985*. Oxford University Press, New York, 1985.

World Bank *Poverty and Hunger: Issues and Options for Food Security in Developing Countries*. IBRD/The World Bank, Washington DC, 1986.

Wu Ta-k'un 'A critique of neo-Malthusian theory'. Peking, 1960. Reprinted in *Population and Development Review*, December 1979.

Yotopoulos, P. *Population and Agricultural Development: 2. The Population Problem and the Development Solution*. FAO, Rome, 1978.

Subject index

Name index